*The Chivalric Romance
and the Essence
of Fiction*

ALSO BY DANI CAVALLARO

The Late Works of Hayao Miyazaki: A Critical Study, 2004–2013 (2015)

Hayao Miyazaki's World Picture (2015)

Synesthesia and the Arts (2013)

Japanese Aesthetics and Anime: The Influence of Tradition (2013)

Kyoto Animation: A Critical Study and Filmography (2012)

CLAMP in Context: A Critical Study of the Manga and Anime (2012)

Art in Anime: The Creative Quest as Theme and Metaphor (2012)

The World of Angela Carter: A Critical Investigation (2011)

The Fairy Tale and Anime: Traditional Themes, Images and Symbols at Play on Screen (2011)

The Mind of Italo Calvino: A Critical Exploration of His Thought and Writings (2010)

Magic as Metaphor in Anime: A Critical Study (2010)

Anime and the Visual Novel: Narrative Structure, Design and Play at the Crossroads of Animation and Computer Games (2010)

Anime and the Art of Adaptation: Eight Famous Works from Page to Screen (2010)

The Art of Studio Gainax: Experimentation, Style and Innovation at the Leading Edge of Anime (2009)

Anime and Memory: Aesthetic, Cultural and Thematic Perspectives (2009)

Anime Intersections: Tradition and Innovation in Theme and Technique (2007)

The Cinema of Mamoru Oshii: Fantasy, Technology and Politics (2006)

The Animé Art of Hayao Miyazaki (2006)

The Chivalric Romance and the Essence of Fiction

DANI CAVALLARO

McFarland & Company, Inc., Publishers
Jefferson, North Carolina

LIBRARY OF CONGRESS CATALOGUING-IN-PUBLICATION DATA

Names: Cavallaro, Dani, 1962– , author.
Title: The chivalric romance and the essence of fiction / Dani Cavallaro.
Description: Jefferson, North Carolina : McFarland & Company, Inc., Publishers, 2016. | Includes bibliographical references and index.
Identifiers: LCCN 2015047087 | ISBN 9780786499830 (softcover : acid free paper) ∞
Subjects: LCSH: Chivalry in literature. | Romances—History and criticism. | Literature, Medieval—History and criticism. | Literature, Modern—15th and 16th centuries—History and criticism. | European literature—Renaissance, 1450–1600—History and criticism. | Fiction—History and criticism—Theory, etc. | Fiction—Technique.
Classification: LCC PN682.C53 C38 2016 | DDC 809.3—dc23
LC record available at http://lccn.loc.gov/2015047087

BRITISH LIBRARY CATALOGUING DATA ARE AVAILABLE

ISBN (print) 978-0-7864-9983-0
ISBN (ebook) 978-1-4766-2358-0

© 2016 Dani Cavallaro. All rights reserved

No part of this book may be reproduced or transmitted in any form or by any means, electronic or mechanical, including photocopying or recording, or by any information storage and retrieval system, without permission in writing from the publisher.

Front cover: St. George and the Dragon, 1455, by Paolo Uccello (PicturesNow)

Printed in the United States of America

*McFarland & Company, Inc., Publishers
Box 611, Jefferson, North Carolina 28640
www.mcfarlandpub.com*

To Paddy, Hazza and Mordecai,
with protean love

Contents

Preface 1

Part I

ONE—Genesis 3
TWO—Form and Structure 28

Part II

THREE—Creative Cornerstones: Chrétien de Troyes and the *Lancelot-Grail Cycle* 57

FOUR—Medieval Masters: Chaucer, Malory, the Lay and the Gawain Poet 114

FIVE—Renaissance Refashionings: Ariosto, Spenser and Shakespeare 152

Bibliography 207
Index 217

I want to learn more and more to see as beautiful what is necessary in things; *then I shall be one of those who make things beautiful.*
—Friedrich Nietzsche (1882)

Everyone who has approached the Arthurian legends with a view to finding out more about them is struck at once by their sheer breadth and complexity. Many turn away at this point, or content themselves with reading Sir Thomas Malory's Le Morte d'Arthur. *Wonderful though Malory's retelling of the legend is, it is only one among many. To have failed to discover the fourteenth-century poem of* Sir Gawain and the Green Knight, *or the mysterious pageantry of the* Vulgate Version [i.e., Lancelot-Grail Cycle] *from which Malory himself drew extensively, is to have missed a wondrous experience.*
—John Matthews (1993)

It must not be supposed that, when realism informed the upper regions of literature, the fantastic was not to be found on the printed page.... Beneath the rational carapace, there was always an imaginative substratum in literature.... And so, to use Professor Tolkien's phrase, the road goes ever onward.... The legends, it seems, will always be a perennial topic of fascination.
—Ronan Coghlan (1993)

Preface

Chivalric romances are intrinsically *acentered*—or *centerless*—texts. As such, they call into question the viability of any controlling force meant to enforce the authority of preestablished values.

Chivalric romances approximate fiction at its purest since they do not claim to house any truths. They thus epitomize the essence of *all* creative literature which is not owned—or colonized—by the ethos of classic realism.

This study focuses on the evolution of the chivalric romance from Chrétien de Troyes (late twelfth century) to William Shakespeare's late plays (early seventeenth century). However, its argument is of immediate relevance to contemporary culture, insofar as it aims to show how the chivalric romance exemplifies an attitude to the world which would greatly benefit present-day citizens and consumers. This is because its centerless structure enables the form to yield a radical examination of the seats of meaning and truth which all societies, in varying degrees, require their members to embrace without reflection or doubt.

It may be tempting, in this regard, to assume that the postmodern text is akin to the type of text characteristic of the chivalric romance. In fact, the two are not the same. The postmodern text is inscribed in a culture of endless recycling where nothing truly new is produced, and the best one can expect is a travesty of novelty. This is a culture of simulacra: surfaces which hide not a secret presence but an absence: the lack of any substance, sense, or indeed identity.

The text associated with the chivalric romance, by contrast, experiments not with an army of entrenched simulacra, but rather a string of intriguing dissimulations. These issue from a playful juggling with actual and apparent meanings redolent of the actions performed by the *eiron* of ancient drama (the root of the word *irony*): a figure whose function is to urge the spectator to question the accepted truth by refusing to take anything at face value. Thus, the chivalric romance offers a mobile world of oppositions without asserting any given principles in a definitive fashion. It asks us, its readers, to make decisions and, where relevant, to act accordingly. Intrinsic to its world view is Socratic irony itself as a denial of conclusive solutions.

The present study proposes that irony constitutes the chivalric romance's motivating force. Irony, in this context, is understood as a *philosophical concept* and as *an attitude to the world* rather than a mere trope. The book's main goal is to bring to light the strategies through which the chosen texts engage with irony at both the literal and the metaphorical levels.

In Part I, the book undertakes a twofold task. Chapter One, Genesis, explores the evolution of the chivalric romance with reference to a selective survey of Arthurian lore. Chapter Two, Form and Structure, examines the salient stylistic traits and thematic predilections evinced by the form, in contradistinction with the epic, and the *chanson de geste* in particular.

Part II provides an in-depth investigation of a range of texts produced between the twelfth and the seventeenth centuries, focusing on their themes, imagery, narrative strategies, and methods of characterization. The leading thread running through Part II is the proposition that the chivalric romance serves a major social function, as both a cherished mode of entertainment, and a fictionalized expression of particular cultural preoccupations. This renders it a versatile vehicle for the exploration of philosophical issues of far-reaching relevance. Since, as emphasized above, the principle of irony is pivotal to the chivalric romance, special attention is given to how the chosen texts engage with this important idea.

The range of authors and texts covered in chapters Three to Five is outlined below.

- Chapter Three: Chrétien de Troyes: *Yvain, or, the Knight of the Lion*; *Lancelot, or, the Knight of the Cart*; *Perceval, the Story of the Grail*; *Lancelot-Grail Cycle* (selection).
- Chapter Four: Geoffrey Chaucer: *The Canterbury Tales, General Prologue: The Knight*; Thomas Malory: *Le Morte d'Arthur* (selection); The Lay: Thomas Chestre: *Sir Launfal*; Anonymous: *Sir Orfeo*; The Gawain Poet: *Sir Gawain and the Green Knight*.
- Chapter Five: Ludovico Ariosto: *Orlando Furioso* (selection); Edmund Spenser: *The Faerie Queene*, Book I; William Shakespeare: *The Winter's Tale*; *Cymbeline*.

Part I

One

Genesis

This chapter's central aim is to chart the development of the chivalric romance with reference to Arthurian lore. It first seems desirable, however, to elucidate the parameters of the exploration here pursued—namely, the terms "romance" and "chivalry" themselves. The definition of the word "romance" provided by the *Oxford Dictionaries* which is most relevant to this study is the following: "a medieval tale dealing with a hero of chivalry, of the kind common in the Romance languages." As an adjective, the dictionary goes on to explain, "romance" designates "the group of Indo-European languages descended from Latin, principally French, Spanish, Portuguese, Italian, Catalan, Occitan, and Romanian." Its origin is the Middle English word "originally denoting the vernacular language of France as opposed to Latin: from the Old French *romanz*, based on the Latin *Romanicus* 'Roman'" ("Romance," *Oxford Dictionaries*).

The *Online Etymology Dictionary*, for its part, offers these definitions:

romance (n.) c.1300, "a story, written or recited, of the adventures of a knight ... designed principally for entertainment," from Old French *romanz* "verse narrative" (Modern French *roman*), originally an adverb, "in the vernacular language," from Vulgar Latin *romanice scribere* "to write in a Romance language" (one developed from Latin)....

romance (v.) late 14c., "recite a narrative," from Old French *romancier* "narrate in French; translate into French." ... Later "invent fictitious stories" (1670s), then "be romantically enthusiastic" (1849); meaning "court as a lover" is from 1938 ["Romance," *Online Etymology Dictionary*].

The present chapter does not claim to provide a comprehensive history of Arthurianism. The extent and variety of the body of lore which underpins that tradition render such an aspiration risible. Any attempt to fulfill it would inevitably deliver nothing more engaging for the reader than a lifeless and tedious inventory of names and dates. Therefore, the chapter seeks instead to provide a panoramic vista of the range of Arthurian materials in which the chivalric romance is grounded. The scope of this overview is essentially illustrative, rather than either taxonomic or encyclopedic.

As a literary form, the chivalric romance originated in Europe between the eleventh and the fourteenth centuries. The literature of this period comprises three clusters of legends. These include the "Matter of Britain" (a.k.a. "Arthurian cycle"), centered on King Arthur and the Knights of the Round Table; the "Matter of France" (a.k.a. "Carolingian cycle"), whose pivotal characters are the emperor Charlemagne and his paladins; and the "Matter of Rome," a cycle combining classical mythology, and episodes from antiquity. Of the three, the first is the one directly pertinent to this book, insofar as it is in its articulation of various facets of the Matter of Britain that the chivalric romance asserts itself as a versatile and colorful form, bound to influence writers and artists of future centuries. However, the Carolingian cycle will also come into play, specifically in the discussion of Ludovico Ariosto's *Orlando Furioso* provided in the final chapter.

As Roberta L. Krueger maintains, "Arthurian romances were not the first vernacular courtly fictions, but their tremendous popularity—in a wide range of linguistic registers, cultural settings, and aesthetic modes—established them as a major force that other romance authors might choose to imitate, adapt, criticize, or even burlesque, but which they did not often ignore" (Krueger, p. 3). Indeed, the ascendancy of Arthurian materials in the romance tradition is still notable in contemporary culture, where it finds varied expression in both literature and cinema. This validates Matilda Tomaryn Bruckner's contention that the "romance is the shape-shifter par excellence among medieval genres, a protean form that refuses to settle into neat boundaries prescribed by modern critics" (Bruckner 2000, p. 13). At the same time, the metamorphic survival of the romance in today's world echoes Krueger's depiction of "the story of medieval romance's evolution" as "one of translation and transformation, adaptation and refashioning, and fertile intertextual and intercultural exchange" (Krueger, p. 1).

An adaptable medium, the romance has endured over time through repeated transmutations, and by embedding many of its salient features onto other literary forms. As John Stevens argues, the romance is "the major secular genre from the time of Chrétien de Troyes (*c.* 1180) to Chaucer (d. 1400). Many of the major achievements of Elizabethan literature either are in the widest sense romances (Spenser's *Faerie Queene*, Sir Philip Sidney's *Arcadia*) or are deeply indebted to romance tradition (Elizabethan courtly comedy, such as *A Midsummer Night's Dream*). What is more, hardly had the fairy-monster 'romance' been knocked on the head by the champions of neo-classical virtues ... than it obstinately began to revive," reaching a new apotheosis with works such as Samuel Taylor Coleridge's "Christabel," and John Keats' "The Eve of St Agnes" (Stevens, p. 15).

As to the reason adduced by the critic for the form's widespread influence, this would appear to lie with its engagement with "experiences" which can be considered of "fundamental and continuing importance to Western man." These find expression in particular "conventions, motifs, archetypes," the most prominent of which include "the mysterious challenge or call; the first sight of the beloved; the lonely journey through a hostile land; the fight with the enemy, often a monstrous creature" (p. 16).

It is crucial to acknowledge that these topoi cannot be easily compartmentalized, let alone dismissed, as formulaic principles to which authors return, time and again, out of unadventurous conformism or sheer convenience. While they are undoubtedly conventional, they are insistently revisited *not* because they are ready-made and expedient, but because they are *ideal* to the formulation of particular experiences and ideas. Stevens develops this proposition, stating that the type of "experience" which the romance strives to capture is itself responsible for giving rise to the form's recurrent formulae, and for perpetuating their relevance across diverse textual constructs. "It is the experience which *creates* these conventions, because it cannot be described so well in any other way. The same experience *re*-creates the same conventions.... Conventions are not arbitrary; they are the creations of human minds seeking forms of expression. The same acts and facts, if treated in a different way in a different spirit, become something different" (pp. 16–17).

Hence, looking down on the romance as a repetitive form, capable only of resorting mechanically to an established body of conventions, fails to grasp an essential aspect of its distinctive modus operandi. The same is true of the fairy tale, a form with which the romance shares many themes and tropes, insofar as the recurrence of certain codes and conventions within this mode is likewise the outcome of the deliberate construction of topoi suitable both to record and to propagate specific types of experience over time.

The following chapter will propose that the chivalric romance is an essentially prismatic form, and that its diversity renders it both centerless and ironic. The present chapter seeks to show that Arthurian lore—the *raw material*, so to speak, to which the romance gives narrative elaboration—is likewise multifaceted, and that this precludes its possession of a stable center, while also suffusing it with irony.

Arthurian lore consists of a tangle of disparate strands which have multiplied and intersected with gusto over several centuries. This kinetic textual constellation is de facto centerless, insofar as the figure around which it revolves, Arthur, constitutes an "absent center," a shifting signifier devoid of a verifiable and consistent identity. Any attempt to construct an origin myth meant to ground the sprawling and hybrid brood of Arthurian legend is bound to meet with disappointment.

At the same time, any effort to marshal into a coherent system the motley ensemble of fictions encompassed by the Arthurian tradition is steeped in irony. Its many filaments always create scope for a multiplicity of positions, clashing perspectives, unresolved tensions, paradoxes, and ambiguities which, in turn, lend themselves to contrasting interpretations. All of this provides fertile terrain for irony to prosper unchecked. William Comfort substantiates this contention, arguing that "scholars have waged war over the theories of transmission of the so-called Arthurian material during the centuries which elapsed between the time of the fabled chieftain's activity in 500 A.D. and his appearance as a great literary personage in the twelfth century." However, insofar as "documents are lacking for the dark ages of popular tradition before the Norman Conquest" (Comfort, p. 6), such scholars may go on speculating evermore without reaching a conclusive answer to their conundrum. As their hypotheses proliferate, and their "wars" rage on, as many ironical disjunctions will crowd around the fables, rumors, anecdotes, myths, and old wives' tales comprised by the boundless galaxy of Arthurian lore.

The answer to the question of whether Arthur existed is both yes and no, which is enough to surround his name with a tantalizing aura of ambiguity and paradox. The historicity of Charlemagne, the leader at the center of the *chansons de geste* immortalized by the Matter of France, is unquestionable, even though the epics themselves have transformed the real-life emperor into the stuff of legend. With Arthur, however, matters are far more problematic, his identity being inextricable from the expanse of tales which have contributed to give it shape over the centuries. Furthermore, as Geoffrey Ashe points out, "the figure of Arthur may be the result of ... medievalizing a tradition that was truly ancient, and have originated in a real person.... An authentic Arthur had exited indeed, a long time before." Yet, most romancers "probably did not care much" (Ashe, p. 3). It is this relative lack of concern amongst medieval authors that has played the key role in ensuring the proliferation of diverse, and even discordant, interpretations of the fabled king.

If Arthur is an absent center, or shifting signifier, so are many of the elements which are meant to give substance to his world. The dramatis personae themselves form a mobile ensemble of possible roles, not fixed figures whose personalities and functions stay unaltered from one account to the next. As Norris J. Lacy and Geoffrey Ashe remark, "depending on the text at hand, Merlin may, for example, be imprisoned by Nimue [a.k.a. Viviane, or Niniane, or the Lady of the Lake], or he may voluntarily retire from the world." A further instability surrounds the infamous love affair at the heart of Arthurian lore: "Guinevere's lover is usually Lancelot but occasionally Bedivere instead" (Lacy and Ashe, pp. xiii-xiv). (Please note, for future reference, that the name "Guinevere" may also be rendered as Gwenevere or Guenevere.)

Arthur's own family life is itself inherently unstable, since the king is varyingly said to have no descendants, just one son, or both a son and a daughter. Mordred is sometimes presented as Arthur's nephew, or as both his nephew and adopted son. Most often, however, he is portrayed as the illegitimate issue of Arthur and his half-sister Morgause: one of the daughters of Arthur's mother, Igraine, by her first husband, Gorlois, alongside Elaine and Morgan le Fay. In some adaptations, Morgause is actually one and the same as Morgan le Fay. Mordred is held to seize the throne, as well as Queen Guinevere, when Arthur, having left him in charge, crosses the Channel with most of his knights to fight the Romans. Some reports maintain that Mordred allies himself with the Saxons, Scots, Picts, and Irish, and kills Arthur at Camlann, receiving fatal wounds himself in the same battle; others reverse the roles, making Arthur the enemy's slayer, and the victim of deadly injuries.

The chief reason for this discursive instability is that medieval literature at large revels in the elaboration of protean worlds. What must be recognized, from a modern perspective, is that this very aspect of the Arthurian tradition—as a pivotal facet of the Middle Ages—is precisely what endows it with its distinctive "vitality and richness," even though it may posit insurmountable obstacles for purists keen on ascertaining the difference between the Arthurian myth's "authentic" as opposed to "inauthentic" components (p. xiv). Such purists will have to resign themselves to the fluidity for which the Middle Ages are renowned—or else turn to a different age for greater solace in the satisfaction of their pigeonholing itch.

The decentering effect triggered by Arthur's elusive figure rebounds— not unlike the butterfly effect of chaos theory—across disparate parts of the romance world: even those which, on the surface, would not appear directly implicated with the mythical monarch. An example of this phenomenon is supplied by the numerous doublings (and redoublings for that matter) which punctuate the chivalric tradition, whereby several key characters feature in distant zones of the romance realm, and with diverse functions.

The signifier "Elaine," for instance, is known to have reached signification in at least seven different incarnations. The two most prominent ones, for the purpose of this study, are Elaine of Corbenic and Elaine of Astolat. As Pelles' daughter, the former is held to have entertained a brief and disastrous liaison with Lancelot, resulting from the knight's having been tricked into sleeping with her (believing she is Guinevere). Ironically, the outcome of this murky affair is the conception of Galahad, the knight destined to achieve the Grail, and hence the holiest of Arthurian champions. Elaine of Corbenic is also known to have revealed the Grail to Lancelot, and is often referred to as the "Grail Bearer," or "Grail Maiden."

Elaine of Astolat, for her part, is reputedly the daughter of Bernard of Astolat (a.k.a. Shalott). Her unrequited love for Lancelot leads to her tragic death aboard a boat, which takes her along the Thames to Arthur's court. This legend has inspired various literary reworkings of its central story, including Alfred Tennyson's famous poem "The Lady of Shalott" (1842). In addition, it has been the subject of numerous paintings, the most famous being John William Waterhouse's haunting depictions of the cursed damsel in the two paintings entitled "The Lady of Shalott" (1888 and 1894), and in the work bearing as its title a line from Tennyson's poem, "'I am half sick of shadows,' said The Lady of Shalott" (1915).

Another well-known name associated with the chivalric romance likewise featuring in different incarnations across the Arthurian tradition is Isolde (a.k.a. Iseut or Iseult). As the daughter of King Anguish of Ireland, and the wife of King Mark of Cornwall, she is said to have been hopelessly in love with Tristan as a result of her having shared with him a fatal potion, and to have died of grief upon hearing of the loved one's death. Tristan's official wife also bears the name Isolde (or Isolde of the White Hands, to be precise). Ever faithful to his true love, Tristan sends for the Irish Isolde upon receiving a lethal wound, hoping to rely on her legendary healing powers, and requests that the ship due to bring her back should sport white sails if the lady has agreed to come to his rescue, but black sails should she have declined. Although the Irish Isolde does not fail to board the vessel, Tristan's wife lies to him regarding the sails' hue, thereby causing the knight's demise prior to the faithful Irish Isolde's arrival at his deathbed.

This legend has provided inspiration for numerous writers over the centuries, an especially original reconceptualization of its key themes being Daphne Du Maurier's 1961 novel *Castle Dor* (a tale begun by Arthur Quiller-Couch). Pictorial interpretations of various aspects of Tristan and

Isolde's tragic love, and the sharing of the formidable brew in particular, also abound, as exemplified by artists as diverse as John Duncan, John William Waterhouse, Aubrey Beardsley, and August Spiess amongst others. The legend of Tristan and Isolde will be revisited later in this chapter in connection with medieval German literature.

Further evidence for the essential centerlessness of Arthurian lore is afforded by the varied nature of its texts. Lacy and Ashe underscore this contention, stating that "some works follow such 'Arthurian' characters as Gawain and hardly mention Arthur himself. Others, such as Gottfried von Strassburg's *Tristan*, are not literally Arthurian at all, and in fact the Tristan legend itself involves the graft of an independent body of narrative material onto the Arthurian legend." Alongside such narrative implants, one witnesses "the opposite phenomenon," whereby "a motif like the wasteland can be split off and exploited for its allusive or mythic value in a non–Arthurian text," such as T. S. Eliot's *Waste Land*, for example (Lacy and Ashe, pp. xiv-xv).

Various sources point to the period around 450–550 as the most likely time setting for the historical Arthur. The historical trajectory reconstructible from these sources indicate that Britain (which then consisted roughly of today's England and Wales alongside the part of Scotland not under the aegis of the Picts) broke away from the Roman Empire around 410. Its native inhabitants were the Britons, a people of Celtic ancestry. Following the secession from Rome, "a different people began encroaching on them. The new claimants to British territory were Angles, Saxons, and Jutes, closely akin and often called collectively Saxons, who came from across the North Sea" (Ashe, p. 4).

In the historical period associated with Arthur, "the Britons still held most of the land," and the legendary monarch is often described as their ruler. In addition, Arthur is "associated with Brittany across the Channel, which began to be colonized at this time by Britons" (pp. 4–5). The advent of the Saxons in post–Roman Britain is generally attributed to the weakness of a ruler named Vortigern, supposed to have "invited" them "to settle in Britain as auxiliary troops" when "he was harassed by enemies from the north." The newcomers' chief is known as Hengist. Before long, Vortigern, a name which means simply "over-chief" or "over-king" (p. 6), was overpowered by Hengist's people, who proceeded to raid the country without restraint. It may well be the case that Brittany came into existence as an overseas settlement as a result of the "flight of refugees" (p. 7) at the time the Saxons were thus pillaging the land. "Finally, the Britons recovered,"

Ashe continues, "thanks to new leaders, and Arthur was the greatest of all. He routed the Saxons and subdued them. His reign was founded on victory over these and other enemies and the restoration of peace. While he lived, the Britons were in the ascendant" (p. 5). However, when the Saxons began to advance once more, after Arthur had gone, they achieved supremacy for good.

All we know for certain about Arthur in strictly *historical* terms, therefore, is that if he ever existed, "he did so at a time when British history was hardly documented at all," as Ronan Coghlan maintains: namely, "a time of historical shadow-lands of which all manner of tales and fables could be told without fear of contradiction." All in all, however, "there is no direct evidence that he ever lived at all" (Coghlan, p. 9).

While there is no definite historiographical evidence for Arthur's existence, there is, however, "an 'Arthur' floating about in Welsh legend," as Derek Pearsall maintains. According to the critic, such a character "is first recorded in *Gododdin*, a commemoration of British heroes who fell at Caetrath (Catterick) about 600 AD, written by Aneirin, a Welsh poet.... In later Welsh legend, Arthur has the reputation of a warrior of superhuman powers, not particularly virtuous, in fact not virtuous at all, and certainly not a Christian" (Pearsall, p. 3). Richard Barber corroborates this line of argument, stating that even though it remains a moot point whether Arthur existed as a historical personage, it is unquestionable that "by the ninth century, there was a traditional hero called Arthur.... The real origins of Arthur," therefore, are steeped in fiction, not historiography, since they "lie in early Welsh literature" (Barber 1991, p. 6).

Coghlan's fascinating journey through Arthurian lore complements this information, explaining that "the first undisputed mention of Arthur occurs ... in the *Historia Brittonum* of Nennius, which appeared about the year AD 800.... Nennius gives a list of twelve battles in which victory fell to Arthur, notably Badon" (Coghlan, p. 10). It is in Nennius, incidentally, that Arthur is first portrayed as "a great patriotic Christian national leader" (Pearsall, p. 3). In the *Annales Cambriae* (a.k.a. *The Annals of Wales*), supposedly composed in the tenth century, we find the earliest reference to Arthur's last battle and its site, Camlann. The *Annales* "inform us that both Arthur and Mordred fell there" (Coghlan, p. 11). The variety of interpretations which the question of Arthur's historicity has spawned is mirrored by the kaleidoscopic profusion of tales and legends to which both the charismatic ruler himself and the adventures of his devotees and foes has given rise. The challenging irony at the heart of this diversity is that the historical construals of Arthur's role available today and the narrative constellations gravitating around his persona are by no means unequivocally reconcilable.

Arthur's significance in the context of Welsh literature is vividly demonstrated by the tale of *Culhwch and Olwen* (c. 1100), a proto-romance found in the prose collection *Mabinogion*, supposedly collated in the late eleventh and twelfth centuries. *Culhwch and Olwen* records a traditional Welsh tale in which Arthur's cousin Culhwch falls in love with Olwen, the daughter of a fearsome giant. Culhwch is told by the giant that he will never discover Olwen's location unless Arthur assists him in his quest. The king dispatches six of his finest knights to assist the young man, and enable him to meet Olwen. However, even though the girl returns Culhwch's attentions, the wedding cannot take place without Culhwch first accomplishing a series of preposterous feats requested by the giant. Only a few of these need completion, however, since the villain is slain, and the lovers are therefore free to marry. As Barber points out, though the tale is "far removed from the knightly world in which we usually expect to find Arthur," it does introduce two elements destined to play a key role in subsequent Arthurian romances: the portrayal of Arthur himself as "the ruler of the noblest court," and of the orchestration of the exploits developing around his figure as intrinsically "marvellous and strange" (Barber 1991, p. 34).

The twelfth century English historian William of Malmesbury confirms Arthur's role in Welsh tradition as the protagonist of numerous fables, while also stressing, however, his standing as a real historical figure. The twelfth century also witnesses the advent of the *Historia Regum Britanniae* (c.1135) by Geoffrey of Monmouth: a work bound to mark Arthur's apotheosis as "the great British hero," as Helen Cooper avers, by supplying "him with the biography that remained current in accounts of the English past down to the time of the sixteenth-century historian Holinshed" (Cooper 1998, p. vii).

Aiming to give England a reputable genealogy, and hence a coherent history as a nation, Geoffrey harks back to the classical tradition. According to Pearsall, his closest models are "the Romans," who "traced their ancestry to the Trojan hero Aeneas, in the story told by Virgil in the *Aeneid*," as well as other ethnic groups who likewise "claimed Trojan heroes as their eponymous ancestors, the Lombards, for instance, claiming Langobardus and the Franks Francus" (Pearsall, p. 8). Geoffrey himself traces Britain's origins back to the legendary city of Troy, and specifically to Brutus (a.k.a. Brute of Troy): the putative successor of the Trojan hero Aeneas, held to have been Britain's founder and first king. The is no mention of this character in any classical text.

The *Historia* is by no means a romance in the literal sense, insofar as it does include frequent references to Welsh history. Nevertheless, its sustained incorporation of fantastic elements, springing from both Celtic lore and the author's own imagination, casts doubt on the work's historical veracity. For one thing, the text abounds "with details of the reigns of kings who never existed and of the numbers killed in battles that never took place" (p. 7). This ruse seems *meant* to invite the reader to question the *Historia*'s factualness. In so doing, Geoffrey steers history towards the province of the romance, ironically purporting to offer a dependable account of real events, while simultaneously admitting without shame to his text's inherent fictionality. Arthur's erection as a national emblem brings together the historical and the romantic dimensions, insofar as it asserts the ruler's historicity, yet denies it through the self-conscious acknowledgement of its grounding in a fiction.

Geoffrey's work invites reflection on the distinction between actual events, and their reconstruction by historiographers. The latter provide conflicting interpretations of the same fundamental facts, fashioned in accordance with the requirements of particular ideologies. Such readings never capture the full bearing of actual events, even though they ask us to accept their contents as objective and reliable. All political regimes rely on edited accounts of the past as a means of shoring up the belief systems they promulgate, to legitimize the adoption of their policies, or to lend credence to schemes of a contentious nature. All written histories, in this perspective, can be said to offer access not to history itself, but rather to convenient textual distortions of time's erratic flow.

In his *Roman de Brut* (c. 1155), the Norman poet Wace "follows the sequence of events in Geoffrey pretty closely but he constantly adapts the story to the fashions of a more courtly and chivalric and self-consciously elegant culture" (p. 13). Most importantly, it is in the *Roman de Brut* that we encounter "the first mention of the Round Table," said to have been "introduced because his barons could not agree on an order of precedence when they sat at table" (Barber 1991, p. 10):

> Arthur fashioned the Round Table
> Of which many tales are told.
> There sit his knights,
> Each one equal to the next:
> They sit equally at the Table
> And are equally served.

> None of them can boast
> That he sits ahead of the next.
> None has a favored position,
> And none is excluded.
> [Wace, lines 9751–9760; cited in Lacy 1997, p. 62].

In Wace's introduction of the Round Table, and explanation of its ethos on the grounds of a potential for discord, one senses the seeds of strife to befall Arthur's court in later works as a result of internecine rifts which the Round Table's presumed courteousness is powerless to hold at bay. For this reason, Wace deserves consideration by any scholar with a keen interest in the evolution of the chivalric romance, and, relatedly, in the gradual metamorphosis of pseudo-histories designed to bolster the myth of nationhood into courtly narratives intended chiefly for entertainment.

As the supreme symbol of fairness, the Round Table emblematizes chivalry itself. At the same time, it epitomizes the spirit of the chivalric romance as a form: just as a circle lacks any definite beginning or end, so the romance shuns linear progression by cultivating instead an aesthetic of interweaving and deferral. It is also significant that whereas in geometry, the circle possesses a center, in the "reality" of the chivalric romance, it does not. Indeed, as noted earlier in this discussion, its supposed center cannot be pinned down with any certainty, since the figure of Arthur, while imparting the body of lore which surrounds it with a sense of unity, simultaneously precludes this very unity by scattering the legend's connotations to the four winds.

Interestingly, when Wace's poem "was taken up by an obscure country priest ... and put into English verse," a different picture emerged. "The *Brut* of Layamon [c. 1200] ... expands the Arthurian section with great patriotic vigour and enthusiasm," focusing on the "heroic and martial" elements of the story and concomitantly marginalizing the "courtly and chivalric atmosphere." Thus, in Layamon's hand, Arthur is portrayed essentially "as a fierce warrior king" (Pearsall, p. 16).

While rapidly gaining popularity both on French soil and in Britain, chivalric lore also "spread northwards to Scandinavia and southwards to Italy and Spain" (p. 18). In the process, a number of German authors came up with their own unique interpretations of various aspects of Arthurian legend. One such writer is Ulrich von Zatzikhoven, the author of *Lanzelet* (c. 1195): an adaptation of the Lancelot tale which diverges to a significant extent from the well-known French version, insofar as it contains no reference to the hero's adulterous attachment to Guinevere. One of the most remarkable peculiarities of Von Zatzikhoven's Lanzelet is the character's connection to "a plurality of wives ... which has been adduced as evidence for the Celtic origin of the story." Indeed, "loose or polygamous marital ties were a feature of Celtic society" (p. 18).

No less significant, in the context of German writing, is Wolfram von Eschenbach's thirteenth century romance *Parzival*. The latter is rendered most memorable by its author's infusion of the chivalric world with a distinctive *ethical* stance. As Barber explains, he "writes of strange adventures and marvels much as Chrétien had done, but he adds to them an exploration of the highest philosophical themes, notably a *coherent* idea of knightly behavior. Within the framework of romance, he portrays a world in which chivalry becomes an ideal fulfilling all man's highest aspirations" (Barber 1991, p. 94; italics added).

The German writer's outlook reverberates with ironical undertones. His search for coherence is somewhat incongruous with the spirit of the typical chivalric romance, when one considers that it is the *in*coherence of much knightly behavior that invests the form's kaleidoscopic adventures with their peculiar verve. In his quest for consistency, Von Eschenbach's poem embodies a mentality in which the romance's rambling fictionality is counteracted by the unifying power of myth. As argued in Chapter Two vis-à-vis Northrop Frye's theorization of the romance, while fiction is happy to be just that, *fiction*, myths aim to portray hidden truths. The *Parzival* bears witness to the human urge to *organize* things—preferably under the canopy of a strict ethos, religion or faith—as a means of imparting human experience with satisfying and morally laudable significance.

Von Eschenbach's myth-oriented mentality is revealed most explicitly by his handling of the Grail legend. This traces the sacred object's origins to the very beginnings of the Biblical universe, purporting that it dropped from the heavens "during the struggle between Lucifer and the angels." Seeking to demonstrate that the Grail "has the power to attract the highest and best in men" (Barber 1991, p. 95), von Eschenbach steers clear of "amorous libertinism," in favor of "high eroticized spiritual devotion" (Pearsall, p. 51). Given the religious undertones of the author's rendering of the Arthurian world, and not solely of the Grail Quest, his eschewal of sensual topics hardly comes as a surprise.

Medieval German literature also includes Heinrich von dem Türlin's *Diu Crône* (*The Crown*), a thirteenth-century poem rendered most exceptional by the fact that it is "the only Grail romance in which Gawain is the successful quester," as well as Hartmann von Aue's romances *Erec* and *Iwein*: adaptations of Chrétien de Troyes' own versions of Erec's and Yvain's adventures.

A particularly innovative interpretation of the romance tradition born in Germany's medieval culture is the poem *Tristan* (c. 1210): a variation on the classic Tristan and Isolde tale, penned by Gottfried von Strassburg. The work evinces subtle narrative ruses which, as Pearsall remarks, "look back to Chrétien and forward to Chaucer" (Pearsall, p. 53). Though peppered with concessions to predictable devoutness redolent of Von Eschenbach's *Parzival*, von Strassburg's *Tristan* lays conventional ethics aside in several key episodes with ironical gusto. This is borne out by Von Strassburg's exploitation of the idea that "the love of Tristan and Isolde was due to a magic potion, administered by mistake," and thus not *really* the result of a consciously indulged illicit passion, as a means of relieving the characters from the strictures of conformist morals. Accordingly, "the vein is often that of daring high comedy, and Gottfried's approach to the high idealized code of sexual love, with its rhetorical self-consciousness, bravura wit and pervasive irony, is very different from that of his contemporary Wolfram" (p. 59).

Barber further underscores the extent to which the *Tristan* seeks to steer the legend of Tristan and Isolde in a new direction, highlighting the romance's transcendence of the code of courtly love (*fin amor*). "The story is subordinated to the study of feeling," argues the critic. It is in the "scene where Tristan and Isolde drink the love-potion," in the belief that it is no more than "common wine," that von Strassburg's subtlety reaches its climax. Indeed, he "leaves us uncertain whether the drink merely confirms a love already begun, or is in itself the *coup de foudre*." However, this is not enough to satisfy the German writer's experimental appetite. Thus, while he is happy to allow the protagonists' love to "be regarded as a supernatural force," he also deploys this idea as a pretext to deliver a saga of "open adultery, treachery and broken oaths as a special case," calling upon magic "as the cause of each transgression" (Barber 1991, p. 75). In this fashion, von Strassburg's ironical genius is able to revel in topics which many of his contemporaries would have deemed immoral by actually appearing to embrace an unimpeachable notion of morality.

A paradigmatic illustration of Gottfried's psychological subtlety is the scene in which, as Leslie W. Rabine observes, "Isolde, having discovered that the dragon-slayer is also the man who killed her uncle, tries and fails to kill Tristan." Here, the "conflict" depicted by Gottfried is not solely one between "abstract, external forces." In fact, "it is also a mythical and historical conflict between the past status and the future status of women" (Rabine, p. 65). The critic substantiates her contention with reference to Gottfried's own text: "those two conflicting qualities, those warring contradictions, womanhood and anger, which accord so ill together, fought a hard battle in her breast.... Thus uncertainty raged within her, till at last sweet womanhood survived over anger, with the result that her enemy lived, and Morold was not avenged" (Gottfried, p. 176; as cited in Rabine).

In order to situate Gottfried's achievement in its broader context, it is vital to recall that the tragic tale of Tristan and Isolde, a legend rooted in Celtic mythology, is one of the most popular romances ever recorded, either orally and textually. In fact, it is generally held to have affected the development of the most (in)famous affair, and related love triangle, in the whole of Arthurian legend: that is to say, the one centered on Lancelot, Guinevere and Arthur. While at first independent of the Arthurian tradition as such, the Tristan and Isolde romance was integrated into the latter following the appearance of the *Prose Tristan* (c. 1240), where the hero officially joins the Round Table. A work whose authorship remains uncertain, though Luce de Gat and Helie de Boron are mentioned (in its prologue and epilogue respectively) as its composers, the *Prose Tristan* was substantially influenced by the *Lancelot-Grail Cycle*, here examined in Chapter Three.

The earliest extant renditions of the Tristan and Isolde romance, both of which are incomplete, date back to the twelfth-century. Their authors are the Norman poet Béroul, and the French poet Thomas. As Jimmy Joe explains, the former's version "was considered to be the uncourtly version, because it was less refined, and some of the scenes and the behaviours of the characters were brutal at times. Béroul may be closer to the original source, since he may have relied on oral tradition. On the other hand, Thomas wrote [a] courtly version of the romance. Thomas was much more interested in the inner thoughts of the characters."

The tale's earliest recountings depict the doomed lovers as passive victims of a malefic sortilege, which serves to exonerate Tristan and Isolde both formally and ethically. The emphasis, in these instances, is on a fatalistic mentality congruous with the otherworldly spirit of the Celtic tradition in which the original tale is supposed to have found inception. In the *Prose Tristan*, by contrast, the role of the magic potion is downplayed. In addition, "instead of King Mark being an innocent victim in the love triangle," he is portrayed as both a "jealous and weak husband" and an unpopular ruler, as well "as a coward and murderer" (Joe).

According to Erich Auerbach, "the series of adventures" offered by the chivalric romance as its structural mainstay "becomes the basis of a doctrine of personal perfection" (Auerbach, p. 118). Alongside the imperative to serve an idealized courtly lady, the quest for the Grail is perhaps the best known means by which many a knight seeks to actualize the ideal pinpointed by Auerbach. When Chrétien de Troyes introduces the Grail theme in *Perceval, the Story of the Grail*, the object is referred to as *a* grail and not *the* grail—that is to say, it is treated as a common noun, not an entity endowed with an already established reputation. Moreover, the object's *nature* remains uncertain, since a "grail" may equally well be a dish, a plate, a stone, or a cup.

Although the Grail Quest has acquired pointedly Christian connotations over time, the topos is rooted in pagan Celtic lore. In "the basic story of the Grail," Coghlan reminds us, "the land has become barren and, at the same time, the king has been fatally wounded in the thigh (or genitals). The aridity of the first has been caused by the injury of the second. The hero of the romance, Perceval ... visits the king in his castle and fails to ask the question ('What is the Grail and whom does it serve?') which would set things right. There is little doubt that behind the tale lies a myth of fertility" (Coghlan, p. 15).

The Grail symbolizes an unattainable object of desire whose authority is quite arbitrary. The knight errant searching for the Grail is de facto tied to a narrative structure of endless deferral, without knowing in unequivocal terms either what function the object is supposed to perform or, more importantly, what it *is*. Its identity remains baffling, elusive, a matter of fruitless speculation. In reading the chivalric romance, one often feels that the Grail is a flimsy shadow, a delusory vision akin to those conjured up by the wizard Atlantes in Ludovico Ariosto's *Orlando Furioso*—in other words, an insubstantial simulacrum whose role is not to conceal a secret presence, but rather to prevent a cavernous absence from revealing itself, and from thereby exposing the unreality of the goals which people pursue with no urge ever to examine their validity.

When Sir Galahad is allowed to reach the coveted prize at long last in some well-known versions of the story, his adventure does not reflect the *typical* chivalric romance, but rather the requirements of a specific ideology: one which, in this particular instance, sanctions the celebration of Christian faith as one of the tasks which it is incumbent upon the romance to perform. In the typical romance, on the other hand, there is no final prize, no safe haven, no last word—because there is *not supposed* to be one. In fact, the removal of inconclusiveness from its chosen formal cocktail would be tantamount to the suppression of its native pleasure.

One of the first works in which the Quest for the Grail was imparted with Christian significance—possibly *the* first, in fact—was *Joseph D'Arimathie* by the French poet Robert de Boron (late twelfth and early thirteenth centuries). In this narrative, Joseph of Arimathea (the man who offered his own sepulcher for the entombment of Jesus) is said to have used the Grail (a vessel central to the Last Supper) to catch the last drops of blood shed by Jesus' body. Joseph's followers are held to have taken the Grail to Britain, and watched over it until Arthur's ascent and the advent of Perceval. The holy relic's specific location on British soil is defined as the "vaus D'Avaron," the valleys of Avaron, or Avalon (the "isle of apples," often identified with Glastonbury, Somerset, where Arthur's actual grave is supposed to have been discovered around 1190). As to the reasons for the conveyance of the Grail to Britain, these remain obscure to say the least, as no obvious association obtains between Joseph and this country. Robert de Boron also provides a variation on the Fisher King topos with his "Rich Fisher."

The Grail legend "reached its classical form" in the part of the *Lancelot-Grail Cycle* known as the *Queste del Saint Graal* (*The Quest for the Holy Grail*, early thirteenth century), here examined in Chapter Three. In this text, "Galahad becomes a Grail Quester for the first time. The author—perhaps a Cistercian—seems to have thought Perceval insufficiently holy to be the real Grail hero, so Galahad has supplanted him" (Coghlan, p. 19). It is worth observing, on this point, that the Cistercians are a monastic order renowned for its emphasis on austerity and manual work, after the teachings of Saint Benedict. Moreover, as Barber explains, "the Cistercians were the one monastic order with a special involvement in secular knighthood, and whether we are looking for a monk or a layman as author, it is to this milieu, at once chivalrous and religious, that he is most likely to have belonged" (Barber 2003, p. 12).

It would be incorrect to presume that the religious redefinition of the Grail myth was either whole-hearted or unconditional, since the many mysteries surrounding its origins called its holiness into question, while the object itself provided the potential lynchpin of an unorthodox sect whose beliefs deviated from the authorized lessons of the Church. At no point, however, was there any reason to mistrust *The Quest for the Holy Grail*'s aims, given its author was "a mainstream Catholic, intent on bending the story to his own purposes" (Coghlan, pp. 19–20). In keeping with its creator's doctrinal obligations, the text strives to reconcile the Christian world picture with the discourse of secular chivalry, despite the latter's individualistic and martial thrust, by harnessing knightly values to religious ends, in much the same way as the Church had enlisted chivalry to its ranks in the First Crusade (1096–1099) to serve its contingent political purposes. As to the extent to which *The Quest for the Holy Grail* succeeded in achieving this goal, this issue will be addressed in detail in Chapter Three.

One of the most famous, albeit controversial, interpretations of the origins and evolution of the Grail myth is provided by Jessie Laidlay Weston's *From Ritual to Romance*. In reading J. G. Frazer's *The Golden Bough*, Weston was "struck by the resemblance existing between certain features of the Grail story, and characteristic details of the Nature Cults" examined therein (Weston, p. 5). Pursuing this hypothesis, she found that the Grail Quest recorded in Arthurian legends finds correlatives in the ancient traditions of "other lands" (p. 16). In addition, while exploring the customs of diverse cultures, Weston came to regard "a form of Nature worship ... as the possible ultimate source from which the incidents and mise-en-scène of the Grail stories" we know today have derived inspiration (p. 28). This reading suggests that the Quest's ultimate roots lie with neither Celtic lore nor Christian doctrine, but rather with cross-cultural fertility rituals designed to celebrate the cyclical healing and regeneration of the vegetation spirits presiding over the land's productivity.

Weston is also eager to underscore the widespread significance of the ritualistic objects associated with the Grail. "Lance and Cup ... were ... connected together in a symbolic relation long ages before the institution of Christianity, or the birth of Celtic tradition," argues the scholar. "They are sex symbols of immemorial antiquity ... the Lance, or Spear, representing the Male, the Cup, or Vase, the Female, reproductive energy" (p. 39). In several ancient traditions, these pivotal fertility symbols feature in conjunction "with other objects.... The Dish, which is sometimes the form assumed by the Grail itself, at other times appears as a tailleor, or carving platter of silver, carried in the same procession as the Grail; ... finally, a Sword appears in varying roles in the story.... These four objects ... form a special group entirely independent of any appearance in Folk-lore or Romance." Moreover, the emblems survive to this day "as the four suits of the Tarot," namely:

Cup (Chalice, or Goblet)—Hearts.
Lance (Wand, or Sceptre)—Diamonds.
Sword—Spades.
Dish (Circles, Or Pentangles, the form varies)—Clubs. [p. 40.]

Chrétien de Troyes' *Yvain, or, the Knight with the Lion* contains an oblique reference to the Tarot tradition in the guise of a reference to "swords and clubs" (Chrétien de Troyes 2008b, p. 142), as the weapons deployed by Esclados the Red's revenge-thirsty henchmen against the eponymous hero. Also worthy of notice, on this point, is an illustration from a French manuscript of about 1300, held in the Bodleian Library, Oxford, entitled *Lancelot, on the quest for the Holy Grail, confesses to a hermit living in a wicker hut in a tree*. In this image, the knight's tunic, his shield, and his horse's caparison bear hearts redolent in style of the traditional card suit.

The continuing association between the Tarot tradition and the quest topos in modern literature deserves notice. A prime example is T. S. Eliot's *The Waste Land* (1920), where a selection of Tarot cards is alluded to as a means of suggesting, through an enlacement of intertextual references, that faint hopes of regeneration may exist even amidst the decay of the modern world. A more recent illustration is provided by Italo Calvino's *The Castle of Crossed Destinies* (1973), where two distinct versions of the Tarot pack are used as the underpinnings of the language, or code, in which a motley crew of mute travelers couch their adventures—all of which bear connections, more or less explicit, with the romance tradition.

It is as a result of its appropriation by cultures "unfamiliar with its Ritual origin," and keen on harnessing it to their own purposes, that the original Grail legend was redefined in accordance with contingent ideological priorities. A paradigmatic illustration of this trend resides with the propaganda surrounding the Crusades. At this point, argues Weston, "the consequent traffic in relics, especially in relics of the Passion, caused the identification of the sex Symbols, Lance and Cup, with the Weapon of the Crucifixion, and the Cup of the Last Supper" (p. 101).

According to Pearsall, "in the England of the late fourteenth century there are two Arthurian traditions." One of these can be regarded as the "native tradition, established ... by Geoffrey of Monmouth," and tends to depict Arthur as "a national hero" (Pearsall, p. 60). The other perpetuates the French strand of Arthurian lore initiated by Chrétien de Troyes. The former is exemplified by the "romance-cum-epic of the alliterative *Morte Arthure* [c. 1360]," whereas the latter finds expression in the stanzaic *Morte Arthur*, composed around the same time and inspired by the closing portion of the *Lancelot-Grail* Cycle, the *Mort Artu* (*The Death of Arthur*). "An important difference" between the two works lies with "the nature of their endings. There are no pious consolations at the end of the alliterative *Morte*

Arthure.... But at the end of the stanzaic *Morte Arthur*, the monasteries take over" (p. 71). This work's overall aim is not to celebrate the epic fortitude of a warrior designed to incarnate the virtues of an entire country, but rather, in keeping with the spirit of its source, to stress the inevitability of the Round Table's fall as a corollary of its adherence to secular, as opposed to Christian, tenets. Hence, a threnodical feel imbues the entire poem from start to finish.

"The year 1485 was the high point in the English history of Arthur," argues Pearsall. "Not only did Caxton publish Malory's *Morte d'Arthur* in that year, but there succeeded to the throne a dynasty, the Tudors, who had Welsh ancestry and who claimed descent ultimately from Arthur." It is not surprising, therefore, that the Elizabethan age should witness the emergence of one of the most famous Arthurian works in English literature in the form of Edmund Spenser's *The Faerie Queene* (1590–1596). Yet, this period also marks the beginning of the chivalric romance's gradual disappearance from the limelight of literary fashion, arguably due to cultural shifts entailing a radical redefinition of the model of conduct promoted by the ruling classes. Consequently, "the idealized knight of the feudal retinue," so central to the Arthurian ethos, cedes its once privileged position to "more politically self-conscious figures such as the idealized Tudor governor and Renaissance gentleman (p. 110). This idea will be elaborated in Chapter Five.

In assessing the romance's reputation in the early modern period, it is also vital to appreciate, as Coghlan underlines, that "in an age when people were becoming, for want of a better word, more 'rational' in their outlook, stories of fairies, hags, giants and dragons seemed outmoded, only suitable for the nursery." Furthermore, the aversion to the fantastic enshrined in this outlook was fueled by commercial and religious factors, insofar as the genre was deemed irrelevant to both the economic priorities of the modern age and Protestant suspiciousness regarding its "vaguely 'papist' connotations" (Coghlan, p. 20). A further factor to be taken into consideration is the impact of colonial expansionism on contemporary perceptions of the boundary between reality and fantasy, "the discoveries in the New World of actual places more fabulous than those formerly fabled" requiring the establishment of "a new and more secure barrier between fact and fiction" than the one afforded by medieval romance (Pearsall, p. 111).

The eighteenth century, as the self-professed Age of Reason, was deeply suspicious of anything otherworldly and magical, and therefore developed the trend launched by the Renaissance by deriding Arthurian lore as the province of gullible peasants. Nevertheless, assuming that the chivalric romance drew its last breath in the Renaissance, to be definitively consigned to oblivion by the Age of Reason, would be preposterous. The form's undying popularity over the ages is in fact paradigmatically borne out by its resurgence in the nineteenth century. With the rampant advance of industrialization, a dissatisfaction with materialism began to spread throughout all strata of society, and, above all, among creative thinkers.

One of the outcomes of this cultural phenomenon was a renewed interest in the chivalric narratives of old, which found expression both in literature and in the visual arts. Alfred Tennyson's *Idylls of the King* (1859–1885) and William Morris' *The Defence of Guinevere* (1858) attest to this assertion, as do the numerous pictorial interpretations of key moments and characters in the romance tradition by the Pre-Raphaelites, as well as later Victorian painters. These include Morris himself, Dante Gabriel Rossetti, Edward Coley Burne-Jones, John William Waterhouse, and Edmund Blair Leighton, among several others.

The rehabilitation of chivalric lore signaled by these works stands in stark contrast with the nineteenth century's devotion to the realist ethos promoted by the great novelists of the period, most famously George Eliot and Charles Dickens. However, it is not entirely surprising when we consider, as Coghlan invites us to do, that "the base upon which the realistic approach to literature stood lay in a belief that science had swept the mystery from life like dust from a room and that scientific development would contain the medication for all humanity's ills"—in other words, a highly questionable premise. Indeed, "the scientists themselves" harbored severe doubts as to "where the boundaries of the possible lay and ... what might lie beyond them." As a result, "the 'realistic sureties' were found to have shaky foundations," which is sufficient unto itself to explain why, by the latter half of the nineteenth-century, "the time" should be "ripe for a renewed interest in Arthurian material" (Coghlan, p. 24).

Tennyson's *Idylls* constitute a particularly intriguing case. Pearsall argues that the Victorian poet "took the Arthurian legend seriously, and was committed to a reworking of it, but in order to write an Arthurian cycle that was acceptable to Victorian public taste." Hence, he proceeded to "moralize the whole story into a fable of good and evil, soul and sense." In the process, he also sought to "create an ideal model of the perfect man (figuring Prince Albert), in whom sensuality was subdued to the higher virtues, or sense to soul" (Pearsall, p. 121). Devising such a paragon, and inscribing it within a coherent and satisfying work of literature, was a tricky task. Spenser had already experienced the complexity of this endeavor a few centuries earlier in his effort to style an ideal gentleman, and very possibly arrived at the conclusion that such a goal was unattainable. The fact that Spenser's hero does *not* finally find the object of his quest would seem to militate in favor of this assertion. In his acceptance of inconclusiveness, the Renaissance poet had honored the very spirit of the original chivalric romances which constituted *The Faerie Queene*'s literary precedents.

In Tennyson's case, the difficulty posed by the task of fashioning a credible ideal in the Prince Consort's image sprang from a logical conundrum. This was posed by the incompatibility between the actual individual he sought to eulogize as the ultimate paragon, and the mythical analogue with whom, in principle, such an individual ought to be identified as a latter-day reincarnation. As Pearsall explains, "Arthur could not be [the] model for the Prince, because of course that would make Victoria into Guenevere, and Lancelot could not be the model, for obvious reasons." Hence, in Tennyson's version of Arthurian tradition, the Prince Consort's model is "a non-existent hoped-for person" whom Arthur and the Round Table never had a chance to encounter in the flesh, and "of course eventually arrived in the person of Prince Albert" (p. 122).

While one would not wish to dispute the literary significance of Tennyson's *Idylls*, the text's overall message points to the ultimate clash between genuine art—which ought to be given to the capture of multifarious, even discordant, aspects of the human condition—and religiosity: a mere flattening of everything which humanity has the potential to achieve, in both its virtues and its foibles, to the imperative to abide by a narrow code. In other words, a form as prismatic as the chivalric romance and Tennyson's project are essentially irreconcilable, insofar as the baffling richness, and inherent incongruousness, of the chivalric romance are bound to conflict with the Victorian poet's more monolithic objective.

The reimagining of the legendary king's role and context proffered in the *Idylls* could be read as an effective erosion of the ironies intrinsic in vintage Arthurian lore, and instrumental in its lasting impact—prime among them the unresolved conflict between virtue and adultery, and the discrepancy between chivalric worth and religious piety. In a sense, Tennyson's project stands out as a typical instance of the Victorian proclivity to simplify the most complex of values in the service of prudish moralism. This tendency reflects a desperate urge to demonize the unclean and the improper as a means of exorcizing the more unsavory facets of Victorian society itself.

As Kurt Vonnegut reminds us, on this point, "what would Queen Victoria really feel in the presence of what she had declared to be obscenities? That her power to intimidate was being attacked ever so slightly, far, far, from its center, was being attacked where it could not matter much as yet—was being attacked way out on the edge. She created arbitrary rules for that outermost edge to warn her of the approach of anyone so crude, so rash as to bring to her attention the suffering of the Irish, or the cruelties of the factory system, or the privileges of the nobility, or the approach of a world war, and on and on? If she would not even acknowledge that human beings sometimes farted, how could she be expected to hear without swooning of these other things" (Vonnegut, p. 214)—let alone, we may add, of any intimation that she and her precious spouse might bear any connection with disreputable elements of British tradition?

It is of the utmost importance to bear in mind that before Arthurian lore was entrusted to the written word, Welsh and Breton minstrels had been divulging orally many of the marvelous tales from which the chivalric romance would draw its material in both courtly and popular contexts. Even with the advent of written romances within aristocratic contexts, it remained popular for courtiers to read these stories aloud within a relatively formalized performative context. This suggests that the appetite for shared participation in the romance's fantastic worlds survived, as did the fondness for public performance. It is as though the chivalric romance were reluctant to disengage itself from its performative past well into the days of its scriptorial articulation. This invites reflection on the extent to which oral transmission might have left its traces on texts meant for reading.

Cooper underlines the romance's imbrication with oral performance, arguing that chivalric tales were "ideally suited to being heard rather than read on the page" for the reason that "the use of the vernacular," which distinguished those fictions from "academic discourse," allied to "their exciting narratives," rendered them "immediately accessible." The oral dimension was further enhanced by the romance's versatility "as material for conversation and argument." To grasp this particular aspect of the romance, it is vital to remember that "debate lay at the heart of much medieval culture," and indeed "across most of the civil institutions invented in the Middle Ages: in the law courts, in the king's council, in Parliament, in the universities." In this context, chivalric narratives offered a lay correlative of "academic debate," by involving listeners who "expected to respond actively to them," and authors who endeavored to foster "such a response" through their themes and techniques (Cooper 2008, pp. 12–13).

Douglas Kelly emphasizes that Chrétien de Troyes himself, the author now considered the creator of the chivalric romance, composed narrative poems meant "for reading aloud, using embellishment that enhances such reading while effectively communicating a story and its lessons" (Kelly, p. 52). Chrétien "used metaphorical and figurative language" to boost the practice of vocal narration, which is effectively the capacity to manipulate reality by concomitantly auditory and rhetorical means. At times, the effect is humorous, as exemplified by the scene in *Lancelot, or, the Knight of the Cart* in which the poet "evokes the bone-crunching lions that threaten to eat Lancelot alive after he crosses the Sword Bridge.... More ominous are the sounds and colours of swordplay in combat in *Yvain*.... Such devices are dramatically effective in oral recitation when they enliven verse, sentence or other small units of discourse such as monologues" (pp. 54–55).

It should also be noted that both in the court and in the town square, oral storytelling did not involve a stark separation between the *show*—the narration as such—and the *non-show*—namely, anything happening in parallel to the narration itself, such as reveling, playing, flirting, arguing, eating, and drinking (often to excess). This is a feature of oral storytelling which would be later replicated in the theater-in-the-round, as opposed to the type of auditorium dominated by the proscenium arch. In the absence of a definitive boundary between the performance and its context, the minstrel, the troubadour, the *cantastorie*, could not take it for granted that their listeners, whoever these might be at any one moment, would be actually *listening* to their words.

It is therefore likely that those narrators/musicians/performers would make every effort to spin a plethora of yarns packed with unexpected turns and new developments in an attempt to keep all listeners as entertained as possible regardless of when, and to how much, each of them might be listening. The passion for digressions, ancillary adventures, and multiple climaxes one witnesses in written chivalric romances is heir to its oral ancestor's deployment of those performative ruses.

At the same time, it is worth recalling that even when the romance tradition was fully established, and Arthur had found renown as the epicenter of a court of knight/lovers and the ladies they worshipped, traditional Celtic tales and quasi-historical accounts of Arthur's rise and fall (especially Geoffrey of Monmouth's) were still well-known, and available to professional raconteurs as bountiful reservoirs of material. "The old and the new were interwoven almost inseparably," argues Barber, "so that the storyteller could move easily from one theme to another, bringing them together like the brilliant colours of a tapestry" (Barber 1991, p. 3).

The permutations incurred by the chivalric romance over a period of roughly four centuries, which constitute this book's object of study, demonstrate that this is not a rigid form, but rather a shape-shifting genus which shows itself capable of adapting with great versatility to the ideological and aesthetic requirements of each new era. This contention is further validated by a number of modern texts which have contributed to the growth of the vast intertextual tapestry into which the chivalric romance has been evolving since the twelfth century, by remolding its conventions in accordance with present-day priorities. Past and present come together in unexpected and forever mutable constellations, like dancers fluidly entwined in a kaleidoscope of colors.

Gérard Genette's essay "Structuralism and literary criticism" is worthy of attention, in this perspective. In this seminal work, the literary theorist proposes that the study of texts lends itself to two principal approaches. On the one hand, it is possible to conceive of past and present as distinct dimensions, and apply substantially different interpretative strategies to each. In this scenario, "'living' literature" constitutes the object of continual decoding, and its reading requires direct engagement with texts in the here and now (hermeneutic model). Texts which are "distant and difficult to decipher" (Genette, p. 70), conversely, are the object of formal and narrative analysis (structuralist model).

On the other hand, argues Genette, past and present may be regarded not as mutually negating, but rather as interacting, dimensions. In this perspective, it is the critic's chief responsibility to encourage an ongoing dialogue between them in the reading of *all* texts, regardless of their chronological positioning. This viewpoint proceeds from the premise that the present does not only encompass texts emanating from the current culture, but also past texts which are somehow relevant to the present. The same work may seem "distant" and "living" at once—distant, in the sense that it dates back to a remote period, and thus lends itself to the structuralist reading; yet living, to the extent that it feels pertinent to a present-day readership, and thus lends itself to a hermeneutic reading.

Even though texts appear to remain the same throughout time at the level of their thematic contents, they alter from one second to the next depending on how they are approached, and on the degree of their contingent relevance to a certain audience. It is therefore necessary to conceive of literature not as sequential collection of "autonomous works, which may 'influence' one another by a series of fortuitous and isolated encounters; it is a coherent whole, a homogeneous space, within which works touch and penetrate one another" (p. 73). This ongoing contact among disparate texts imparts all literature with life by precluding its classification in terms of tedious labels and dates, and releasing it instead to infinite metamorphic options. Arthurian literature epitomizes Genette's positions to a paradigmatic degree. Remote by virtue of its historical roots, yet alive due to its inexhaustible relevance, it yields a textual forest of interpenetrating elements: a vast arboreal cartography of overlapping roots, boles, and branches, which propagate by means of incessant graftings and regraftings.

Two

Form and Structure

The animating force at the heart of the chivalric romance is the spirit of adventure. The typical romance hero is not involved in a series of grim battles upon which the fate of his native soil is supposed to hang, such as those one encounters in the epic. On the contrary, as Derek Pearsall observes, he "chooses to go out from a secure bastion of wealth and privilege (such as the Arthurian court) to seek adventures in which the values of chivalry and service to ladies ... will be submitted to test and proved" (Pearsall, p. 21). Erich Auerbach further validates the proposition that the spirit of adventure is the pivotal mechanism driving the knight's quest. Unlike the typical warrior of the *chanson de geste* ("song of heroic deeds"), which constitutes the prototypic epic text in the Carolingian tradition, the romance hero "sets out without mission or office; he seeks adventure, that is, perilous encounters by which he can prove his mettle. There is nothing like this in the *chanson de geste*. There a knight who sets off has an office and a place in a politico-historical context" (Auerbach, p. 133).

So central is the pure spirit of adventure to the wanderings of the typical romance protagonist that the purpose of his quest often becomes subordinate to the action. In fact, the knight errant's exploits do not of necessity pursue any clear goals. Nor do they move towards simple resolutions. Hence, the concept of teleology is of scarce relevance to their unfolding. Open-endedness is instead pivotal to the romance world. Events conjoin in an erratic fashion, thus producing unexpected situations which bear witness to the arbitrariness of fate, and to the ascendancy of serendipity in human life. The form's passion for mystery, magic, and the supernatural fuel these stylistic preferences at every turn.

The ensuing pages examine three pivotal characteristics of the chivalric romance: namely, its centerless structure, its self-conscious profession of fictionality, and its propensity for irony. In a nutshell, the three features can be described as follows:

1. Since adventures proliferate unhindered within its mold, the chivalric romance lacks a stable center: i.e., an identifiable point of reference meant to keep the text's diversity at bay, and corral its disparate elements within the bounds of a single, dependable, meaning.
2. The chivalric romance does not present itself as a purveyor of truth. Quite the opposite, it tends to lay bare its fictional nature with more frankness than most other forms, thus encapsulating the essence of fiction as such.
3. The chivalric romance is infused with the genius of irony. Its polychromy and diffusion foreclose the viability of conclusive interpretations. At the same time, the juxtaposition of conflicting meanings enjoins readers (and listeners) to confront the ironical suspension of truth in their own lives.

As W. P. Ker points out in the influential volume *Epic and Romance* (1957), "whatever epic might mean, it implies some weight and solidity; Romance means nothing if it does not convey some notion of mystery or fantasy.... Beowulf might stand for the one side, Lancelot or Gawain for the other" (Ker, p. 14). While in the conventional heroic narrative, characters "always have good reasons for their own fighting," the "wandering champions of romance" often seem driven only by an irrational "readiness" (pp. 15–16). Hence, the epic is defined by gravity and a solemn sense of the heroic. The romance, conversely, is characterized by a supernatural atmosphere, which may well seem *flimsy* in comparison with the weightiness of epic.

Pearsall reinforces Ker's position, attributing the contrast between the romance's relative levity and the epic's seriousness to the two forms' allegiance to divergent social groupings. While the epic uphold the values of a fundamentally "warlike and male-centred society," the romance "exists," first and foremost, in order to "reflect, celebrate and confirm the chivalric values by which its primary consumers, the noble or knightly class, live or purport to live" (Pearsall, p. 21). It is with the "transplantation of Arthur from England to France," argues the critic, that the traditional ethos enshrined in the "national epic" gives way to the alternate world view of the "courtly romance" (p. 20).

William Comfort lends further credence to the arguments outlined above, maintaining that "epic poems ... portray a warlike, virile, unsentimental feudal society, whose chief occupation was fighting, and whose dominant ideals were faith in God, loyalty to feudal family ties, and bravery in battle. Woman's place is comparatively obscure" (Comfort, p. 10). Where the epic foregrounds combat, the romance dramatizes the aristocracy's engagement in amorous dalliance, courtly games, hunting, jousting, and—above all else—the *search for adventures* which might give the zealous knight a chance to prove his puissance. Even when fighting becomes pivotal to the action of the romance, therefore, it is undertaken in the service of a private code of courtesy rather than a collective cause laden with political significance. Moreover, much of the time, deadly duels and tournaments come about not as a result of voluntary initiative but in accordance with the arbitrary convolutions of fate.

In assessing the different ideological drives animating the epic and the romance, it is crucial to appreciate that the epic was committed to the shaping of national identities: a crucial priority in an era in which the notion of the nation-state was just beginning to penetrate the *Realpolitik* of several European countries. Furthermore, the epic's contribution to a political cause was systematically enhanced by the suggestion that its heroes' actions conformed withGod's will, no less than with an earthly monarch's orders. It is not surprising that the epic should have been "exploited by the Church throughout the period of the crusades," as a means of campaigning on behalf of a "muscular Christianity" (p. 10). The *chanson de geste* proved handy in the advancement of Christian values, given its assiduous casting of heroes whose mission was the protection of Christendom from the encroaching infidel. The romance served no such purpose. For one thing, the Celtic materials at the core of the chivalric romance are pervaded by an atmosphere of eeriness and enchantment which may well appear "inconsistent with the essential teachings of Christianity" (p. 11).

The debate surrounding the relationship between the epic and the romance will be revisited later in this chapter. What is first worth recalling, on the matter of Celticism, is that the Britons, the native inhabitants of Roman Britain, were a people of Celtic stock. Well before the appearance of the chivalric romance as such in the twelfth century, Arthur had already established himself as an important figure in Celtic lore. An exuberant mix of motifs dovetailing in their shared taste for the fantastic, the absurd, and the bizarre, Celtic literature and mythology are essentially the patrimony of peoples connected to a world picture which some might deem "uncivilized." What is here meant by this contentious word is the attribute of an outlook as yet unfettered by oppressive notions of order and stability rooted in an obsessive preoccupation with the achievement and maintenance of political power over and above any other aspect of human endeavor—in other words, the chief concern driving practically the whole of Western society since the Renaissance.

The influence of Celtic literature and mythology constitutes a pivotal force in the evolution of Arthurian lore. In assessing the romance's Celtic affiliations, it is especially useful to consider the Celts' druidic past. As Geoffrey Ashe explains, "essentially, the druids were shamans or medicine men, but in their heyday they were far more, an elaborately trained priesthood, counselors to rulers, custodians of poetry and mythology. Women as well as men could join the order, though their concern perhaps was more with the magical side.... As Christianity took a firmer hold, it squeezed out belief in the gods and goddesses of the druidic era. But Celtic Christians viewed the old divinities and their myths with a tolerance and even attachment that few of their co-religionists shared.... A great deal of pagan mythology survived in storytelling, and sometimes gods and goddesses reemerged disguised as kings, queen, enchanters" (Ashe, pp. 20–21).

Infusing many aspects of the romance world, and especially its appetite for a distinctive type of otherworldliness, the Celtic spirit is often noticeable even in the form's most religious manifestations. The *Lancelot-Grail Cycle*, for example, purports to offer a Christianized version of the Arthurian legend, yet the romance entitled *The Story of Merlin* has the feel of a dark fairy tale with a taste for the fantastic, the outlandish, and even the monstrous. As argued in the chapters to follow, especially vis-à-vis the topos of the Grail Quest, the chivalric romance evinces an unresolved tension between secular and religious leanings. That the tension should remain unresolved is quite congruous with the form's penchant for irony. It is also a corollary of its genetic makeup. Indeed, as long as Arthurian materials are involved, there will always be traces, however spectral or disguised, of an ancient Celtic substratum, and therefore of a fundamentally pagan outlook.

Roger Sherman Loomis underscores the ascendancy of Celtic lore in the romance tradition, stating that "the marvellous element" at its core is "a heritage from the mythology of the Irish and the Welsh, which was preserved by bards and story-tellers long after the introduction of Christianity. It is this well-recognized survival of paganism among the Celts" that generates the enveloping "atmosphere of wonder" typical of the chivalric romance, as well as its trappings. Among the latter, Loomis identifies the following as the most distinctive: "revolving castles, sword-like bridges, springs haunted by fays, isles inhabited only by women, enchantresses who take the form of birds, hags changed by a kiss into damsels of peerless beauty, vessels of inexhaustible plenty, vessels moved by no visible agency, banqueters who preserve a youthful appearance in spite of their many years" (Loomis, p. 111). The list could stretch much further, but this would be only at the detriment of the present argument's momentum. Further details of characteristic magical locations, props, and characters are therefore held in reserve for the analyses of specific texts undertaken in the chapters to follow. What does, however, deserve notice at this stage is the broader philosophical significance of the chivalric romance's imbrication with fantasy.

The fantasy at stake in the chivalric romance is not just *any* fantasy but one specifically defined by the *magical* Weltanschauung. Magic, in this context, must be understood not merely as legerdemain, or a bundle of tricks, charms, hexes and spells, but as a *philosophy*: a *discourse* governed by the principles of endless transformation and transformability. In other words, magic constitutes a way of thinking, and of articulating thought in language. Its animating force is the imagination, which the romance espouses as a prismatic and eclectic power. Echoing Colin McGinn's words, the romance demonstrates that the "imagination is a faculty that runs through the most diverse mental phenomena.... We need imagination to have mental images, to dream, to believe, to represent possibilities, and to mean" (McGinn, p. 5).

By emplacing the imagination as its driving force, the romance uses magic to look at the world from fresh perspectives. Vital to this task is the recognition of the untapped realms which extend in all directions beneath the surface of the visible. To participate in magic means to accept, and commit oneself to, the invisible. By investing its personae with the capacity to beget magical phenomena, the romance intimates that *all* imaginative people, and not just born witches and wizards, are drawn to the invisible as their fundamental treasury.

Rainer Marie Rilke beautifully captures this idea: "we are bees of the invisible. We madly gather the honey of the visible to store it in the great golden hive of the invisible" (Rilke, p. 48). Friedrich Schlegel throws into relief the affinity of magic and the domain of the invisible by declaring that "poetry is the finest branch of magic," insofar as it constitutes an "invisible spirit" (Schlegel, p. 80). The world opened up by magic is a holistic land of infinite connectivity in which everything intermingles with everything else.

Fostering magical thinking, the chivalric romance yields a space-time in which the marvelous co-exists at all times with mundane routines. Its magic is able to envision the invisible, to endow the amorphous with palpable shape, and to place illusion and reality on the same level. Concurrently, the romance reminds us that it is essential to value the magical realm's irreducible alterity and inscrutability, rather than attempt to tame it by rationalizing its wonders.

The romance's approach to the discourse of magic also bears notable analogies with Vilém Flusser's stance on the subject. According to the philosopher, "the universe of traditional images, as yet unclouded by texts, is a world of magical circumstances; a world of eternal recurrence in which everything lends meaning to everything else and everything signifies everything else: a world full of meanings, full of 'gods.'" Flusser's characterization of "creativity" is also relevant to the romance's standpoint, insofar as it portrays that quality as an imaginative contribution to the making of reality. Creativity, for Flusser, is "the production of previously non-existent information" by means of imaginative efforts to "restructure ... preceding items" (Flusser).

The world of magic is often described as "pre-scientific." However, a more accurate definition would be *pre-mythological*. This is because in many cultures, it is mythology that has supplanted magic, by replacing the outlook typical of magical thinking—and hence the belief that the cosmos emanates from the interaction of spirits immanent in all natural forms—with a stance which accords human beings a central position in a cosmos ruled by remote deities.

No-one could deny that the discourse of magic is highly codified, as attested to by disparate traditions and their practitioners: from Persian magi to Siberian shamans, from Native American witch doctors to Afro-Caribbean voodoo masters, from Celtic druids to Pharaonic magicians, from European alchemists to Shintō *kannushi*—to mention no more than a diminutive number of possible examples. Yet, since magic honors the principle of ceaseless metamorphosis, it is predicated on a vision of the universe as *fluid*. Mythology, by contrast, has insistently sought to promulgate stable meanings by inscribing its beliefs in texts invested with quasi-divine status.

Science has followed a more hybrid trajectory. While the Enlightenment enthroned science as the sole means of arriving at objective truth, genuine science is untrammeled by the vaporous pretensions of Rationalism, and remains open to ongoing revision. In a sense, the scientific mindset is closer to the magical than to the mythological one in its own intrinsic affinity with the view of the universe as an open-ended process, always susceptible to reinterpretation and redefinition.

The interplay of magic and technology deserves consideration. "Ever since the Middle Ages," argues Eddo Stern, "the discourse of magic emanating primarily from the pagan remnants of the Roman Empire and that of the new scientific reason have battled for sovereignty over the human soul's epistemological allegiance. The science and magic of farming calendars, home remedies, astronomical maps and alchemical concoctions are only a few examples of preoccupations that originated in the context of magical belief systems and were gradually transitioned to fall under a scientific rubric during the Middle Ages" (Stern, p. 259). Nowadays, "technology operates to realize what was previously in the hypothetical realm of magic. There is definitely some connection in the way both magic and technology create a sense of wonder as they seem to expand upon the notions of what is or has been feasible in the realm or the real." Stern cites A. C. Clarke's oft-cited aphorism—"any sufficiently advanced technology is indistinguishable from magic"—in support of his hypothesis (p. 260).

Marina Warner backs this idea, stating that "modernity did not by any means put an end to the quest for spirit and the desire to explain its mystery" (Warner 2006, p. 10). Technological developments further corroborate this proposition: "as the vast army of modern inventions began to change our experience of the world—from the telescope and the microscope onwards—their advent interacted with imagery from antiquity and theology which had dominated thought about the stuff of the spirit." Therefore, the "patterns of data and thought" which are still imprinted on the human brain are permeated by "the figures of the inner world, unavailable to the senses" (p. 12).

Even the most casual reader will be quick to notice that chivalric romances harbor a fascination with *monsters*: a handy term to designate a rich gallery of multifarious creatures—by no means always *ugly*, as Faërie's denizens indicate—which signal a troubling departure from so-called normal humanity, at the same time as they raise questions about the solidity of the concept of humanity itself. As Stephen King points out, "it is not the physical or mental aberration in itself which horrifies us, but rather the lack of order which these aberrations seem to imply" (King, pp. 55–56) In other words, monstrosity terrifies us because it reminds us that the systems on which we routinely rely as a means of asserting and perpetuating agreed notions of stability and lawfulness are not so reliable after all, since the monstrous Other is at liberty to infiltrate them unhindered. Monsters can be said to incarnate a culture's anxiety about its precariousness: an apprehension which often afflicts, ironically, the very societies which go to the greatest of lengths to proclaim their impregnability.

The knight's destruction of one or the other manifestation of monstrosity which he encounters along his journey does not guarantee the permanent restoration of the order which the Other has challenged. In fact, the monster's ability to materialize out of the blue in any conceivable context (Arthur's court included) alludes to its virtual ubiquity. The materialization of *one* monster symbolizes monstrosity's knack of appearing *anywhere and anytime* without scruples.

Monsters fulfill a major role in unveiling the discrepancy between the ideal of the knight as a perfect superman, and the reality of the knight as a flawed human. Indeed, romance monsters tend to expose the inherent vulnerability, imperfection, and incompleteness of both the human characters they confront, and the social order which these people are supposed to uphold. This capacity is quite consonant with the etymology of the word "monster": namely, the Latin *demonstrare*, which translates as "to reveal," "to disclose." Like the dread it so often induces, the monstrous other holds illuminating potentialities, insofar as it awakens its human counterpart to his or her own inadequacies.

Jeff Rider corroborates this proposition. "Like the other worlds of modern cinema, television, and print," argues the scholar, "the other worlds of romance were laboratories of fears and longings whose monstrous, elegant and fantasized elaborations medieval audiences enjoyed in the same way that we do those of our media.... Other worlds are thus repositories of everything 'we' lack and are not" (Rider, p. 129).

On the other hand, in making the romance hero aware that neither the world he inhabits nor his private self are exempt from failure, the monster implicitly incites him to strengthen the social order which its very monstrosity appears to threaten. Furthermore, by challenging the knight to face Otherness at its most fearsome, the monster prompts him to develop defensive strategies which are bound to prove precious in countless confrontational situations. According to J. B. Twitchell, to lay oneself open to horror, a concept which monstrosity epitomizes to a proverbial degree, is an attempt "to practice controlling one of our primary impulses—the impulse to flee" (Twitchell, p. 5). Thus, monsters throw human limitations into relief, but also ignite humanity's instinct for self-protection. They do not make conclusive inroads into the structures which humans erect so as to assert their concept of order: on the contrary, they abet the consolidation of those formations. "Night visitors prepare us for daylight," states Twitchell (p. 7).

It is also worth noting, in this perspective, that the monstrous masks and costumes of the Carnival serve an analogous fashion, declaring in emblematic and ceremonial form the human determination to survive danger. As Warner maintains, "the magical attempt to secure safety takes two predominant forms: either the participants impersonate the danger itself ... and thus, cannibal-like, absorb its powers and defeat its ability to inflict harm; or they expose themselves and by surviving the ordeal, prove their invulnerability" (Warner 2000, p. 112).

Chrétien's romances provide illustrations of both trends. The eponymous hero in *Lancelot, the Knight of the Cart* epitomizes the former. In agreeing, albeit with a moment of hesitation that will cost him dear, to ride the cart reserved for criminals, he embraces the identity of a pariah—a social monster—and opens himself to a fate of opprobrium. Yet, this action also boosts his knightly excellence by enabling Lancelot to harness the unlawful Other's powers to his panoply of virtues. Yvain from *Yvain, or, the Knight with the Lion* exemplifies the latter. His willingness to confront the monstrous bull-master (a harmless, albeit hideous, creature comparable to a noble savage), and, with much greater consequence, the supernatural knight who rules over the magical spring, Esclados the Red, he reveals his capacity to prevail over the Other through either civil conversation or brutal combat, as the situation might necessitate.

A character like the eponymous hero of *Le Chanson de Roland* stands for a static world picture in which individual thoughts, feelings, and actions abide by the predetermined rules of a seemingly inflexible political/religious system. "*Roland*'s world," states Eugene Vance, "is one of hierarchies, and ascendance is the ethical imperative of that world; and, with ascendance, comes the merger of individual heroic will with that of a heroic God in whose belligerent image Roland wills to fight" (Vance, p. 11). Grand political matters are of scant interest to the romance author, while God frequently features as little more than a figure of speech. At times—in Chrétien's *Yvain, or, the Knight with the Lion*, for instance—the deity is addressed with a degree of light-heartedness verging on disrespect. In the romance at large, loyalty to the king exceeds in importance the knight's allegiance to any preternatural power. Even this rule is relative, however, since the royal personage often comes across as a master of the revels rather than a political figurehead, and evinces unpalatable human foibles and quirks, in spite of his putatively unmatched virtues. In fact, his power may dissolve altogether when challenged by a representative of Faërie's alternate universe.

The chivalric romance disengages itself from the values which dominate the world of the *chanson de geste* in order to evoke a world of fortuity, contingency, and randomness. Not even the most formulaic incident, in this context, is ever wholly predictable, since the very notion of predetermination, if it figures at all, is there to be flouted, played with, and distorted at will. Thus, the world of the romance "is primarily one of imminent, horizontal relationships between things and people, and a true perception and proper judgment of those relationships here and now is a precondition of ethically responsible action" (Vance, p. 11).

This philosophy is reinforced by the form's take on daily reality. While the epic strives to elevate its heroes' adventures above all ordinary concerns and habitual customs of an obviously *un*heroic nature, "it is typical of romance to be much occupied with the everyday paraphernalia of the world it creates," as Gillian Beer explains. "The descriptions of clothes and feasts ... give body to its ideal world. They make it physically present" (Beer, p. 3). The lofty ideology of the epic gives way to a code of conduct which, strict though it is, remains firmly grounded in the here and now.

At the same time, the romance's divergence from the plots perpetuated by the epic could hardly be more blatant. Nevertheless, it is important to bear in mind that in their heyday, the two forms often shared the same audiences. As Simon Gaunt explains, on this point, "although it is likely that some early *chansons de geste* were transmitted orally and addressed to a broad non-courtly audience, many surviving texts are preserved in luxurious compilations that were clearly commissioned for a wealthy lay audience. In other words, their likely public was the same courtly audience that listened to romances and indeed sometimes *chansons de geste* and romances are preserved in the same compilations" (Gaunt, pp. 48–49).

Gaunt's elucidation of the dynamics of reception met by the epic and the romance over time suggests that the two forms might have been involved in mutual cross-pollination. Indeed, the coexistence of epic and romance narratives within the covers of a single text evokes a cultural scenario in which the generic boundaries treasured by post-medieval literary communities do not obtain, and different forms are therefore at liberty to cohabit in harmony, or perhaps merge as complementary—rather than antithetical—sources of entertainment in their receivers' minds and senses. One may go so far as to propose that in the large collections described by Gaunt, epic and romance rub off on each other through symbiotic interplay, to the extent that a reader's (or listener's) responses to the romance might be affected, albeit subliminally, by familiarity with the epic, and vice versa.

In *Faust*, Goethe distinguishes between the "small world" and the "wide world" to polarize two attitudes to life centered on the principles of reduction and expansiveness respectively. The "small world" designates a cocooned existence guarded by unexamined assumptions, and a good dose of self-righteousness. The "wide world," by contrast, points to the desire to look beyond one's immediate situation, and stretch one's purview of things into the inscrutable. Goethe's distinction carries crucial repercussions in all areas of human existence, posing questions of an ethical, aesthetic, and broadly political nature for anyone willing to pay it heed.

On the surface, the epic, by dealing with big deeds centered on large groups, should be synonymous with the "wide world," but is actually caught up in contingent pursuits, such as the establishment of a national identity, or the defence of a specific belief system, and is hence circumscribed by the local, even parochial, priorities of a "small world." The romance, conversely, may appear to treat small-scale quests which revolve around individuals, and seem motivated by trivial events or desires. Hence, it should belong in a "small world." In fact, it ushers in an expansive world view, proposing a bold unlimiting of human experience through the trope of errantry. The knight errant's adventures are constantly expanding from within through endless digressions and detours. The text thrives on open-endedness, supplying no final answers but yielding instead an ironical suspension of both belief and disbelief. Thus, an ostensibly limited world turns into a boundless realm of forever growing possibilities akin to Goethe's "wide world."

As Beer points out, the typical romance pivots on "a complex and prolonged succession of incidents usually without a single climax" (Beer, p. 10). David Lodge sees the form's incorporation of multiple climaxes as pivotal to its identity. Contrasting the epic and the romance by recourse to an erotic metaphor, Lodge proposes that the "epic" tends to "move inexorably to … an essentially *male* climax—a single, explosive discharge of accumulated tension. Romance, in contrast, is not structured this way. It has not one climax, but many, the pleasure of this text comes and comes and comes again. No sooner is one crisis in the fortunes of the hero averted than a new one presents itself; no sooner has one mystery been solved than another is raised; no sooner has one adventure been concluded than another begins. The narrative questions open and close, open and close…. Romance is a multiple orgasm" (Lodge, pp. 322–323). This makes the poly-climactic romance a female form, in contrast with the mono-climactic, and hence implicitly male, epic.

Lodge's allusion to the sexual undertones of the romance brings to mind Roland Barthes' *The Pleasure of the Text*, and specifically the philosopher's theorization of the kind of writing (*écriture*) likely to induce the form of pleasure known as *jouissance* (a term translatable as "bliss," or "orgasm"), as opposed to the meeker *plaisir*. While the text which grants mere pleasure is one which "contents, fills, grants euphoria," and is thus conducive to "a *comfortable* practice of reading," the text of *jouissance* "unsettles the reader's historical, cultural, psychological assumptions, the consistency of his tastes, values, memories, brings to a crisis his relation with language" (Barthes 1975, p. 14).

A useful illustration of the romance's affiliation with the spirit of *jouissance* can be found in the narrative delivered by the character of Suor Teodora in Italo Calvino's *The Non-Existent Knight* (1959): a text which testifies with unparalleled vibrance to the timeless propagation of the chivalric romance. Calvino's nun—herself depicted as the author of a romance—is an intriguing and unusual narrator who luxuriates in the production of a text which posits the act of writing as virtually synonymous with love-making.

A key move performed by the romance so as to weave a text of *jouissance* is the avoidance of the law of causality whenever possible, in favor of bizarre and coincidence-riddled incidents. At the same time, realism and the supernatural freely intertwine, as do adventure and love, pleasure and strife. As Paddy Bostock suggests, the strategies and tropes characteristically deployed by the romance enhance its idiosyncratic tastes. The following are most notable: "there is little use of foreshadowing or anticipation of events.... Instructors or helpers are common.... Women characters have the typical forwardness of fairy mistresses.... The concept of doubles, as representative of the extreme edges of the hero's personality, is common. The hero's quest often takes him to the 'chapel perilous' where he will learn crucial information" (Bostock, pp. 79–81).

The strategies and tropes delineated above assist the generation of a tantalizing reading experience of the kind described by Barthes vis-à-vis the text of *jouissance*. Their cumulative effect is to absorb the reader into a realm in which all sorts of familiar and trusted boundaries are suddenly disrupted. By shunning the use of foreshadowing and anticipation, the author or teller is free to create spectacular *coups de théâtre* which bear no causal or logical connection with anything which has happened before. Peppering the narrative with magical personae such as mentors, aides, ladies redolent of fairy concubines, and doubles is bound to abet to great effect the form's eschewal of both logic and reason. It is quite fitting, in this perspective, that so many tales should feature eerie test-centered climaxes pregnant with mystical undertones.

The traditional chivalric romance is underpinned by the mechanism of deferral. This pivots on the employment of a wandering—or errant—figure as the narrative's leading thread. According to Vance, an epic like *La Chanson de Roland* equates "the marvelous" to "an esthetics of force," by positing it as a secondary accessory of martial prowess. The romance, on the other hand, links it to "the quest for *sens* or *senefiance* and even with the very process of *écriture* ... understood as a pleasure in subtlety" (Vance, p. 20). It is worth noting, in this context, that *sens* is translatable as both "meaning" and "direction," while *senefiance*, in Old French, means both "sign" and "significance." Vance's association of the romance's handling of the "process of *écriture*" as a special kind of "pleasure" echoes Barthes' coupling of *écriture* and *jouissance* in texts which subvert the reader's expectations by rejecting the obvious and the conventional.

Let us consider how the key terms in Vance's argument might concatenate in the romance form. A knight's search for "meaning" is not guided by strict laws of the epic ilk. Lacking any obvious trajectory and destination, the search for "meaning" is also an attempt to discover a "direction": an effort which the knight's peregrinations continually renew and, on the whole, leave unresolved. Furthermore, the knight's quest is a search for a "sign"—i.e., a mark or pointer which might offer some guidance in this directionless world—at the same time as it lures the character with the promise that he would be accorded "significance" if his venture were to prove successful. Therefore, meaning and direction (*sens*) constitute the aims of the romance hero's twisty wanderings, while sign and significance (*senefiance*) represent their potential results. The two pairings—meaning and direction, sign and significance—bear a common trait of pivotal import in the romance world: *forever deferred realization*.

Beer reinforces the idea that the chivalric romance reflects a meandering temperament, arguing that this genre is distinguished by "a peculiar vagrancy of imagination" (Beer, p. 4). This approach to storytelling may well be deemed frustrating (or even indefensible) by modern readers who have grown so accustomed to the so-called realist novel as to expect satisfying casual linkages, and neatly rounded-off endings. Nonetheless, it is inseparable from the narrative premises from which most romances proceed: i.e., the idea that their protagonists' quests are devoid of precise objectives, and the concurrent assumption that were any such targets to materialize, their achievement would be susceptible to endless postponement.

A paradigmatic illustration of this structural trend is provided by the *Lancelot-Grail Cycle* (a.k.a. the *Vulgate Cycle,* or the Prose *Lancelot*): a series of five volumes chronicling the history the Holy Grail, Merlin's adventures, the troubled affair between Lancelot and Guinevere, the quest for the Holy Grail, and Arthur's death. At one point, King Arthur meets a grievously wounded knight, who implores the monarch to find someone willing to relieve his suffering, and avenge him. The narrative then abandons the wounded knight for quite some time, lingering instead on the arrival at Arthur's court of the Lady of the Lake and the young Lancelot, on the latter's investiture, and on his first meeting with Guinevere. When the tale returns to the wounded knight, this is to tell us how Lancelot removes the weapons lodged into his wounds, and promises to avenge him, which gives it an excuse to digress into a lengthy series of independent adventures. As Eugène Vinaver explains, it is only "after an interval which in any modern edition would occupy about a hundred pages" that "we are told of Lancelot's first battle on behalf of the wounded knight" (Vinaver, p. 17). The topic is again left behind, however, as the text chooses to focus on other matters instead.

What is extraordinary about this narrative—as indeed about several others in its category—is the extent to which, even when its author appears to have forgotten his priorities, he actually retains them very much at the forefront of his mind, albeit in an oblique and, upon casual inspection, imperceptible fashion. Thus, all of the themes which the text intersperses with the plight of the wounded knight turn out to have been "carefully interwoven with one another, entwined, latticed, knotted or plaited like the themes in a Romanesque ornament.... When eight hundred pages after the first appearance of the wounded knight and some time after the last occurrence of the theme we meet the knight again," and are apprised of his identity at last, the reader's mind can grasp in one go all of the theme's "scattered fragments," perceiving sense where only random deviations and curious detours seemed to obtain at first (pp. 17–18). Among the devices used to facilitate this result, special credit is owed to *entrelacement*: i.e., narrative interlacing, a term coined by Ferdinand Lot in his seminal *Étude sur le "Lancelot" en Prose* (1918).

The verb "to err" is preferable to the verb "to wander," in this perspective, insofar as it alludes to the knight's propensity not only to roam and ramble, but also "to blunder." The knight errant goes astray in both a literal and a figurative sense, as he rides along from one adventure to the next, one test to the next, one love to the next. Patricia Parker underscores this idea in her portrait of the romance as "that mode or tendency which remains on the threshold before the promised end, still in the wilderness of wandering, 'error' or 'trial'" (Parker, p. 4). The spaces through which the knight errant journeys in his search for adventures, such as the wasteland and the tangled woods, symbolize the principles of suspension and deferral central to the chivalric romance as a form. These recurring loci provide ideal stages for the character's endless drifting, while also emphasizing his susceptibility to spells and delusions bound to exacerbate the incidence of potentially fatal bungles.

The chivalric romance's typical hero is not just someone who tends to get sidetracked as he journeys along, and thus averted from his purpose, as a result of his inner disposition or (ill) luck. Were this the case, his displacement would be only one aspect of the text's subject matter. In fact, the knight errant is set adrift by the very force which drives the narrative. The text's architectonics itself demands that he be caught up in uncontrollable and ever-shifting currents. Seen from this angle, errantry is not just a corollary of content, but rather a formal and structural event pregnant with affective and philosophical implications.

The knight errant is *meant* to err because the text in which his adventures are couched is *not meant* to provide decisive resolutions. In fact, one senses that if the romance were to afford any clear guarantees of success, the unique kind of satisfaction it yields would evaporate. As Vinaver observes, one of the most salient (and amusing) things about the medieval romance is the way its personae "behave as though" shifting from one adventure to the next according to no logical principle "were an accepted mode of living, requiring no apology or explanation, and as though they themselves were involved, not, as we would imagine, in a series of unhappy accidents but in an enviable pursuit, to be sought after and enjoyed." In this fashion, the chivalric romance defies any attempt to identify a clear "rational principle behind it. The knights-errant whom we try to follow as they make their way through a forest—that ancient symbol of uncertain fate—are apt to abandon at any time one quest for the sake of another, only to be sidetracked again a moment later" (Vinaver, p. 8).

The wandering knight's predicament recalls Jacques Lacan's portrait of the human condition itself as one of capricious drifting. "Life," argues Lacan, "is something which goes ... *à la dérive*. Life goes down the river, from time to time touching a bank, staying for a while here and there, without understanding anything" (Lacan 1972, p. 190). The romance emphasizes the wayward and giddy rhythms of life at each turn. Errantry and erraticness combine to shape the destiny of its characters as one of perpetual mutability and displacement. Furthermore, the classic knight errs ad infinitum because the ultimate goal which his quest requires him to pursue symbolizes an unreachable objective: that is, an unfulfillable object of desire. This is the human thirst for total gratification, happiness, or peace: in other words, concepts which exist only *as such*—as disembodied ideas—and will never find satisfaction in real life.

This state of affairs brings to mind Lacan's proposition that human desire cannot be satisfied, because it is at root a longing for wholeness: an objective which the individual, in order to operate in adult society, must relinquish altogether. Since words are not material *things*, but conventional symbols of a purely arbitrary nature, they are bound to lack substance. Words *destroy* things as such. Upon entering the Symbolic Order of language, human beings themselves are reduced to the status of incorporeal words. Each individual becomes an "I": a mere *shifter*—i.e., a part of speech which carries no intrinsic value, and only makes sense, therefore, with reference to the context in which it is used. To live as a socialized grown-up, one has no choice but to depend on signs which negate the possibility of plenitude to the extent that they mark the absence of the things they designate: they operate on the basis of a lack, a systemic denial of completeness.

The subject's insertion in an order whose very functioning is founded upon the principle of absence entails that no experience can ever supply anything other than an unreliable approximation to true plenitude—an insubstantial specter akin to the knights and destriers of the Wild Hunt often found in Celtic lore. This is an eerie jaunt led by a king (sometimes Arthur himself), in which a ghostly bunch of mounted huntsmen ride across the skies, searching for an unnamed object with crazy zeal, their eager hounds in hot pursuit—in other words, a phantom quest, undertaken by a likewise spectral cast, unfolding in an unfathomable dimension, and encrypted in indecipherable symbols.

The chivalric romance uses the code of courtly love (*fin amor*) as a handy means of ratifying the destiny of unfulfillment to which humans are fated, sanctioning that the knight must worship the object of his desire from a distance, and wander for her sake from one adventure to another in the knowledge that no conclusive success is available. In the scenario of uncompromising lack depicted by Lacan, courtly love performs a consolatory function. In the code's twisted logic, the impossibility of ever achieving the desired goal is posited not as a random mishap, but rather as a vital prerequisite. This involves that courtly love cannot provide plenitude because it is *not intended* to do so. To give a courtly-love tale a fully rounded ending in which the knight pleases the lady whom he seeks to serve, and the two live happily ever after would deprive it of its *quidditas*—its "courtly-loveness," as it were. Lacan indeed portrays courtly love as "an altogether refined way of making up for the absence of sexual relation by pretending that it is we who put up an obstacle to it" (Lacan 1985, p. 141).

The part of the forever loyal, albeit forever unrequited, admirer may not seem a particularly desirable role, yet the knight has no choice but to play it since, "for all his heroic qualities," he "is nothing without the love of his lady. She is his inspiration and without her love he is incapable of action" ("Romances of Chivalry"). Thus, while chivalry requires qualities such as martial prowess, courage, honor, and indifference to material rewards, these assets would fade into insignificance without a refined sense of *courtesy*: namely, the steadfast cultivation of courtly manners like elegance and bonhomie, which is expected to manifest itself primarily as gentility towards women.

It must be stressed, however, that the romance also cultivates an intentional discrepancy between the figure of the idealized woman as a *dramatic role*—i.e., a formula designed to serve the text's formal demands—and the *actual character* of the courtly lady—which may leave rather a lot to be desired. (Queen Guinevere illustrates this point most conspicuously.) Indeed, in placing the courtly dame on a pedestal in order to bolster its erratic tempo and its inconclusiveness, the romance is by no means advancing a moral message centered on the ethical superiority of a *real* type of woman—let alone alluding to woman's symbolic connection with a Christian "angel," despite the courtly lady's angelic connotations.

Once in a while, a knight does manage to achieve his supreme goal, and gain the favors of the beloved. Not even on such occasions, however, is there any guarantee of ever-after happiness. A good example is the lay of *Sir Launfal*. At the end, the protagonist is rewarded by his admission to the loved one's glorious court. However, the realm to which he is spirited by the lady and her entourage at the close of his ordeal is the land of Faërie, a mysterious Otherworld which humans may only inhabit at their own peril. Once drawn into Faërie's enchantment, few people make it back home even if they want to Furthermore, excessively prolonged commingling with Faërie's denizens may cause the human visitors to remain interminably spellbound, or even lead them to madness. It is one thing for a human to catch a glimpse of the Gentry's world by peeking into their chandelier-lit great halls through a door left ajar between this world and the Otherworld, for instance, or espying a Fairy Cavalcade with its sinuous lines of exquisite creatures on their steeds. Even a nocturnal visit to a stately manor, and participation in a sumptuous fairy feast, may leave the human guest unscathed.

Yet, it is quite another to hope to partake of Faërie's lifestyle ad infinitum without laying oneself open to mysterious hazards.

The code of courtly love, writes Richard Barber, "was derived from the literature of Southern France, where, from the beginning of the twelfth century, the troubadours had elaborated on the theme of the superiority of the lady and the moral worth to which the worshipping lover could attain, investing the beloved with an aura of divinity" (Barber 1991, p. 55). As Norris J. Lacy explains, "the 'theory' of courtly love is contained in *De amore* ('On Love') by Andreas Capellanus, a twelfth-century contemporary of Chrétien who described 'courts of love' that adjudicated questions of amorous duty and service. Andreas also included a long list of love's 'rules,' in which he affirmed that love and marriage are incompatible and described the actions and reactions appropriate to lovers" (Lacy 1997, p. 71). What is most intriguing, for the purpose of the present argument, is that the ideas contained in *De amore* should have caught the collective imagination as though they resulted from earnest philosophical speculation, when the tract was only ever meant as a purely *ironical* commentary on the vagaries of sexual relationships.

John Stevens stresses that it is vital to appreciate the uniqueness of courtly love as "a distinct variation of romantic love" in eminently *social* terms—i.e., as a function of the values and aspirations of a very specific cultural stratum and its milieu. What distinguishes courtly love from other forms of idealized amatory practice consists chiefly of "its aristocratic connections, its identification with the way of life of a particular class. This is romantic love for the very best people. Not only that, it is romantic love made sociable, fit for the dinner-table and the drawing-room. It is, indeed, the essential paradox of courtly love, that an intensely private experience is made the ground of social well-being" (Stevens, pp. 39–40). Its association with courtly love reinforces the chivalric romance's intrinsic commitment to the Janus-faced spirit of irony. The normally conflicting demands of intimacy and conviviality coexist in a spirited dialectical tension rarely found in later elaborations of romantic love.

It is also noteworthy, with regard to the romance's penchant for ironic contradictions, that the code of courtly love pandered to a fantasy of wish fulfillment which did not correspond to any actual state of affairs. Indeed, the culture in which *fin amor* thrived was one in which "the actual relations between the sexes were rigidly prescribed by the Church and by feudal practice, rather than by the sentiments of the individuals concerned" (Comfort, p. 8). Both authors and audiences would have been well aware of the discrepancy between courtly love and Christian ethics, cherishing the former as a lawful (at least within certain limits) means of indulging in an alternate set of standards, desires, and aspirations.

Despite the prominence of the code of courtly love as one of the romance's most distinctive appurtenances, it would be quite erroneous to assume that romance writers embrace that ethos in a mechanical fashion, without ever examining its foundations, objectives, and both private and social implications. In actual fact, even the supposed founder of the chivalric romance, Chrétien de Troyes, approaches courtly love in a critical mode, albeit with genial tolerance. Peter Haidu expounds this proposition in his study of *Perceval, the Story of the Grail*, where he maintains that Chrétien offers "courtly relationships ... for observation and judgment, not acceptance or identification. They are materials, not purposes; their pretensions are the characters' not the author's." Thus, Chrétien "is not a courtly writer in the sense that he propagandizes the ideals of courtly love, but only in using them as literary subjects toward which he suggests an attitude which is primarily ironic" (Haidu, p. 262).

Critics have often posited the automatic celebration of the ethos of courtly love as one of the chivalric romance's chief attributes. Chrétien's stance explodes this supposition. If unquestioning adherence to the philosophy of *fin amor* were indeed a prerequisite of the form, this would be pivotal to its progenitor's oeuvre. The fact that Chrétien is already interrogating the validity of courtly love makes one wonder whether the allegiance to that code might in fact be a figment of modern critics' imagination more than a real trait of the chivalric romance as such.

In chivalric romances informed by Arthurian lore, one witnesses a gradual Christianization of originally pagan motifs, the Grail in particular, which reflects a particular ideological climate. It is in this context, as intimated earlier, that Sir Galahad is promoted to quasi-divine status. Nevertheless, the overall thrust of the texts examined in this study is of a secular kind. Their stories do not pretend to harbor universal truths associated with celestial forces. In fact, they locate both the causes of their characters' ordeals, and the measures taken to resolve such predicaments, with the human. Unlike classical drama, where providential powers are held responsible for punishing hubris, and administering the law of nemesis, chivalric romances as yet uncontaminated by Christianity leave gods out of the game. Supernatural entities abound, but they belong to the domain of Faërie, or else to a venerable dynasty of witches and warlocks with decidedly pagan properties and leanings. This is equally the case in Chrétien de Troyes' early romances, and Shakespeare's much later adaptations of the form.

What deserves notice, in assessing the relevance of the chivalric romance to modernity, and indeed to today's world, is that the "secular moment" it marks is a relatively short-lived one. Not long after the end of the time span here covered, providentialism returns to the scene. In Milton, for example, or in the works of Corneille and Racine, deities are as influential as they were in Aeschilus or Sophocles. As to what might have triggered such a shift, one possible answer is the incremental transition towards the ideology of the Enlightenment, or Age of Reason. This is somewhat paradoxical, given that reason is construed as a human endowment—indeed as evidence of the individual's very *existence* as a human (*cogito, ergo sum*).

It is not so bizarre, however, if one considers that the gradual deification of reason per se comes to posit this faculty as akin to a *god-within-man*: an earthly correlative of heavenly providence, and even proof of the existence of divine forces behind the human knack of ratiocination. At the same time, it is feasible that humanity, having appropriated a superior power, might have become prey to the fear of having thus committed the sin of hubris, and hence exposed itself to the prospect of nemesis. It would be logical, were this the case, for humans to seek to honor the putatively transcendental agents of providence, by showing that the idolization of Reason is not tantamount to a sacrilegious discarding of the divine per se in the service of secularism.

With the ascendancy of realism in the nineteenth century, providentialism finds new ways of asserting itself, not least in the guise of the realist text itself (be it literary or visual), as a presence comparable to a superior power, and capable of functioning as the ultimate receptacle of truth. Taking a huge leap forward to the present day, one discovers that providentialism is still very much with us in the form of a crusading fundamentalism of often rabid intensity. Combined with the reduction of diverse cultural phenomena to a pageant of simulacra, this often seems to preclude the likelihood of many (if *any*) truly challenging voices and texts making their imprint on the contemporary scene.

C. S. Lewis describes the medieval romance as a "polyphonic narrative" (Lewis). It is worth noting, in this regard, that polyphony, as a musical term, refers to the combination of several parts which elaborate independent melodies, yet harmonize with one another. In the chivalric romance, accordingly, various characters, events, narrative threads, and climaxes develop with seeming autonomy, but are actually integrated within a coherent ensemble. Most importantly, the form's polyphony gives the chivalric romance an essentially *acentered*—or *center-less*—narrative structure.

This situation invokes Jacques Derrida's philosophy, and in particular, its commitment to a sustained critique of the concept of center as the guarantee of meaning and truth. While praising classic structuralism for its analytical approach to human culture, Derrida questions its tendency to invest all manner of structures—which are at base fluid systems made of many disparate elements, and whose functioning depends on the capacity to mutate and evolve—with a single, fixed center, feasibly in an attempt to keep the system's volatility at bay. "Transcendental signifiers" such as Truth, God, Being, and Reason have proved most popular in many societies as apposite incarnations of such a privileged point. "The function of this center," argues Derrida, "was not only to orient, balance, and organize the structure ... but above all to make sure that the organizing principle of the structure would limit what we might call the *play* of the structure" (Derrida, p. 109).

The center is meant to anchor the structure by keeping at bay its mobility and mutability. These two phenomena underpin the structure's "structurality": namely, its fundamental quality. As "the point at which the substitution of content, elements, or terms is no longer possible," the center is the point where the structure loses its fundamental quality. It lacks the very feature—structurality—which, as a structure's most representative point, it logically ought to incarnate without fail: "the center, which is by definition unique," represents "that very thing within a structure which, while governing the structure, escapes structurality.... The center is, paradoxically, *within* the structure and *outside* it." This entails, in a fabulous twist of logic of which the most proficient medieval romancer would be proud, that "the center is not the center" (Derrida, p. 109). Transcendental signifiers, in this perspective, can only be accepted as reliable principles through an act of faith—i.e., through dogmatic acceptance of their validity. The chivalric romance refuses to sustain the faith-based ideology which grants centers unquestioned (and ultimately illogical) value through its exuberant flouting of any center whatsoever.

The Romanesque ornament mentioned by Vinaver as an apt visual correlative for the chivalric romance again comes to mind, insofar as in this kind of motif, "the expansion is not, as in classical ornament, a movement towards or away from a real or imaginary centre—but towards potential infinity" (Vinaver, p. 13). The effect is abetted by the fact that the romance writer does not only recount the events which find realization on the page: on the contrary, he simultaneously alludes to "endless possibilities of further growth"—namely, to the *unrealized* events lurking in the margins and between the lines. As a result, the text suggests that "everything we see or read about is part of a wider canvas, of a work still unwritten, of a design still unfulfilled" (p. 15).

We are thus reminded that all texts, regardless of their amplitude and preciseness, are bound to bow to the principle of selection, and hence organize their narratives as sequential, syntagmatic, strings of utterances. No text, therefore, could ever presume to capture the entire paradigm from which its words and images are chosen. However, some texts may at least venture to *hint* at the countless options potentially at their disposal. Pure fiction—as epitomized by the chivalric romance—accepts the inevitable limitations of writing, and its attendant dependence on the syntagmatic chain. Yet, it is at the same time capable of alluding to an inexhaustible network of unrealized potentialities: of unwritten stories waiting to be written, and indeed straining to cross over from the text's borders and blank spaces into its visible patterns of signs.

Its passion for multiplicity makes the chivalric romance an intrinsically *ironic* mode. Indeed, multiplicity entails the inclusion of divergent viewpoints, meanings, and voices. The typical textual operations seen in the chivalric romance recall the actions performed by the *eiron* of ancient drama (the root of the word *irony*): a character whose job is to exhort the audience to interrogate all apparent truths by declining to take anything at face value. At the same time, they echo the spirit of the Socratic method, the *elenchus*: a paradigmatic refutation of definitive solutions.

As Jonathan Lear observes in his review of Alexander Nehamas' *The Art of Living*, the *elenchus* "tended to induce the experience of emptiness in others: an interlocutor would begin thinking he knew what justice or courage or piety is, and in the course of the conversation would be reduced to confusion and self-contradiction." In engendering this state of perplexity, Socrates' aim was "to lead his conversational partners to a recognition that although they took their lives to be incredibly important, they did not really understand what they were doing, or why, or why it was a good idea for them to be doing that rather than something else." To avoid confronting the questions raised by Socrates' method, his puzzled interlocutors would typically hole up in "the concerns of daily life"—mundane affairs they felt capable of pursuing unthinkingly, on the assumption they had a full grasp of their import. Ironically, such preoccupations were just a means of shirking an embarrassing reality: the fact that they "had no idea what a truly successful life might be," let alone "what 'getting ahead' meant" (Lear 1998).

The romance author's tendency to handle irony in accordance with the spirit of the Socratic *elenchus* brings to mind Thomas Mann's manipulation of that strategy. As Alexander Nehamas maintains, "Thomas Mann's irony deprives his readers of any final ground.... It does not reveal the ironist's real state of mind, and it intimates that such a state may not exist at all. It makes a mystery of its author as well as of his characters.... It is an irony that goes back to the very origins of the concept" (Nehamas). Like Mann, the romance writer uses irony to deny his readers any safe footing in the narrative, by cloaking his feelings and intentions in a shroud of ambiguity. Like Mann's, his messages tend to be understated and unobtrusive—so much so that they often glide by unheeded, and thus penetrate the reader's mind as nearly inchoate suggestions.

It is worth noting, incidentally, that Mann himself revisits the world of the chivalric romance in *Tristan* (1903), a novella informed by the myth of Tristan and Iseult, especially as presented in Richard Wagner's opera. Mann's *Tristan* revolves around an ironic juxtaposition of the romantic heroism embodied by Wagner's personae, and the actions of a decidedly *un*heroic present-day threesome.

The romance author does not try to impose a personal viewpoint on the narrative even when he appears to be disposed to lecture his readers or listeners about favorite topics, such as the mysteries of love, with oratorical relish. In fact, on these occasions, he adopts so grandiloquent a tone, and so florid a lexicon, as to make it patent that he does not expect the audience to take his declarations too—or at all—*seriously*. We are here presented, therefore, with a further level of irony.

The reason for which the romance author has no desire to assert his personal opinion is that, in a sense, he *has* no such thing. Having inherited his material from not one but many voices, fleetingly embodied in myriad bards over time, he is not the owner of a single personality. This kind of author conforms closely with Roland Barthes' *scriptor*, a figure theorized in the 1967 essay "The Death of the Author." In this groundbreaking text, Barthes argues that it is impossible, upon reading a text, to establish its writer's intentions beyond doubt. To be precise, such a task is not only unfeasible but also misleading, insofar as no text has a singular point of origin in an author (and his or her biography), as traditional literary studies have for long claimed to be the case. On the contrary, a text's meaning lies with *language itself*, the impact of such language on the text's readers, and the resulting interpretations. Since these are bound to vary enormously from one reader to the next, and indeed in the experience of even a single reader from one day to the next, the writing agent "is born simultaneously with the text, is in no way equipped with a being preceding or exceeding the writing, [and] is not the subject with the book as predicate" (Barthes 1977, p. 143).

In lieu of the term *author*, with its instantaneous association with the concept of *authority*, Barthes proposes the word *scriptor*: an entity that does not predate the text and its meanings, but actually comes into existence alongside the text it produces, aiming neither to explain it, nor grounding it in some given truth. The word "scriptor" is suffused with medieval nuances, given its etymological connection with "scribe" and "scriptorium"—two terms which are indeed *inscribed* across the art and act of writing throughout the Middle Ages.

At the same time as it echoes Barthes' position on authorship, the nonindividualistic standpoint communicated by the chivalric romance brings to mind John Keats' reflections on the "chameleon poet," formulated in a letter to Richard Woodhouse of October 27, 1818: "it is not itself—it has no self—it is every thing and nothing—It has no character—it enjoys light and shade; it lives in gusto, be it foul or fair, high or low, rich or poor, mean or elevated—It has as much delight in conceiving an Iago as an Imogen. What shocks the virtuous philosopher, delights the camelion [*sic*] Poet" (Keats 1818). Keats himself experimented with the romance form in the poem "La Belle Dame Sans Merci" (1819), a ballad redolent of the Breton lay in both its treatment of the supernatural and its economy of form. The legend dramatized in Keats' poem was to meet much favor among nineteenth-century artists, as attested to, for example, by Frank Dicksee's and Henry Meynell Rheam's paintings of the same name, both of which were completed in 1901. Also notable is John William Waterhouse's pictorial rendition of the story (1893).

According to Jonathan Lear, irony should not be regarded just as the proclivity "to make certain forms of witty remarks, perhaps saying the opposite of what [one] means, or remaining detached by undercutting any manifestation of seriousness" (Lear 2011, p. 9). Real irony is one of the main tools we need, as members of the human species, to *become* human in a full-fledged sense, by experiencing to the fullest every disturbance in our lives which upsets, or threatens to upset, the "norms" to which we commit ourselves, and "adhere to" on a day-to-day basis (p. 4). These are only a convenient scaffold for the "practical identities" we need to assume in order to function within particular societies (p. 5).

Irony entails the ability to recognize the disruptive, destabilizing, and ambiguous moments in one's life which suspend the value of those norms and identities. It is what enables us to respond commodiously to the challenges of the uncertain, instead of dodging them so as to find refuge in the fake certainties of a rule-governed existence. More importantly still, irony consists of "the capacity to occasion an experience of irony"—that is to say, "the capacity for deploying irony in the right way at the right time in the living of a distinctively human life" (p. 9). Key to the development of this aptitude is the ongoing preparedness to question one's activities and beliefs through an imaginative "disruption" of their premises (p. 31). Genuine ironists do not simply utter ironical statements; they also deconstruct their world's accepted truths through their everyday conduct.

The chivalric romance corroborates the idea that irony is not just a rhetorical trick intended to convey a certain stance to the world, but rather the crux of an overarching existential attitude. This is demonstrated by the tendency, prevalent among the form's chief exponents, to present two conflicting scenarios within a single fictional edifice. On the one hand, they weave yarns which throw into relief the huge lengths to which the knight will go to constitute himself as a respectable (indeed enviable) member of courtly society by conforming to its codes with punctilious care. On the other hand, they endeavor to expose, no less emphatically, the knight's all-too-human frailty, and hence the spectacular extent to which he fails to incarnate the ideal of excellence to which he aspires. As Comfort maintains, "the twelfth-century 'honnête homme'" (i.e., the ideal gentleman with refined social graces) embodies an imaginary nonpareil, not a flesh-and-blood character. "For the glaring inconsistencies between the reality and the ideal," argues the critic, "one may turn to the chronicles of the period" (Comfort, p. 6).

The romance's embroilment with a tangible social context will be revisited shortly. It is first necessary to note that the ironical disparity between chivalric etiquette and the knight's vulnerability begs a crucial question: if code-directed identities are bound to fail, what kind of existence will maximize a person's potential for being human, and living as a human? The answer which crops up again and again, in legion forms, across the spectrum of the texts here studied is redolent of Lear's argument. It indeed portends that the ironical temperament is key to such an existence, and that its goal is both to recognize the ruptures of the ordinary as formative challenges, and to help us bring about such ruptures by questioning the artificial truths which shape social behavior.

Far from employing irony merely as a trope so as to imply something by appearing to say its opposite, the chivalric romance elevates it to the status of a structural mainstay in order to intimate that no irrefutable meanings obtain *anywhere*—either in surface utterances or in their implied antitheses. The use of irony as a mere literary device is founded on the assumption of an ascertainable meaning—albeit one that is seemingly denied by the statement used to convey it. The chivalric romance, by contrast, refutes the existence, indeed the *plausibility*, of definite meanings.

Addressing audiences with a refined sensitivity to rhetoric and casuistry, the romance raconteur is able to return irony to its pure Socratic value as a means of interrogating the viability of truth itself—and, behind truth, of order, stability, and an unequivocal sense of belonging. He poses questions which preclude any definitive answers. Readers and listeners hellbent on finding any such answers will soon find themselves in the tragicomic position of Socrates' interlocutors, as seekers after incontrovertible certainties which the *elenchus* simply precludes.

By means of irony, the chivalric romance delivers a vibrant realm of oppositions and tensions, without endorsing any established values with conclusiveness. This is a reality akin to Derrida's "world of signs without fault, without truth and without origin, which is offered to our active interpretation" (p. 121). Concurrently, the chivalric romance anticipates Derrida in taking it for granted that language never says what it means, and never means what it says. Through its admixture of disparate elements which many other forms would deem incompatible, it revels in inconsistencies. There are no certainties in its universe, but only interminable *play* in the Derridean sense of the term.

Frederic Jameson argues that no text escapes the social system in which it is produced, insofar as its author is bound to be influenced by the environment in which he or she operates. The romance's entanglement with an identifiable context is borne out by its handling of the conflict between good and evil, which is couched as a magical rather than a moral issue. This topos reflects a predicament rooted in a specific culture, which may be described as a difficulty in negotiating the transition from the past to the future. Jameson sees the society in which the romance develops as one torn between two dimensions it cannot quite understand (*any longer*, in the case of one dimension, and *not yet*, in the other). This society tends to project the intractable enigma it faces onto the mysterious world of magic and the supernatural in an effort to situate it, to give it a home, at least at the intuitive level (Jameson, pp. 135–163).

Acknowledging that all texts are conditioned by the context in which they come into being is of critical importance. Nonetheless, one should also appreciate that there is a difference between the type of text which allows itself to be *possessed* by the ideology of its day, and the type of text which *questions* such values. This critical act is not synonymous with attacking the status quo, which would make the text subservient to its social context by implication, as an entity derivative from, or parasitical upon, the dominant ideology. In other words, it would be a product of that system, capable of "being" only by criticizing its tenets. Rather, the truly questioning text is one which invites recognition of the lacunae, contradictions, and ambiguities inherent in human society—and in human identity—by embodying *within itself* the inevitability of those expressions of diversity and inconclusiveness.

The key strategy brought into play by such a text is the aforementioned capacity for irony: the ruse whereby conflicting meanings are presented not as mutually exclusive, but coexistent. A text embracing irony as its pivotal force neither marries nor opposes ideology, by accepting the tyranny of social context in either the compliant or the snubbing modes. In fact, it may well appear to have nothing to do with an empirically verifiable world. Whatever its setting, the ironical text weaves its tapestry from conflicting voices and principles and, instead of striving to smooth over their differences, or quash one set of possibilities in favor of another, fosters their coexistence, and unresolvable disparity.

Its preference for improbable situations has gained the romance a somewhat negative reputation as a form which bears no connection with reality. As Richard Kaeuper points out, its status as "imaginative literature" has led several critics to regard its chivalric tales as "dreamlike, a thin veil pulled over the realities of the harsh world, and completely divorced from grinding social tensions and violence" (Kaeuper, p. 97). In fact, the romance abounds with vivid depictions of "combat and war" which emphasize "the detailed effects of sword strokes on armor and the human body beneath." Moreover, this descriptive trend did not stem from a gratuitous preference for graphic violence, of the kind one may associate with gory horror movies. Rather, it reflects political and ethical concerns of great consequences, which can be encapsulated in the following questions: "what violence is licit, what illicit? Who decides and exercises violence? Does God bless any violence?" (p. 98).

As a result, "to read chivalry in romance simply as a set of personal qualities in a knight risks reducing chivalry to a 'micro' force; it was, in fact, a 'macro' force doing major social work" among "the dominant strata of lay society for roughly half a millennium (say, from the eleventh to the sixteenth centuries)." There is a "fierce side" to chivalry which studies of the romance often gloss over—or simply ignore—as irrelevant. Nevertheless, to understand the cultural import of the form in its multifaceted complexity involves grappling with chivalry's—*unromantic*—status as "a code of violence in defense of a prickly sense of honor" (p. 99).

Thomas Bulfinch underscores the less than palatable connotations of medieval chivalry in his assessment of the dubious lawfulness of knightly behavior. Much as knights might have been construed by troubadours and poets as selfless personifications of integrity, loyalty, and fairness, historical accounts of a less elegiac orientation make it patent that chivalry as a corporate body was embroiled with an unsentimental, and indeed often brutal, exercise of power. "The justice administered by such an instrumentality," states Bulfinch, "must have been of the rudest description. The force whose legitimate purpose was to redress wrongs, might easily be perverted to inflict them." Romances themselves, despite their fictive nature and idealizing thrust, point to this unsavory reality in their commitment to the honest depiction of "manners." This is especially true of the numerous passages revealing that "a knightly castle was often a terror to the surrounding country; that its dungeons were full of oppressed knights and ladies, waiting for some champion to appear to set them free, or to be ransomed with money; that hosts of idle retainers were ever at hand to enforce their lord's behests, regardless of law and justice; and that the rights of the unarmed multitude were of no account" (Bulfinch, p. 11).

The romance is entangled with a tangible, tough, and dangerous world, which its often grisly content epitomizes with uncompromising vigor. However, at the same time as it embodies an unsentimental historical reality, the romance also stands out as the archetype of imaginative literature. Hence, its very essence is imbued with the spirit of irony. The present study seeks to emphasize that even though the fantastic worlds of the romance allude to a tangible social context, this factor neither weakens nor devalues the form's intrinsic fictiveness. In fact, through the creation of imaginary worlds filled with supernatural personae and occurrences, the romance foregrounds its allegiance to fiction on two counts. On the one hand, it utilizes such characters and events to spin manifold fictional adventures. On the other hand, it hints with satirical incisiveness to the likewise fictional nature of the society which its courtly audiences wish to think they inhabit, in temporary denial of the brutal protocol which it knows real knights to follow.

The chivalric romance tells us something vital about the nature of fiction per se as the prime reflection of the human propensity to fantasize, invent, and narrativize the fruits of its imaginings in texts. "Romance is the structural core of all fiction," declares Northrop Frye. "Being directly descended from folktale, it brings us closer than any other aspect of literature to the sense of fiction, considered as a whole, as ... man's vision of his own life as quest" (Frye, p. 15). Relatedly, it is the form in which the boundary between reality and imagination is most effectively demolished, or disregarded altogether. According to Frye, "in romance, neither the waking world nor the dream world is the real one," which renders "reality and illusion" alike "mixtures of the two" (p. 55). Both the real world and the world of imagination escape clear-cut definition, insofar as they tend to interpenetrate and influence one another in myriad ways.

While "myths are usually assumed to be true, stories about what really happened" (p. 16), insofar as human beings, once they have created "a mythological universe," always need to convince themselves that "it is also the actual universe" (p.14), "fabulous" narratives of the romance type foreground their fictionality hands down. They are neither ashamed of their fabulous nature, nor particularly interested in binary oppositions such as the one between "true and false." This is because they do not feel obliged to assert a specific vision of the world, let alone enforce its "authority" so as "to prevent anyone from ... questioning" its "truth," in the way myths do (p. 16).

The chivalric romance does not purport to act as the vehicle for the communication of extratextual "truths." Therefore, while influenced by its socio-historical context, it does not kowtow to the ethos of classic realism, and its conception of the text as a mimetic reflection of a tangible state of affairs. In fact, it wears its fictionality on its sleeve, basking in its right not only to make things up, but to do so with unbridled zest. To this extent, the chivalric romance deserves credit as an enduring tribute to *the essence of fiction* as a whole.

Part II

THREE

Creative Cornerstones: Chrétien de Troyes and the Lancelot-Grail Cycle

Chrétien de Troyes

Since the Renaissance, Western culture has been given to differentiate between historiography and fiction on the basis of cognitive criteria to which Chrétien de Troyes' age was deliberately oblivious. The medieval indifference to the dividing line between fact and fiction epitomizes the aesthetic of hybridity which also characterizes medieval iconography. This evinces no stark separation between the sacred and the profane, as borne out by cathedrals whose ornamentation abounds with gargoyles, demons with blood-dripping fangs redolent of pagan wood deities, enticing virgins, and many other patently *unholy* motifs.

This type of art is representative of a passion for the grotesque, and a carnivalesque—even unruly—profusion of composite shapes as yet untouched by the revival of notions of luminosity, balance, symmetry, and purity of form launched by humanism in its worship of classical antiquity. The Middle Ages, moreover, have fostered diversity in the musical and poetic realms, witnessing the genesis not only of sacred melodies of the highest order, but also of irreverent poetry of the kind collected by Carl Orff in the cantata *Carmina Burana* in 1935–1936.

Reflecting a widely held opinion, William Kibler and Carleton Carroll state that Chrétien de Troyes "was the inventor of Arthurian literature as we know it. Drawing from material circulated by itinerant Breton minstrels and legitimized by Geoffrey of Monmouth's *Historia Regum Britanniae*, ...

Chrétien fashioned a new form known today as courtly romance" (Kibler and Carroll, p. 1). The phrases "courtly romance" and "chivalric romance" are pretty much synonymous, insofar as medieval courtly culture, as anticipated in Part I, pivoted on a code of conduct designed specifically for the knight. It should be noted, in this regard, that the word "courtliness," which is practically synonymous with "chivalry," derives from the Old French *chevalerie*, "chivalry," which itself derives from *chevalier*, "knight"—a word whose root is *cheval*, "horse." *Chevalier* is etymologically associated with the Italian *cavalliere*, or *cavallaro*, i.e., "knight," the root of which is the common Latin word for "horse," namely, *caballus*.

William Comfort further emphasizes the seminal nature of Chrétien's romances, arguing that to him "is due the considerable honour of having constituted Arthur's court as a literary centre and rallying-point for an innumerable company of knights and ladies engaged in a never-ending series of amorous adventures and dangerous quests" (Comfort, p. 7). Indeed, even though major texts based on Arthurian lore had been in circulation, alongside oral stories, well before Chrétien's appearance on the scene, it is to his imagination that we owe the genesis of the chivalric romance as such, and of a distinctive formulation of the very concept of adventure.

What separates Chrétien's tales from the legends they draw upon and adapt is not simply the flair with which they impart established characters and themes with unprecedented meanings, even though this asset cannot be overestimated. Rather, it is the writer's knack of turning legend into art by infusing the old stories with the spirit of irony. This ability pivots on the exposure of insoluble conflicts between secular and spiritual aspirations, on the one hand, and between amorous and martial duties, on the other: the key topoi around which most romance yarns tend to revolve.

Comfort claims that Chrétien may be accused of a "lack of sense of proportion," and of "carelessness in the proper motivation of many episodes." He goes on to maintain, in a rather peremptory style, that the poet "*ought to* have handled his material more intelligently, even in the twelfth century," since "the emphasis is not always laid with discrimination, nor is his yarn kept free of tangles in the spinning" (p. 7; italics added). It could be argued that the flaws detected by Comfort in Chrétien's oeuvre are in fact irrelevant to the world of the chivalric romance. It could even be claimed that the critic *ought to* have realized it, given his intimate familiarity with the form as an academic and translator.

Chretien's art transcends the idea that texts should evince rational orchestration, apportion prominence to particular events and characters with judicious selectiveness, and ensure that plot lines unfold in a tidy and orderly manner. In fact, Chretien's fictional worlds recall dreams in which many small blocks concatenate in their own peculiar way. Most of the time, connections are of a wholly paratactic nature, as distinct narrative units are juxtaposed and joined together by the simple principle of *and*. This should not be taken as symptomatic of an overall lack of refinement. On the contrary, Chretien's structuring method ensues from a deliberate aesthetic decision, as well as an ideological aversion to the law of causality.

If proportion and tangle-free plotting are immaterial to the imaginative universe fashioned by the twelfth century French author, this is because, as Erich Auerbach maintains, "the true element of the courtly romance" is its "Fairy-tale atmosphere." However, as noted in the previous chapter, its immersion in a make-believe quasi-reality does not mean that the romance is totally divorced from society. In fact, it is "interested" not only "in portraying external living conditions in the feudal society of the closing years of the twelfth century but also and especially in expressing its ideals" (Auerbach, p. 127). Chrétien embraces this task with passion, missing no opportunity to poke ironical fun at the knightly class' failure to live up to the ideals celebrated by the very romances he composes. The romanticized conception of chivalry—as the espousal of noble principles and gallant conduct—belies the *real* knightly order's embroilment in a reality of violence and greed, and preparedness to protect its immediate interests with unscrupulous brutality at the slightest provocation.

Chrétien's take on the vaporousness of chivalric idealism demonstrates that the romance is by no means devoid of realism. Sure enough, the type of realism evinced by his works is not of a documentary or reportorial type. Yet, this does not render it any less striking. In fact, his subtle filtering of reality through the lenses of irony, symbolism, and metaphor enables Chrétien to reach to the core of things and look at them for what they are, not what a particular dogma or ethos proclaims they *ought to* be.

As noted in Chapter One, the figure of Arthur operates as an absent center by virtue of its concurrent existence and nonexistence. While serving this function, "Arthur" also captures the absurd spirit of the concept of center as theorized by Jacques Derrida, here outlined in Chapter Two. Chrétien's portrayal of the legendary monarch attests to the character's role as a paradoxical hub: a vital point of reference which, like the center critiqued by Derrida, is simultaneously pivotal and peripheral: representative of the system it is supposed to govern, yet isolated from it.

Norris J. Lacy underlines Arthur's relative marginality in Chrétien's opus. While Camelot plays a cardinal role in their plots, its sovereign is not granted parallel centrality. The fabled court "remains the ideological and geographical center of the characters' world." For example, "Perceval lives a bucolic life in the woods until he learns of knights and the court, and he is then irresistibly drawn to Arthur." The king himself, however, is by and large portrayed "as a secondary character" (Lacy 1997, p. 69). A putative bastion of chivalric excellence in much of the body of lore sustaining his myth, he actually comes across as a whimsical kid motivated by rather selfish desires on numerous occasions. He also seems prone to boredom, chagrin, and laziness. In this respect, Chrétien's representation of Arthur's personality serves to bolster a far-reaching critique of courtly culture as a whole, by intimating that posturing and pretense are crimes to which not even chivalry's noblest scions are altogether immune.

Lancelot, or, the Knight of the Cart exemplifies the flaws in the royal person in the scene where Arthur, hearing that Lancelot has been abducted, reveals the obligatory public angst, but clearly prefers to dwell on his private delights. "This news is not pleasing to the King, and he is very sorry and full of grief," the narrator informs us, "but his heart is so lightened by the pleasure he takes in the Queen's return, that his grief concludes in joy. When he has what he most desires, he cares little for the rest" (Chrétien de Troyes 2008a, p. 236). This is not exactly the kind of ruler to whom one would entrust the fate of one's land at times of strife—a constant in Arthur's realm—and certainly nothing like the prototype of the selfless leader one encounters in the typical epic.

Yvain, or, the Knight with a Lion further underscores the divergence of courtly reality from the principles meant to guide its denizens' conduct in its representation of the Arthurian fellowship itself. As Tony Hunt maintains, "the Arthurian company depicted in the romance is revealed to be very much less ideal than is suggested in the prologue and the elements of contemporary feudal reality incorporated in the protagonist's adventures are also less than reassuring." The knightly personnel at the king's disposal no doubt leaves something to be desired, accommodating as it does eccentricities and flaws which, while humanizing their bearers, also testify to their *un*-ideal standing.

Indeed, "Arthur's court finds room for an ineffectual knight, Calogrenant; ... a bilious seneschal, Kay; ... and a chivalric butterfly, Gauvain [*sic*], whose inopportune absences from court are the result of an overzealous and somewhat indiscriminate sense of chivalric duty to ladies." As for the monarch, his actions blatantly contradict the ideal behavior expected of an orthodox ruler. This is borne out by Arthur's decision to withdraw with his spouse "at the height Pentecostal festivities," no doubt in search of private pleasure, when he should in fact be concerned with the entire community's enjoyment (Hunt, p. 164).

The effectiveness of Chrétien's social critique stems from his adoption of a composed attitude towards his materials. This allows trenchant comments on the chivalric world to reach the page without ever deteriorating into sanctimonious pulp. According to Matilda Tomaryn Bruckner, this stance owes much to Chrétien's use of "narrators" who tend to "remain uninvolved in the story they tell: their distance from the narration allows the play of irony that clearly distinguishes romance from the modes of epic or saint's life" (Bruckner 2000, p. 16). At all times, the narrative voice is portrayed as a mindful presence which never allows itself to lose sight of its role, and hence of the likely impact of particular storytelling ploys on audience.

Self-distancing is enhanced by Chrétien's incorporation of an ongoing self-reflexive metacommentary on the art of storytelling. *Perceval, the Story of the Grail*, in particular, abounds with self-reflexive remarks, thus offering many telling illustrations of their use in Chrétien's narrative at large. A few examples are sufficient to prove the point:

> And the boy told the story
> You've been hearing.
> To tell it
> Again would be stupid and boring:
> Who wants a twice-told tale?
>   [Chrétien de Troyes 1999, p. 44].

> The knights first washed their hands,
> Then seated themselves at table....
> No one needs to know just what
> They ate....
> They dined and they drank, till they stopped,
> And that's all I'll say on the subject.
>   [p. 50].

> They fought on equal terms
> And I could describe it all,
> But it isn't worth the effort:
> One word is as good as twenty
>   [p. 85].

> They fought fiercely and hard.
> But why tell it all?
> I've no interest in wasting
> My time.
>   [pp. 124–125].

> And here the story breaks away from Perceval,
> About whom the tale turns silent:
> I'll speak a good deal of Gawain
> Before Perceval is mentioned again.
> [p. 206].

This last illustration of Chrétien's self-referential flair is spiked with the cheeky intimation that he knows full well how accomplished a storyteller he is, and where he aims to go with his story at any one point in its development.

According to Hunt, *Yvain, or, the Knight with a Lion* as a whole can be regarded as an extended reflection on "the problems of romance composition," and could therefore be said to operate "as a self-reflexive experiment" (Hunt, p. 167). The preamble illuminates this aspect of Chrétien's narrative in a capsulated fashion by means of Calogrenant's tale, and its distinctive storytelling attributes. "Calogrenant's quest with its literary prologue," states the critic, "represents in embryo (*mise en abyme*) the courtly tale or *conte*, whilst his self-definition as ... 'a knight in search of what he cannot find,' namely 'adventures to test my prowess and mettle,' is also a *mise en abyme* of the knight errant" (p. 168). It could also be argued that Calogrenant's awareness that he is unlikely ever to find the ultimate object of his quest encapsulates in a self-reflexive fashion the forever deferred fulfillment of desire in the chivalric romance as a form.

Even Chrétien's most casual readers are likely to prove receptive to the writer's penchant for turning everyday objects, such as garments or foodstuff, into vivid entities of palpable aesthetic merit. In Chrétien's allusions to culinary and vestimentary items, we see evidence not only for his wonderful descriptive flair, but also for the visceral pleasure he derives from their corporeality. His romances indeed give the impression that the author cherishes the many materials he mentions, and even *savors* their unique feel, qua materials. This passion is matched by an enthusiastic approach to color, epitomized by the description of the multi-hued robes and tunics worn by many of the ladies whom a weary knight first espies upon arriving at a new castle. These polychromatic images suggest, with stunning unobtrusiveness, that the knight should be at least partly restored even by such sight before any chance of rest and victuals. The clothes he is given to wear once his armor has been removed are also depicted with meticulous care. In this instance, too, one feels that the garments' beauty has the capacity to restore their wearer no less potently than material comforts and sustenance.

It is important to bear in mind, in this perspective, that the romance writer's distinctive appetite for material details is a corollary of his not only aesthetic, but also philosophical, priorities. As Geoffrey Ashe asserts, "romances ... cared little for authenticity.... They updated.... They considered their patrons and readers ... and told stories that those patrons and readers could understand, stories about things belonging to their world, however anachronistic the result.... A story would emerge in the garb, so to speak, of the author's own time" (Ashe, p. 3). In Chrétien's hands, descriptive details never becomes too formulaic, no matter how many times the same fabrics, ornaments, accessories, gems, or dishes get mentioned. This is because they are not treated as *mere* descriptive details—that is to say, as dispensable supplements or atmospheric touches—but rather honored as aspects of the narrative worthy of no less consideration than a story's adrenalizing battles, or its amorous banter.

One of most memorable images in Chrétien's entire opus occurs in *Perceval, the Story of the Grail*, in the scene where a goose is lightly injured by a falcon, and falls to the snowy ground, causing its body to impart its "oval shape" upon the snow, while also leaving "three drops of blood." "The blood-dyed color suffused inside it.... Blood and snow so mixed together created a fresh color, Just like [Perceval's] beloved's face"—i.e., Blanchefleur's exquisite visage (Chrétien de Troyes 1999, p. 133). Commenting on this unusual segment of Perceval's adventures, John Stevens remarks: "the full meaning of this episode is never discussed by Chrétien, who has supremely the tact of leaving things alone for the imagination to work upon, as poets in all ages do and must."

It is worth stressing that with these reflections, Stevens draws our attention not only to a salient characteristic of the French romancer's art, but also, by implication, to what constitutes authentic art per se. In the specific context of the argument pursued in this study, this lies with the cultivation, and frank admission, of a work's fictionality: its difference from so-called reality, and, no less importantly, its right to champion this difference in defiance of classic realism. The work's endeavor to stimulate the reader's own imagination reinforces its allegiance to fictionality, providing scope for the fiction contrived by the author to proliferate into an unchartable galaxy of *other fictions*, issuing from the minds of the work's readers. This is the genius of true art of which the chivalric romance incarnates the very essence.

The injured goose episode in *Perceval, the Story of the Grail* shows how "the world of everyday," in this case epitomized by "a few drops of blood on the winter's snow," is capable of conveying "a meaning beyond the commonplace" in the hands of a teller as skilled as Chrétien. Yet, even "the most fantastic 'marvels' in the hands of a prosaic fiction-monger can leave the heart as cold and unresponsive as a piece of fish on a stone slab.... There is often a sense in the greater romancers that quite ordinary events, ordinary things, have a significance quite beyond themselves" (Stevens, p. 97).

The episode thus also demonstrates that in Chrétien, the realm of the marvelous is by no means coterminous with the otherworldly. Indeed, many of the images which his writing evokes open up a vista of enticing marvels without making the slightest reference to any supernatural agencies, such as fairies or monsters of the kind found elsewhere in the chivalric romance. The marvelous, we are reminded, lies in store in the *most mundane* of things when we have eyes to recognize it, and a willingness to revel in its mystery.

The *entrelacement* for which, as noted in Chapter One, the chivalric romance is renowned finds paradigmatic expression in Chrétien's *Yvain, or, the Knight with the Lion*, a work reputed to have been composed between 1177 and 1181 (Schweke, p. 3). The author's preference for enchained exploits, which often appear motivated by no force other than the protagonist's desire for adventure, is bolstered by an elegant application of the structural principle of deferral: another pivotal attribute, as we have seen, of the romance as an art form. What has just now been described as "elegant" would plausibly be deemed *maddening* by modern readers keen on linear plotlines and straightforward resolutions, but this is evidently not the type of reader—or indeed audience—addressed by Chrétien.

The story's opening segment declares its passion for both *entrelacement* and deferral. Having held a sumptuous banquet on the day of Pentecost, King Arthur uncharacteristically absents himself from courtly games and wordplay, preferring instead to join Guinevere in the bedroom in search, though this is not spelled out, of more private pleasures. The knights who congregate outside the royal couple's chamber to exchange tales are soon joined by the queen just as the gracious Calogrenant is in the process of recounting his own adventures. While the knight is reluctant to continue the narration in the queen's presence, Guinevere presses him to do so.

No sooner has the romance begun to unfold than deferral has already had a chance to assert itself as pivotal to the drama. This narrative preference is borne out by the narrative's movement from the great feast, though the courtly pursuits following the banquet, the description of the knightly gathering outside the royal chamber, and Calogrenant's first attempt at storytelling, to Guinevere's intervention, her exchange with Kay, and her request that the narration be resumed. Deferral operates in conjunction with *entrelacement* insofar as Calogrenant's story sows the seeds for the entwined adventures centered on his cousin Yvain which follow. These adventures will turn out to be interwoven with that early narrative both thematically and structurally. At the same time, they will also invite comparison between Arthur's court as portrayed in the romance's inaugural portion, and the various aristocratic contexts encountered by Yvain in the course of his quest.

In addition, the sarcastic humor and cutting remarks issuing from the mouth of the proverbially impertinent Kay avert attention from Calogrenant's early narrative, focusing it instead on the issue of chivalric etiquette and, by implication, also on the complexity of the court's hierarchy—a system which controls the knights' interaction with one another and each member of the royal pair, in spite of the Round Table's putative effacement of any kind of pecking order. The early scenes of *Yvain, or, the Knight with the Lion* indicate that gender relations are an important facet of this social structure. Guinevere's role among the knights assembled outside the royal bedroom deserves special notice.

On the one hand, the queen's privileged status allows her to be present in a knightly gathering to which other, less prominent, women would feasibly have not have access. Thus, Guinevere is not only accorded the power to attract Arthur to the bedroom on a solemn occasion: she is also deemed entitled to assert her presence among her husband's knights without the least trace of timidity. Furthermore, she is able to steer the course of their conversation to her liking by deciding whether or not Calogrenant should continue with his story. On the other hand, Guinevere's power is reduced by Kay's ironical suggestion that she ought not to abuse the authority given her by her fortuitous presence among the knights. Though rebuked by Guinevere for his ungallant treatment of the gentle Calogrenant, Kay, as a man, still feels entitled to remind her where she—as a woman, albeit an influential one—belongs. "If we are not better for your company," Kay tells the queen with circuitous insolence, "at least let us not lose by it" (Chrétien de Troyes 2008b, p. 134).

As Yvain hears from his cousin Calogrenant of the latter's defeat by a formidable knight, later named Esclados the Red, he leaves Arthur's court, determined both to avenge his wronged relative, and to prove his own valor by searching for adventures come what may. Having managed to come face to face with the knight responsible for Calogrenant's humiliation after confronting a series of interconnected tests, Yvain overpowers and kills Esclados the Red. His martial triumph is soon followed by an amorous victory of no less significant magnitude: he is able to marry the dead foe's wife, Laudine, through the intercession of her handmaid, Lunete. Out of gratitude to the knight for the kindness he once showed her at Arthur's court, when the other knights appeared indifferent or disdainful, Lunete presents Yvain with a magical ring which enables him to hide from the guards hunting for their master's murderer, and uses persuasive rhetoric to turn her mistress' hatred for the assassin into undiluted devotion.

As Jessica Schweke notes, Lunete "fills a role usually open only to men," insofar as Laudine allows herself to be influenced by the girl's arguments, and "complies with her ... counsel much more than she does with that of her seneschals" (Schweke, p. 10). At the same time, the methods by which the maid persuades her mistress to abide by her advice are somewhat questionable from an ethical point of view, insofar as Lunete is prepared to massage the truth whenever appropriate, and, if worse comes to worst, to resort to downright deception. Chrétien's writing does not condemn the girl—not explicitly, at any rate. By recourse to irony, it *both* criticizes women's ploys *and* provides justification for their conduct. On the one hand, it suggests that even the best of women cannot be trusted for, noble as their motives might be, they are most likely to fall back on mendacity to back their cause. On the other hand, it intimates that the weaving of plots and tales behind the scenes is often the only means by which a woman inscribed in a strict patriarchal society may affect a given course of action.

Once he has gained Laudine's favor, and wedded her in great pomp, Yvain leaves the homestead to engage in yet more, unrelated, exploits at Sir Gawain's behest. Laudine allows her new husband to join his fellow knights upon the condition that he will return to her within a year, which Yvain solemnly vows to do without hesitation. To seal the pledge, Laudine bestows upon the knight yet another magical ring, meant both to protect him from harm, and to remind him of his promise. Having engineered Yvain's failure to return to the marital nest by the promised date, with little explanation other than his commitment to chivalry, Chrétien's plot turns to a wonderful dramatic pretext for yet more—loosely connected—action: madness. Indeed, the realization that he has lost his wife's affection beyond redemption (or so it seems), drives Yvain insane, and further allows him to give vent to his manic self-loathing with a fervor anticipative of Ariosto's Orlando.

The hero's recovery of his wits is itself the center of a separate and exquisite quasi-amorous adventure. Yvain would go to unimaginable lengths to regain the heart of his beloved—if the term "unimaginable" could ever hold any meaning for an author so brimming with inventiveness as to seem able to deliver plot twists and incentives for unexpected action with practically every sentence. As it happens, with the exception of Yvain's rescue of Laudine's maid, Lunete, from death at the stake, a fate ratified by the lady herself, the exploits undertaken by Yvain prior to his climactic reunion with the beloved have little—if anything—to do with either Laudine or the land over which she presides. Rather, they just seem to crop up as opportunities for displays of prowess, and to be embraced *as such* without any ulterior motives other than the attainment of fame.

If errant adventurousness is something which a knight is expected to accept not only as his own raison d'être, but also as an end in itself, the achievement of renown is no less axial a trait of the chivalric code: as Yvain emphasizes, there is no point in completing any daring task, unless knowledge of its accomplishment is conveyed to those capable of identifying its performer, and of according him due recognition.

Looking back at the romance's inception, it could be argued that Calogrenant's defeat by Esclados the Red works as a narrative device to set the main narrative in motion, and thus inaugurate a quest to be accomplished though a chain of interlaced segments. Notably, the tests become harder and harder as the text unfolds. However, in keeping with the romance's preference for multiclimactic structures which eschew any grand pinnacles of the epic ilk, Yvain's quest does not build towards a cumulative climax. Rather, each episode has its own culmination, and all of the various climaxes are, therefore, presented as provisional. The romance's final conclusion itself, though satisfying, is not made to serve as a conclusive resolution for the romance as a whole. Instead of providing a cumulative rounding-off of the entire fictional experience, it only resolves the specific combat it dramatizes. Thus, Yvain's overpowering of his last enemy is portrayed as a localized zenith, not a massive release of all the tension accumulated over the development of the entire narrative.

Its deliberate inconclusiveness makes the tale's ending deeply ambiguous—or, to be more precise, it imparts it with the aura of a scene which can be read *both* as an ending and *not* as an ending at one and the same time. In fact, *Yvain, or, the Knight with a Lion* as a whole appears to be built around the principle of ambiguity. The hero himself comes across as a duplicitous character, amenable to interpretation as the incarnation of knightly virtue, on the one hand, and a common liar, on the other. The fight against Esclados the Red demonstrates his puissance. Nevertheless, the roundabout means by which he seeks to steal a look at Laudine calls his virtuousness into question. The pretext he adduces to satisfy his secret desire is that he would "gladly look out through some window or aperture at the procession and the corpse" (Chrétien de Troyes 2008b, p. 144).

The voyeuristic nuances of this scene are rather unpalatable, as their effect is to pollute the potential purity of the knight's feelings towards the dead man's wife. It is not the melodramatic tone in which Yvain describes his thrall to Love that casts doubt on the honesty of his disposition. After all, it would be foolish to expect a romance to depict a knight in love as anything other than a cardboard figure, or even a caricature. Rather, it is the unnecessary circuitousness with which he choreographs his moves. The dubiousness of Yvain's moral credentials is intensified by Laudine's conjectures: frustrated by the vanity of her men's hunt for the murderer, and by her own inability to "see the man who must be so close" to her, the lady concludes that "some demon or spirit has interposed himself" between them, hence placing her "under a spell" (pp. 143–144). Yvain's association with a malevolent supernatural agency intensifies his character's ambiguity, implying that the powers whence he derives strength are not the chivalric ideals he is supposed to uphold, but rather dark and dishonest forces.

Furthermore, Yvain's dubious morality is attested to by the inconsistency of his aims. The quest he sets out to pursue is centered on the desire to avenge Calogrenant, which means that once this objective is fulfilled, Yvain ought to return to the fellowship to which he belongs, and face the chivalric duties entailed by his position. Nevertheless, the epiphanic experience of love at first sight displaces Yvain's original goal, urging him to focus on the achievement of personal gratification instead.

The role accorded to magic in *Yvain, or, the Knight with a Lion* serves to intensify the sense of undecidability surrounding the protagonist's portrayal. Chrétien makes use of magic as a potent means of expressing courtly culture's yearning for what it knows to be impossible in both physical and ethical terms. In so doing, it underlines the romance's fictiveness—and the unabashed pride it takes in its fictiveness. It reminds us that the romance, as a form sui generis, is not only a chronicle of imaginary adventures, but also, and more importantly, a jubilant embodiment of fiction at its purest, to the extent that it does not claim or pretend, unlike myth, to encapsulate dependable truths about the human condition. When it reflects the actual social and political preoccupations of its epoch, which it often does, it is nonetheless forthright in the exposure of its intrinsic fictionality.

The magical ointment which enables Yvain to regain his sanity exemplifies the romance's knack of both asserting its fictionality, and alluding to a real situation of broad cultural significance. As Jeff Rider observes, "the fairy salve" serves as "a narrative device which moves the story forward, signals that it is a fiction, tells us that such medicaments and such women do not exist in 'our' world, and, simultaneously, represents a desire to have the one and be the other." The imaginary realms in which such incompatible possibilities ironically coalesce are both "narrative devices and the repositories of everything 'we' lack and are not, and of everything 'we' would like to have and to be" (Rider, p. 129).

As argued in Chapter Two, Jacques Lacan posits courtly love as the epitome of the forever deferred fulfillment of human desire. This proposition reaches a veritable apotheosis in the ending of *Lancelot, or the Knight of the Cart*, a romance believed to have been composed between 1175 and 1181. Informed throughout by the structural principle of deferral, this text takes the concept a stage further by applying it to the finale itself. Indeed, this leaves the audience with no clues to the future development of the relationship between Lancelot and Guinevere. All we know is that the queen must conceal her impulse to reveal her love without restraint, lest her feelings should become known to the vigilant eyes of her retinue or even the king himself. "Reason closes up and binds her fond heart and her rash intent," declares the narrator, "and made it more reasonable, postponing the greeting until it shall see and espy a suitable and more private place where they would fare better than here and now" (Chrétien de Troyes 2008a, p. 248).

As Bruckner observes, this scenario is foreshadowed in the tournament episode, which gives the adulterous pair "their first opportunity to come together in Arthur's kingdom," their earlier tryst having taken place in the quasi-magical realm of Gorre. "Their indirect, displaced reunion in that public arena ... anticipates the difficulties of future rendezvous," argues Bruckner, emphasizing the extent to which Guinevere's "circumspection" in the closing scenes forces "body and heart" apart in the service of protocol, and genteel façades. This entails that "no closure will be found in the romance for the love story initiated between Lancelot and the queen, only expectations for something more, expectations the public no doubt shares with the lovers, though we all remain uncertain about what form their future may take" (Bruckner 2008, p. 149).

As Rowan Bridgwood contends, "one of the most enduring factors of the Arthurian tradition" consists of "Lancelot's joint depiction as the best of worldly knights and the catalyst for the collapse of Arthur's court.... Chrétien introduces the notion of Lancelot's attributes as courtly lover as detrimental to other aspects of his knighthood." However, his fatal flaw is largely responsible for the knight's undying attraction. The character's portrayal indeed throws into relief Lancelot's all-too-human frailty, demonstrating that "adherence to one code of chivalry prevents success in another," and that a knight torn between martial and amorous duties is therefore *destined* to fail.

The reader's recognition of this unsavory state of affairs is bound to kindle his or her sympathy with the knight and his predicament. Ultimately, "it is this very fallibility that makes [Lancelot] such an enduring character." One of Chrétien's chief means of exposing his protagonist's schizophrenic situation is the humorous "undercutting" of "courtly love motifs." His depiction of "Lancelot's dedication to courtly love in moments when he is disarmed—in physical or moral weakness or defeat—resulting in the insinuation that it is Lancelot's role as lover that makes him so ineffectual in other areas of knighthood.... Lancelot has, in a sense, become emasculated, and Chrétien depicts his love as the cause for his emasculation" (Bridgwood, pp. 481–482).

The fight between Lancelot and Meleagant, the queen's abductor, corroborates this argument. The hero will stop at nothing to destroy his mortal enemy as long as he feels sustained by Guinevere's approval and inspiring presence. Yet, Chrétien informs us that as soon as Meleagant's father begs the queen "to let them be separated," and she agrees to comply with his plea, Lancelot "ceased to fight and renounced the struggle at once" (Chrétien de Troyes 2008a, p. 234), as though he had no will of his own, and only existed to serve his beloved's demands.

This scene reinforces the impression that Lancelot is caught in a paradoxical situation, predicated on the ironical coexistence of mutually exclusive values. The knight's identity is correspondingly split: the epitome of energy and ardour one moment, he descends into inertia the next, with no transitional adjustment in between. On the one hand, Lancelot's subservience to the philosophy of courtly love ennobles him by revealing his capacity to embody one of the romance's defining ethical systems to an unparalleled degree. On the other hand, inasmuch as it requires his utter passivity, that very ethos also debases Lancelot: it expects him to relinquish his commitment to a parallel ethical system which demands the demonstration of courage and martial dexterity at any given opportunity.

At several key junctures in the romance, Chrétien depicts love as an affliction comparable to a terminal disease of soul and body alike, thereby calling into question both its aesthetic and its societal credentials with ironic glee. The following passage epitomizes this trend: "he of the cart is occupied with deep reflections, like one who has no strength or defence against love which holds him in its sway. His thoughts are such that he totally forgets himself, and he knows not whether he is alive or dead, forgetting even his own name, not knowing whether he is armed or not, or whither he is going or whence he came. Only one creature he has in mind, and for her his thought is so occupied that he neither sees or hears aught else" (p. 199). The devastating, though elegant, derision here levelled against the greatest Arthurian champion of all times dwarfs Lancelot's standing, suggesting that his blind devotion to courtly love has ceased to be a virtue, and degenerated instead into dangerous folly.

Scenes of this kind intimates that Lancelot, as Armel Diverres maintains, is failing in "the basic discipline made up of *mesure* [judiciousness, restraint] and *raison* [reason, wisdom] which Chrétien seems to consider inherent to courtly love in a chivalrous society" (Diverres, p. 35). This is no minor flaw in a culture where a true knight is always expected to harbor a flawless balance of amatory savvy and martial prowess, and ensure that even at the height of passion and ferocity, his actions will evince equanimity and good sense. Fanni Bogdanow corroborates this point, stating that "Lancelot is not acting in the rational manner in which a knight should; but he is not just a knight; he is a knight who is a *fin amant* [courtly lover], and Chrétien's intention, it seems, is to parody the excesses to which *fin amor* can lead a knight.... The great paradox around which Chrétien builds his *Charrette* is that *nuls om ses amor re no vau*—no man can merit esteem without love—and yet love forces Lancelot at times, against reason, to submit to the greatest humiliations" (Bogdanow, p. 56; p. 53).

The conflict between incompatible value systems is also central to the episode surrounding the eponymous cart. In this case, as Douglas Kelly maintains, "Lancelot's hesitation before mounting the cart contrasts.... Reason with Love. After a brief hesitation Lancelot follows his heart and springs into the cart. Chrétien thus confronts two standards for evaluating Lancelot's action: Reason's based on chivalric honor and Love's based on amorous devotion." Lancelot embraces the standard of Love but this choice, as it turns out, is not quite enough to satisfy Guinevere's unappeasable thirst for chivalric perfection: his instant of hesitation before boarding the cart proves sufficient to trigger the queen's vitriolic scorn, and refusal to be rescued by Lancelot in spite of everything he has endured for her sake.

To emphasize the opposition between Reason and Love, the author shows how Gawain, unencumbered by passion, rejects the pressure to jump into the notorious vehicle on the grounds that he can rely on the support of a strong horse: "a reminder that he is a knight (*cheval-ier*) and that knights ride horses, not carts" (Kelly, p. 58). The discrepancy between the law of the heart and the law of reason renders the two systems downright incompatible as the romance progresses. In dramatizing Lancelot's and Gawain's choices with reference to those incompatible principles, Chrétien deploys irony with masterful subtlety. The irony goes further, however, as Gawain himself becomes the butt of ironical humor: his belief that a true knight must ride a horse at all costs, and that to reach the queen, all he has to do is follow the despicable cart turns out to be fallacious, as he gets nowhere near Guinevere by means of this seemingly clever strategy.

There are also times when courtly love, in spite of its standing as the secular equivalent of a religion, degenerates into utter absurdity. According to Derek Pearsall, it is feasible that Chrétien's tendency to deflate the conventions of *fin amor*, indicated by his somewhat derisive exposure of "the extravagances" of Lancelot's "all-consuming passion," might be a result, at least in part, of his consciousness of the disparity between his own social status, and the morally suspect nature of the erotic code idealized by courtly culture. "Chrétien might have resorted to irony," argues the scholar, "in order to deal with a certain wistful embarrassment that he might have felt, as a cleric, in glorifying adultery, even at a lady's command" (Pearsall, p. 29).

The ludicrousness of courtly love is vividly illustrated by the episode in which Lancelot is offered vintage erotic opportunities which any *proper* knight would not only welcome but *honor* as akin to a social and ethical obligation. Lancelot himself is torn between the imperative to adhere to his society's amorous code, which requires him to accept his hostess' advances, and his true feelings, which make him more inclined towards faithfulness to his beloved, yet does not fail to recognize where his chivalric duty lies. A gem of Chrétien's comic genius, the scene deserves extensive citation:

> "Sire, my house is prepared for you, if you will accept my hospitality, but you shall find shelter there only on condition that you will lie with me; upon these terms I propose and make the offer." Not a few there are who would have thanked her five hundred times for such a gift; but he is much displeased, and made a very different answer: "Damsel, I thank you for the offer of your house, and esteem it highly, but, if you please, I should be very sorry to lie with you." "By my eyes," the damsel says, "then I retract my offer." And he, since it is unavoidable, lets her have her way, though his heart grieves to give consent [Chrétien de Troyes 2008a, p. 201.]

The conclusion to which Lancelot so swiftly arrives, in spite his initial determination to remain loyal to his true love, demonstrates that a genuine Arthurian champion ultimately has no choice but to obey to the law of *fin amor*. The phrase "though his heart grieves to give consent" feels almost like a perfunctory concession to the affective sphere he would like to follow, yet knows to be alien to his role. Furthermore, the scene lays notable emphasis on the emotional volatility of both sexes, giving rise to a palpable sense of fluctuation which imparts the narrative flow itself with a wave-like rhythm of unique vibrance.

The text's manifest message is that emotions and judgment can coexist: the mark of a worthy knight consists of his capacity to abide by both simultaneously. Beneath this message, however, lies a contrasting proposition: love and reason are by and large mutually exclusive, and proficiency in the amatory arts often clashes with martial responsibilities. A perfect knight *should* no doubt excel in all areas of the chivalric code, but perfect knights, alas, are hard to find—assuming, that is, they *exist at all*. The Chrétien behind the apparent message is the courtly poet devoted to the chivalric code, whilst the Chrétien behind the latent message is the ironist reluctant to endorse chivalry in an unequivocal fashion, and keener instead on exposing the disparity between abstract ideals and practical conduct.

Simon Gaunt suggests that "Lancelot is a secular saint.... When he steps into the cart, like many saints in contemporary texts, he rejects the path expected of him and instead makes himself into an outcast who derives strength from an inner faith in the value of an abject course of action" (Gaunt, p. 52). It is worth noting, however, that not even this potentially holy connection is left unscathed by Chrétien's penchant for irony. In fact, Lancelot's ordeal intimates that a secular knight's vicissitudes might be even more challenging than those endured by real saints. No doubt the pious figures immortalized in medieval hagiographic writing have a tough time in their endeavor to satisfy God: an arbiter whose goalposts famously keep moving, just as his actions have a proverbial reputation for unfolding according to mysterious laws. Yet, in dramatizing Guinevere's dissatisfaction with Lancelot's performance, Chrétien's irony intimates that even the Christian God might be easier to satisfy than the deified lady of courtly love.

The erotic scenes in Chrétien's romance signal an additional connection with the hagiographic tradition to the extent that "in many saints lives the union of the saint with Christ is figured through erotic metaphors" (p. 52), comparable to those employed by Chrétien to describe Lancelot and Guinevere's lovemaking. Nonetheless, the romance ethos and the hagiographic mentality are barely reconcilable, since the doctrine of courtly love can easily be regarded as a blasphemous perversion of *real* faith outside the circle for whom romances where being read and cherished. The prestige enjoyed by monastic institutions in the literary culture of Chrétien's era made the implicit comparison of sexual passion to religious devotion a particularly delicate matter. "When [Lancelot] steps into a cart," observes Gaunt, "it is Love (for a woman), rather than love of God that pushes him into this act of humility.... If Chrétien invites us to think of Lancelot as a secular saint, he also implicitly invites us to think about how problematic this notion is: he worships the queen, we are told, with more ardor than he does a holy relic" (p. 53).

Chrétien evokes a pervasive impression of mutability throughout the development of *Lancelot, or, the Knight of the Cart* in order to keep his readers/listeners on their toes. In the process, he provides no straight answers, only enigmas. Even the protagonist's identity is unclear when he is first introduced. This sets the tone of the adventures to follow. The sense of uncertainty is reinforced first by the puzzle surrounding Lancelot's moment of hesitation upon boarding the cart, and, later, by the sibylline mood of the cemetery scene which, with uncanny irony, proclaims the knight's uniqueness at the same time as it presages the end of the Arthurian era. These, and the many other, enigmas which pepper the romance indicate that Chrétien's narrative art invites ongoing interpretation and debate. It is this capacity to engage the audience directly in the process of semiosis that gives the text the power also to enlist, at one and the same time, our deepest emotions and most intimate desires.

The romance has come to be seen as an escape from reality over the centuries, the reputation of romance novels from the Gothic to the present having fueled this inclination to a significant extent. Yet, the romance is actually grounded in a specific historical context. Bruckner upholds this idea in her analysis of the status of the romance author by comparison with the transmitter of heroic tales. "Unlike the jongleur," argues the critic, "whose voice speaks for the collectivity commemorated in the exploits of their shared heroes, the epic deeds of Roland or Charlemagne, the romancer appears as a clerkly figure whose school training enables him to instruct a particular segment of society by telling stories that take place at some distance from both narrator and public, whether chronologically, linguistically, or geographically. This shift emphasizes the role and the specific character of the storyteller, who is simultaneously a writing author and an inscribed narrator speaking directly to an audience of 'readers'" (Bruckner 2000, p. 14). Even when the romance audience consists of listeners, rather than readers, it is still a relatively homogeneous group, meeting within a private space.

Lancelot, or, the Knight of the Cart provides a good illustration of the dynamics of narration and reception in Chrétien's society. "In the opening lines," the romancer "introduces ... the patron, the first and primary member of his courtly and aristocratic public. The naming of Marie de Champagne as commissioning patron for the *Charrette* reminds us that not only courts and kings, but ladies, queens, and countesses, play an important role in the reception of romance" (p. 15).

Most crucially, Chrétien's handling of "the persona of the narrating voice as filter for the tale told" (p. 18) operates as an implicit reminder that meaning is never immediate—i.e., *unmediated*, direct—but rather inevitably *mediated* by language. In the world of narrative, relatedly, meaning is always *textual*. The etymology of the words "text" and "textual" is worthy of notice, in this context. These derive from the Latin word *textus*, "things woven," which is in turn the past participle of *texere*, "to weave." As a product of the medieval world, the culture wherein *tapestry* achieves an arguably unprecedented status, the romance as a textual form boasts a close and illustrious relative within the visual arts of the same period.

A central facet of the fictional tapestry woven by Chrétien in *Lancelot, or the Knight of the Cart* lies with the fluid interpenetration of *this* world and an *Other*world. The romance shows with unrivaled relish the extent to which the alternate, preternatural, worlds of romance may be employed to accommodate forbidden fantasies—and, more vitally, to permit their fulfillment. As Rider emphasizes, on this subject, "Chrétien ... is careful to situate Lancelot and Guenevere's night of ecstatic, blood-drenched, adulterous and treasonable love-making in Gorre"—a land as fantastic as Arthur's realm, Logres. Its accommodation of a surge of illicit passion shows that an Otherworld like Gorre, though imaginary, is by no means divorced from reality, since it actually allows for "the representation and imaginative satisfaction of ... materially and morally unrealizable desires" (Rider, p. 129). At the same time, Gorre's otherworldly connotations are intensified by its implicit association with the Classical Underworld. Indeed, Lancelot's foray into Gorre to rescue Guinevere echoes Orpheus' descent into Hades in the hope of bringing Eurydice back to the world of the living. (The romance is also indirectly connected with the lay *Sir Orfeo*, discussed in the next chapter.)

Throughout the tale, the interpenetration of this world and an Otherworld functions as a narrative device pregnant with thrilling possibilities. The hero's crossing of the formidable sword bridge, a task which entails both considerable physical pain, and rare self-discipline, encapsulates the topos to memorable effect. Several critics have remarked on the folkloric and literary employment of the image of the hazardous crossing as emblematic of a transition of more than purely geographical import. Esther C. Dunn, for instance, argues that a risky passage is one of the main conventions typical of the journey to the Otherworld (Dunn). Not only the sword bridge in *Lancelot, the Knight of the Cart*, but also the drawbridge marking the entrance to the Fisher King's castle in *Perceval, the Story of the Grail*, exemplify this trope. The latter, it should be noted, is opportunely "lowered for [Perceval's] use" when he reaches the fortress (Chrétien de Troyes 1999, p. 97), and is already "down" by the time the knight is ready to leave. Nonetheless, it delivers unexpected dangers just as he reaches its end, at which point, it is suddenly "raised" (p. 108). This scene implies that a knight errant's way *out* of the Otherworld may be no less perilous than the way *in*.

As Howard Rollin Patch points out, the transition from this world to an Otherworld is often connoted by the presence of liminal zones of an aquatic nature: "most descriptions of the Otherworld involve a world cut off from the every-day world by some sort of water barrier (Patch, p. 604). Sarah Cramer elaborates this idea, noting that "a hero *must* cross over water in order to reach the Otherworld. Yet there is also a symbolic significance. Water is, after all, a symbol of both life and death and helps one to understand how a journey to the Otherworld also can be a symbol of death and rebirth" (Cramer).

Perceval, the Story of the Grail abounds with examples of Chrétien's use of water as a means of separating a location off from its wide setting, and thus allude to its special, and very possibly magical, qualities. This applies to both the Perceval-centered and the Gawain-centered portions of the romance. The castle of Belrepeire is a case in point, being described as "well / Located but surrounded by the sea / And the waves" (Chrétien de Troyes 1999, pp. 54–55). The overall effect is frequently enhanced by the inclusion of vessels redolent of Charon's vessel in the Classical rendition of Hades. A good example of Chrétien's use of boats permeated with supernatural (and even miraculous) connotations is the "heavy barge, / Loaded with wheat and other foodstuff," steered by supernatural intervention to the castle of Belrepeire just as its defenders are running out of supplies, and thereby aiding the Perceval-led defence of its bastions against Clamadeu's assault (p. 80).

According to David Quint, the use of the enchanted boat in the chivalric romance, as opposed to the epic, epitomizes the difference between the two forms, while also symbolizing the romance's meandering preferences. In the romance, argues the critic, "such ships embody the adventure principle that is a ubiquitous, perhaps essential feature of romance narrative:

counterbalancing an equally constitutive quest principle, it accounts for all the digressions and subplots which delay the quest's conclusion and which come to acquire an attraction and validity of their own.... In epic narrative, which moves to a predetermined end, the magic ship signals a digression from a central plot line, but the boat of romance, in its purest form, has no other destination than the adventure at hand. It cannot be said to be off course. New adventures crop up all the time, and the boat's travels describe a romance narrative that is open-ended and potentially endless" (Quint, p. 179).

One of the most outstanding aspects of Chrétien's *Lancelot, or, the Knight of the Cart* consists of its capacity to communicate the sheer delight taken by the writer in the multiplication of the story's ramifications—not only the ones we see realized on the page, but also the *potential* ones he could have pursued instead, and remain palpable, within the text's interstices, as its ghostly alter ego. According to Eugène Vinaver, the digressive temperament characteristic of the medieval romance "would not call for 'unity,'" the priority pursued by modern aesthetics, but rather for "expansion and diversity" (Vinaver, p. 12). Chrétien's romance embodies these structural priorities to a paradigmatic degree, while also conveying a lusty appetite for capaciousness, absurdity, and waywardness. With its expansive narrative mold, the text overrules the epic's single-minded, corporate, mentality by dwelling on the vagaries of individual experience, reveling in erotic interludes, and mocking chivalric ideal with satirical, albeit unobtrusive, glee.

Chrétien wrote only the first 9,000 verses of *Perceval, the Story of the Grail* (probably written between 1135 and 1190). The romance has acquired the extraordinary length it boasts today courtesy of various "Continuations." The text deserves inclusion in this context on account of both its thematic significance as an important component of the Grail myth as a whole, and its proficient handling of the stylistic device commonly described as the "cliffhanger." While it is undeniable that the use of this device was quite unintentional, considering its cause was the author's death before he had a chance to complete the poem, the effect is nonetheless remarkable. In fact, many readers have admitted to finding their experience of Chrétien's unfinished text more regarding, on the enjoyment plane, than the perusal of complete accounts of the notorious quest.

Perceval, the Story of the Grail is the first romance in which Perceval is cast in the role of the Grail knight. In both literature and cinema, the character is often portrayed as clumsy, blundering, and poorly socialized. Naomi Wise, accordingly, calls Perceval a "bumbling hero" (Wise, p. 52), while Norris J. Lacy, Geoffrey Ashe, and Debra N. Mancoff describe the young knight as "naïve, charming and slightly absurd" (Lacy, Ashe, and Mancoff, p. 344). Ann McCullough terms him "socially inept" (McCullough, p. 48), and Caroline D. Eckhardt sees him as the classic "country bumpkin" (Eckhardt, p. 205). Moreover, as Paula Leverage states with reference to Wise, "Chrétien's romance itself has been called 'a story of the blunders of a teenage knight'" (Leverage, p. 133; citation: Wise, p. 48). Leverage's own thesis is that Perceval, instead of being merely silly or juvenile, is in fact "autistic," and that the character's "failure to ask the question essential to the Fisher King can be understood," therefore, in the light of "a general cognitive deficiency" (Leverage, p. 145).

Numerous moments in Chrétien's romance "suggest that Perceval is deficient in reading minds" (p. 135). He also evinces an "inability to engage in conversation" (p. 137), and a "detached" stance towards other people's "emotions," including his own mother's (p. 138). These facets of the knight's personality and behavior, according to Leverage, are redolent of autism. Thus, "he cannot ever fit into the knightly culture because his low level of function in mind reading does not allow him to emulate and replicate the mental states of others by which process he might better understand how to engage with the community to which he aspires" (p. 139).

A telling example is provided by the scene in which "Sagremor rides up to Perceval and demands that he come to the king." At this juncture, the knight "appears not to hear him." He is so engrossed in the contemplation of the blood-speckled snow which reminds him of his darling Blanchefleur as to show no consciousness of anything else which might be happening around him. While "Perceval's reverie ... is usually interpreted as symbolic of his initiation into the world of love, and of chivalry motivated by love," Leverage contends that Perceval's conduct in this scene, where he seems "completely withdrawn and absorbed in his own thought," is suggestive of a "cognitive deficiency." This reaches its culmination in his failure to "ask the key question about the grail procession, which he must ask if the Fisher King is to be healed" (pp. 142–143).

According to Peter Haidu, Perceval actually exemplifies neither the maladroit nor the autistic personality, but rather "a type which became increasingly popular in the Middle Ages, that of the 'wild man.' Primitiveness was seen differently in this tradition than in modern thought. Where we often tend to consider the 'natural' elements in man as anterior and more essential to his being than the restraining effects of civilization, the medieval tradition saw the state of wildness rather as a fall from the normal human condition, the result of psychological turmoil or a peculiar upbringing," though not as an "irremediable" one (Haidu, p. 119). Wildness involves "asociality: ignorance of common objects, forms of behavior, conceptions of individuality and propriety" (p. 120), and other aspects of the normal world which any socialized person would take for granted, or at least grasp without inordinate effort.

Haidu's assessment of Perceval's character is based on a close analysis of the character's responses to the sensory stimuli released by his environment. The romance's first segment offers a succession of interrelated contrasts. The first of these consists of the opposition between "the sound of birds" and "the sound of armor," in the scene where Perceval is seen to ride through the forest and enjoying nature's blissful tunes as the clangor of knightly armor colliding with the surrounding vegetation suddenly surprises him. The second contrast is the one between "the sound of armor" and "the sight of armor," as the boy's attention is gradually transferred from the noise—and its association with satanic agencies—to the vision of its actual source—and attendant shift to the opposite end of the spectrum, as the knights are equated by Perceval to angelic or indeed divine beings.

"The brilliance of knighthood" and "the flat ignorance of Perceval" are next contrasted, as one of the knights asks the boy for information, and Perceval, appearing not even to hear his queries, questions him insistently about his chivalric trappings: i.e., items he has never seen before. Having come to regard chivalry as the most desirable state to which a human being could ever aspire—just on the basis, ironically, of one brief encounter with a small sample of its scions—Perceval announces his intention to become a knight to his ageing mother, thereby eliciting her mournful account of the misfortunes which have befallen their family precisely as a result of its aristocratic/chivalric status.

In this case, Perceval's idealistic perception of chivalry's unmatched magnificence is contrasted with his elder's emphasis on "knighthood's cost in death and sorrow." The woman's decision to lead a retired life in a remote rural area, and to bring up her one surviving son in total oblivion to anything knightly, denotes "sorrow leading to a willful search for innocence," whereas in Perceval's interaction with the knights, "innocence" is portrayed "as ignorance and brutal rudeness." In all of the oppositions outlined above, the two contrasting terms are connected by means of irony, insofar as "each is shown to bear values other than it seems to possess at first" (p. 128).

The episode centered on Perceval's encounter with the five knights, who happen to be riding through the forest in pursuit of enemies, is the first scene in Chrétien's romance to feature the titular hero. The author's unique humor comes instantly to the fore as one of the text's most distinctive assets. The scene indeed offers a glorious case of speech at cross purposes. As one of the knights questions Perceval repeatedly about his possible sighting in the area of another knightly posse leading three girls, the innocent youth is utterly transfixed by the sight of objects he has never seen before: a lance, a shield, and a hauberk. These appear to hold visceral appeal for him, as though they were somehow *meant* or *destined* to occupy a special place in his future life.

The insistence with which Perceval interrogates the knight, thereby ignoring the questions posed to him by the latter as though they carried no meaning whatsoever for either his ears or his brain, recalls the attitude of an uncultured child. What the youth seeks is an explanation of the function of each object kindling his curiosity, which the courteous knight deigns to provide with notable forbearance. Perceval's unselfconscious persistence brings to mind *Blackadder*'s Baldrick, as borne out by the snippet of dialogue in which the rustic boy, commenting on the knight's hauberk, remarks: "may stags / And does never get / These mail shirts, or I'll never kill / Another; I'll give up hunting!" The inane exchange reaches its apotheosis as the boy inquires: "Were you born with this shirt?" (Chrétien de Troyes 1999, p. 10).

The scene's comical impact, built in a crescendo of glee, stems from the clash of two incompatible frames of reference, and related forms of discourse. Chrétien is here presenting us with comedy at its most basic—at least apparently. In fact, the humor is soon rendered more subtle by the layering of comedy with the genius of irony. This becomes evident as the knight who has been questioning Perceval declares that he was knighted five days ago by King Arthur himself. This suggests that Perceval and the knight, at first presented as antithetical characters in all respects, are not actually as dissimilar as we might have thought, both of them being newbies of sorts. Just as Perceval is just beginning to grasp the meaning of hitherto unseen objects, so his interlocutor is only in the propaedeutic phase of his career as a member of the chivalric caste. Ironically, the two characters turn out to be alternate versions of the same human state: greenness. The literal association of both Perceval and the errant knight with the image of the luxuriant forest in the scene just examined reinforces this chromatic metaphor with graphic energy.

A further illustration of Chrétien's distinctive humor is provided by the scene, set in a luxurious tent which the youth initially takes to be a church (again assuming a beautiful thing must be holy), in which Perceval kisses a girl and seizes her ring—clearly against her will—before proceeding to gobble a venison pie accompanied by wine before departing. Once again, the comedy springs from the character's absolute misinterpretation of unfamiliar objects and situations. In addition, the scene serves to stress Perceval's limited linguistic understanding: his mother, prior to his departure from the reclusive abode, told him he *could* take a kiss and a ring from a girl (if offered, that is), but in the tent, he interprets his old woman's words as meaning he *must* do so come what may.

Yet another instance of Chrétien's humor comes with the episode dramatizing Perceval's defeat of the Red Knight threatening Arthur's dominion, which takes place shortly after he has made his first appearance at the great court. As Haidu remarks, it is ironical that "Arthur's court," which "represents the locus and epitome of courtly knighthood," should be "defended by the antithesis of its own values" (Haidu, p. 145)—that is to say, an uncouth boy for whom chivalry still remains, despite his strength in combat, nothing other than a distant mirage. This impression is reinforced by the later episode in which Perceval receives both hospitality and training from the suave Gornemant De Goort. In this case, "the contrast between the youth's self-assurance in his knighthood and the lack of knighthood it betrays to Gornemant's unexpressed standards is one of the most subtle examples of Chrétien's juxtaposition of two disparate worlds of awareness" (p. 149). Hence, the host's advice regarding proper courtly behavior clashes with his pupil's penchant for literalism to hilarious effect.

Likewise memorable moments of comedy emanate from Chrétien's affectionate exposure of Perceval's linguistic inadequacy. Given the opportunity to sit next to the sublime Blanchefleur shortly after his arrival at the city of Belrepeire, for example, the boy recalls Gornemant's counsel to use speech with prudence, and refrains from uttering even a single word, thus behaving not quite as the paragon of courtesy he wishes to be, but rather with a peculiarity which invites lively speculation amongst the onlookers. It is for the very reason that Perceval is *desperate* to be a knight, and be *perceived* as one, that he unknowingly conducts himself in a risibly *un*chivalric fashion.

In fact, the text gives us reason to wonder whether Perceval *ever* succeeds in embodying the knightly spirit: he might develop skills which the rustic youth seen at the start of the romance could not ever have imagined, yet never seems to *internalize* the code of chivalry, and act it out with effortless know-how. Therefore, by the time the romance comes to its abrupt end, Perceval is still only a *potential* knight: the values which feel natural, despite their blatant artificiality, to those he seeks to mimic remain extrinsic to his essence.

As the romance develops, we realize that this state of affairs is not purely comical: it is also tinged with a sad irony. While Perceval's desire to become a consummate member of the chivalric ranks is never quite fulfilled, it nonetheless distances him from his roots in nature—his primitiveness, so to speak. On the one hand, the chivalric code can never become so intimate a part of Perceval's being as to feel like an innate endowment. On the other hand, the boy becomes increasingly unable to behave in accordance with nature's own laws. This is exemplified by the scene in which Blanchefleur approaches Perceval's bed—with the intention, at least in principle, of apprising him of her land's plight—and lies next to him wearing nothing other than a flimsy nightdress throughout the night. In the presence of this overt offer of sexual favors, Perceval remains a paragon of chastity.

At this juncture, as Haidu observes, "it is not only by comparison with social assumptions that [Perceval's] persistent innocence is risible, but by comparison to nature" (p. 161). The apparent meaning of Chrétien's irony is that Perceval is too natural, and that his inability to embody the knightly code emanates from this naturalness. The latent message is that the chivalric values he has managed to grasp, courtesy toward women chief among them, prevent Perceval from behaving in a natural manner. If, on one level, he is too natural, on another, he is not natural enough.

A tantalizing inversion of the dramatic formula described above is supplied by the dramatization of Perceval's experiences in the Fisher King's otherworldly domain, and responses to the mysterious events unfolding before him. Commentators have devoted unending attention to the youth's silence in the face of the Grail pageant, and attendant failure to heal the Fisher King, as though these were the result of *unnatural* politesse. Keith Busby, for example, contends that "Perceval remains silent, remembering Gornemant's advice," to conform to an acquired code as opposed to "his own inclinations" (Busby, p. 34). This evaluation of the boy's behavior is based on the supposition that Perceval is repressing his natural instincts in the service of an unnatural etiquette, which de facto renders his comportment itself unnatural. Lacy corroborates this interpretation, arguing that Perceval's silence bears witness to a "conflict between a character's natural (and therefore good) impulse and an action dictated by an artificial and learned code of behaviour" (Lacy 1980, p. 5).

Not a single one of the critics consulted in the preparation of this study has suggested that Perceval's conduct may actually be quite *natural*. In fact, it might be salutary to ask ourselves whether we would really dare break the imposing atmosphere of solemn proceedings such as those presented by the Grail procession to pose questions about their meaning. Even in a less formal context, such as a theatrical performance, it is unlikely that many of us would suddenly pipe up from the auditorium to ask what an action is supposed to signify, or which character is eventually going to benefit from its enactment, let alone inquire about a director's intentions. In this respect, the interruption of a ritual like the Grail procession could be seen as synonymous not with wisdom, but with nosy insolence; not with charitable intent, but with selfish curiosity.

Perceval's treatment of Blanchefleur can be read as unnatural. Hence, it is ironically inconsistent with the youth's reputation as an overly natural person. The Fisher King episode inverts the formula: though interpreted as unnatural by several generations of commentators, it is quite natural if viewed as a basic expression of politeness. What aggravates the immature knight's predicament is the fact that he has embraced a protocol he cannot fully grasp, and therefore does not really know any more what is polite and what is not. At times, he might seem uncouth, but there are also times when he seems just too polite for his own good.

Critics keen on interpreting Chrétien's last romance as a redefinition of a fundamentally secular Arthurian world through the infusion of religious messages into the mix have been inclined to stress Perceval's remissness in inquiring about the Grail sequence as symptomatic of his sinfulness. Moreover, they have blamed the youth's descent into this state on his progressive refinement as a would-be knight. For these critics, Perceval's impiety is a corollary of his self-distancing from the religious tenets instilled in him from a young age by his disillusioned mother, which is borne out by his neglect to visit any religious establishments for five years after his departure. It is because of his transgression of orthodox Christian mores, this line of argument suggests, that the boy fails to grasp his responsibility in the hailing of the Fisher King, and in the restoration of the land to prosperity (i.e., a state of grace).

Some commentators have substantiated the religious reading by averring that even the part of *Perceval, the Story of the Grail* centered on Gawain reveals a shift towards religion. They propose that insofar as Gawain is the epitome of secular chivalry, this part of the text could be expected to deal solely with worldly matters. However, since it portrays this normally brilliant knight as ineffective, it actually conveys a spiritual message by implying that his ineffectiveness results from his inveterate secularity. In this fashion, those inclined to decode the romance in a religious key claim that it is Gawain's very worldliness that alienates him from any chance of success. Undeniably, Gawain does not bring any of his secondary tasks to fruition, let alone his initial goal, and thus fails to achieve *anything* much in the course of the story as we have it. However, the knight's failure to complete any quest cannot be unequivocally attributed to any personal flaw, since it could be a simple corollary of the text's incomplete nature.

It could, however, be argued that there are no overt spiritual lessons in Chrétien's last romance. Even the episodes in which supposedly Christian teachings are inculcated into the innocent Perceval, their mystical messages are presented in so condensed a fashion as to look rather platitudinous: more like snippets of a pre-digested catechism than any seriously internalized truth. For instance, the explanation of the meaning of Good Friday proffered by the penitents whom Perceval meets on that date seems rather perfunctory, which makes it sound very much like a potted history of the Passion, and related events from the Gospel.

In scenes of this ilk, it is not so much the veracity of the lessons as the chronic credulity of their receiver that is thrown into relief. The suggestion is that just as in the forest Perceval was so susceptible to the knights' glamor as to resolve to emulate their career and forget all about god and his angels, when he is faced with the hermit's chastizing words, he likewise imbibes everything he sees and hears without discrimination. As for Gawain, his incapacity to achieve any objective is not a consequence of his lack of faith in religion. His problem is that by now, he has grown into so consummate an exemplar of chivalry at its most formulaic that his behavior has become entirely mechanical, and hence as lacking in judgment as Perceval's.

Moreover, the hermit episode delivers an ironical interrogation of religious dogma, bearing witness to Chrétien's refined humor at its subtlest. The pious man seals Perceval's resolve to return to the faith taught him by his mother by whispering into his ear "a prayer full of the sacred names God is known by, the highest and holiest names," enjoining the youth never to recite the words "except when facing the greatest danger" (Chrétien de Troyes 1999, p. 205). Though seemingly endowed with religious significance, the scene is redolent of a magical rite. At the same time as he appears to accord religion the highest ranking, therefore, Chrétien ironically debunks its authority by equating it to the very system of belief it is supposed to have displaced.

Lancelot, or, the Knight of the Cart offers a further illustration of Chrétien's penchant for yoking together religious and secular discourses with latently sacrilegious irony. This consists of the scene in which great crowds gather in order to witness Lancelot's fight against Meleagant, the arrogant prince responsible for Guinevere's abduction. "The grounds," we are told, "were filled with people from the kingdom of Logres. For just as people are accustomed to go to church to hear the organ on the annual feast-days of Pentecost or Christmas, so they had all assembled now" (Chrétien de Troyes 2008a, p. 222). An unequivocally worldly event is thus equated to two of the most hallowed dates in the Christian calendar. It is also intriguing that the reason adduced by the narrator for the custom of visiting the house of god on Pentecost or Christmas should be people's desire to "hear the organ": not exactly the most devout of objectives.

Yvain, or the Knight with the Lion exhibits a comparable taste for irreligious parody in the passage describing the titular hero's perception of the object of his desire. "Never before in a work of beauty was Nature thus able to outdo herself, for I am sure she has gone beyond the limits of any previous attempt.... If she should try to make a replica, she might spend her time in vain without succeeding in her task. Even God Himself, were He to try, could not succeed, I guess, in ever making such another, whatever effort he might put forth" (Chrétien de Troyes 2008b, p. 146). Chrétien clearly feels at liberty to refer to his society's supreme deity as though he were in the same league as ordinary artisans, or even storytellers like himself, whose task consists of creating things of beauty out of the raw materials supplied by words. God's own ways remain proverbially mysterious. By contrast, the tools deployed by romancers like Chrétien are no mystery, since these authors are given to foreground their means and methods without reservations, through their self-conscious profession of fictionality. It is *through* language, and *in* language, they persistently remind us, that both loveliness and its diametrical opposite, the monstrosity in which the romance so often revels, find fruition, and survive the test of time.

With subtle irony, Chrétien calls attention to the inadequacy of all established codes, secular and religious alike. Time and again, his romances bring into focus the fallibility of courtly etiquette by exposing the disparity between knightly ideals and knightly comportment. While engaging in this critique with assiduousness throughout his career, Chrétien does not fail to include religion in the menu, intimating that spiritual values are as questionable as worldly ones: as soon as either one or the other set of standards is swallowed whole, reason and discernment dissolve.

Like the titular hero's exploits in *Yvain, or, the Knight of the Lion*, Gawain's adventures in *Perceval, the Story of the Grail* are informed by the structural principle of deferral, as one episode triggers another before reaching completion. The salient thing about this technique is that each new task embraced by Gawain in his metamorphic quest comes across as sufficiently interesting unto itself to make one forget the old one—or, at any rate, make one willing to shift one's attention to its perusal without regret. (Italo Calvino's *If on a Winter's Night a Traveler* [1979] springs to mind as an apt contemporary analogue.)

To begin with, Gawain resolves to leave Arthur's court in order to relieve the siege of Mont Esclaire. This objective is pushed to the background of the action as Guinganbresil, seneschal of the King of Escavalon, accuses Gawain of having murdered the king's father, and is hence guilty of treason, daring him to journey to Escavalon to answer the challenge to his violated honor. However, during the journey to Escavalon, Gawain is again deflected, this time by a grand tournament held at Tintagel to which he contributes in order to champion a little girl, thereby defeating the valiant Meliant de Lis, suitor to her hot-tempered sister.

In Tintagel, the strategy of deferral asserts itself once more as one of Chrétien's prime narrative ruses, since the tournament itself is not immediately presented as the focus of the romance. Much attention is instead given to speculations surrounding Gawain's social standing and intentions. In the scenes in which the knight refrains from taking part in the grand contest played out before him, despite his credentials, the loquacious female spectators infer that he must be after his own profit. The passage demonstrates that the romance's fantastic aura does not automatically imply a lack of socioeconomic relevance. At the same time, the women's conjectures, which they voice as they watch the jousting knights and the inactive Gawain, are also eerily prescient of contemporary financial inequity. "He must be a merchant," some comment, while others surmise: "he's here to sell his horses." A number of suspicious spectators are convinced that Gawain merely "imitates" the "appearance" of a knight, when all he truly seeks is "to keep from paying a merchant's / Taxes" (Chrétien de Troyes 1999, pp. 160–161).

When the knight eventually reaches Escavalon and is there offered hospitality, he hardly gets down to martial business right away, preferring instead to indulge in gracious dalliance with the king's sister. Recognized and attacked by the blood-thirsty rabble, Gawain and his new sweetheart defend themselves in a series of comical vignettes (the apotheosis being the one where the knight and lady protect themselves by flinging hefty chess pieces, and using the chessboard as a shield). Ironically, it is Guinganbresil himself who comes to the rescue. Just as Gawain's initial quest seems to be approaching its resolution at last, we are informed that insofar as the knight is guarded by the monarch's hospitality, his judgment will have to be postponed for a year. Meanwhile, the knight must pursue a novel objective: the Bleeding Lance prophesied to precipitate the fall of the Kingdom of Logres. This task enables Gawain's adventures to intersect with Perceval's, the spear constituting a pivotal element in the Grail parade witnessed by the young knight in the course of his own adventures.

Gawain's quest is again rerouted as he chances upon a damsel grieving over a mortally wounded knight, who cautions him not to cross the Galloway border lest he should meet certain death. With a classic flourish of insouciant obstinacy typical of the seasoned knight errant, Gawain defies the dying knight's warning and rides into Galloway by means of a perilous crossing of the kind often associated by romance writers with the transit from this world into an Other world. He thereby reaches a grand city, there to acquire the unsolicited company of a spiteful girl whose only aim is to ride with him till she sees him "suffering pain, misfortune, / And sorrow" on her account (Chrétien de Troyes 1999, p. 217). Returning to the spot where he had left the dying knight, Gawain deploys his impressive medical knowledge to heal him, but instead of gratitude, he receives a grievous insult as the patient proceeds to steal Gawain's trusted steed, Gringolet, and to abuse the creature through reckless maneuvering.

The treacherous knight, whose name turns out to be Gregorias, resents his savior on two counts. Firstly, Arthur's nephew has been responsible for his humiliation following his rape of a girl "for the sheer fun and pleasure of it" (p. 225). Secondly, Gregorias is Guinganbresil's brother, and therefore holds Gawain guilty of treason—which causes the narrative to loop back to the scene set in Arthur's court where Gawain's quest effectively begins. The perfidious Gregorias goes on persecuting Chrétien's hero, instructing his nephew to pursue Gawain, and bring him the knight's head come what may, thereby allowing the romance to indulge in yet another digression.

One might expect Gawain's adventures to have reached a climactic destination with his arrival at the Castle of Marvels (a.k.a. Castle of the Rock of Champguin), where the knight undergoes the most wondrous experiences in his journey so far. There can be little doubt that the episode evinces all the narrative credentials of a major climax. Not even now, however, does Gawain seem able, or prepared, to stay put. The spirit of adventure which, as noted, motivates romance heroes over and above the thirst for any one designated goal proves just too potent for the paragon of Arthurian chivalry in its most accomplished, albeit also most urbane, incarnation. Thus, defying the local interdiction on free movement in and out of the magnificent fortress, Gawain requests his hostess' permission to explore the grounds, there to meet another string of adventures culminating with the meeting with Grinomalant, and hence the prospect of yet another bracing test of his knightly puissance (Gawain's father having supposedly been responsible for the death of Grinomalant's own, and Gawain himself for that of one of his cousins).

Gawain's exploits demonstrate that Chrétien knows well how to exploit the strategy of deferral to produce textual gaps meant to stimulate the reader's own imagination. Though we will never know what the stories which the author has left untold might have contained, we are at liberty to formulate alternate tales. This allows the text to expand from within as the strands connecting any two, or more, incomplete episodes proliferate in our own heads. However, deferral is not Chrétien's sole means of stoking the reader's creativity. In fact, he also capitalizes on descriptive elements which, albeit vivid, are so succinct as to make it incumbent upon the audience to speculate about their narrative and philosophical implications.

A good example of this proclivity is provided by the depiction of the great hall of the Castle of Marvels, where "art and enchantment" are said to collude to unique effect. The "feats of magic" sustaining the Champguin establishment have been put in place by an "astronomer priest" (Chrétien de Troyes 1999, p. 238), the living epitome of an age in which astrology and astronomy fluidly coalesce, as do alchemy and the natural sciences, or indeed magic and medicine. Chrétien is eager to show that these creative coalitions are not purely a matter of convenience. While they do serve utilitarian agendas, they also yield a sophisticated aesthetic which underpins many stunning artifacts. One such work is the prosthetic limb worn by the "cripple" whom Gawain meets on "the stairs in front of the palace." Captivated by the uncommon beauty of an artificial "leg" made of "silver / Wound around with gold / And besplanged all over with golden / Rings and precious stones," Gawain describes it simply as "incredibly lovely," as though even his refined rhetoric were at a loss for words in the face of so unusual a masterpiece (pp. 241–242).

Chrétien's output as a whole capitalizes on the integration of multiple narrative threads which echo one another through reiterations, correspondences, and variations. In *Perceval, the Story of the Grail*, his final romance, Chrétien takes this technique a stage further by interlinking two discrete plot lines—and two protagonists. As Bruckner observes, "at the traditional moment of crisis, which requires the hero to take a second series of adventures, Chrétien doubles the accusers who arrive at Arthur's court and sends both Perceval and Gauvain [*sic*] out on quests…. In the midst of Gauvain's adventures, the narrator recounts Perceval's visit to his hermit uncle, which takes place after five years of fruitless adventures. A strange time warp into the future opens, but just as this single episode promises to reorient Perceval's quest, the narrator loops back to Gauvain's story, whose adventures continue to accumulate" (Bruckner 2000, p. 16).

Chrétien's employment of two heroes within a single text bears witness to the author's appetite for experiment. Having invented the chivalric romance virtually from scratch, the writer was not satisfied with following the same basic narrative pattern from one text to the next. His works are therefore distinguished by an ardent desire to stretch the text's boundaries through more and more complex strategies of deferral, which ultimately result in jubilantly self-unraveling plotlines. Rupert Pickens reinforces this proposition, arguing that in his last work, Chrétien "explodes romance as he pushes the form he has developed previously beyond all expectations. He does this by amplifying the role of Perceval's double so that he approaches parity with him" (Pickens, p. 176).

The romance sets up a solid connection between its two heroes by means of a stark contrast. "Perceval at the beginning of the romance," argues Busby, "was a young lad without a past, without a reputation, and without an identity; much of the poem is concerned with the acquisition of these." Gawain, on the other hand, faces "the opposite" difficulty insofar as he has a "long history, both within the text and without" (Busby, pp. 53–54). A further contrast between the two co-protagonists is borne out by Gawain's adventures at the Castle of Marvels, compared with Perceval's at the Grail Castle. "Whereas Perceval fails to ask the questions, heal the Fisher King, and restore the land to prosperity," states Busby, Gawain "passes the test" by showing himself able to sit unharmed on the Perilous Bed (a.k.a. Bed of Marvels), "frees the inhabitants, and becomes lord of the castle." Nonetheless, the atmosphere which pervades Gawain's visit to the Castle of Marvels is no less mysterious than the aura surrounding Perceval's Grail Castle experiences. For one thing, even after Gawain's successful performance vis-à-vis the Perilous Bed, "it is still not clear whom he has liberated from what, for no more details are forthcoming about the inhabitants or the nature of the enchantments" (pp. 78–79).

While capitalizing on contrast as a major structural ploy, Chrétien also connects Gawain's exploits with the Perceval segment of the story by recourse to parallelisms and similarities. Some of these are explicit, while others are so subtly woven into the fabric of the narrative as to become perceptible only with the benefit of repeat readings. An important affinity between the two components of *Perceval, the Story of the Grail* is their shared emphasis on the topos of lineage. Both the Grail King and the hermit are Perceval's mother's brothers, and, therefore, Perceval's uncles. The Fisher

King is Perceval's mother's nephew and hence Perceval's cousin. However, he may also be her husband—i.e., Perceval's father—which would make Chrétien's hero the issue of an incestuous relationship.

As Joseph J. Duggan observes, Perceval's "mother has told him that his father was wounded between the legs and as a consequence both his land and his treasure went into decline. Perceval's cousin explains that the Fisher King has been wounded between the haunches, and he lives in ... a wasteland.... Is it possible that the Fisher King, then, is Perceval's own dead father and the Grail King his grandfather? If this is so, then Perceval would be the offspring of incest between his mother and her nephew" (Duggan, p. 299). Queen Ygerne, a character symbolically associated with the Land of the Dead, is presented as the mother of both Gawain's unnamed mother and Arthur, which makes Arthur Gawain's uncle, and Ygerne his grandmother. Clarissant is Gawain's sister, and Chrétien's hint at the possibility of a prospective sexual liaison between them echoes the incest theme already central to the portrayal of Perceval's line.

According to Duggan, one of Chrétien's most notable skills is the capacity "to construct episodes that in some way resonate with each other." This is borne out by the use of implied relationships between the Perceval and the Gawain strands, which serve to clarify some of the more esoteric aspects of the romance. Gawain's "adventures in Champguin," argues the critic, "illuminate obscure characteristics of Perceval's Grail experience. The Grail Castle is inhabited by Perceval's kin just as Gawain's family live on the Rock of Champguin.... Access to each is facilitated by a man in a boat. In both castles, the newcomer is subjected to a test" (p. 298).

The portion of the romance devoted to Gawain's exploits is no less infused with irony than its Perceval-centered correlative. In the romance's handling of courtly love, in particular, Gawain is as much a target of Chrétien's ironical humor as the gauche Perceval. In the course of the romance, none of Gawain's liaisons is consummated. As Haidu comments, for one reason or another, he never passes beyond the earlier, incomplete stage ... of the flirtation with its verbal exchanges of love and ... kisses and caresses. The 'love' Gauvain [*sic*] enjoys is a formalized social [pastime] with no satisfaction other than the pride of another unconsummated conquest" (p. 215). This scenario is ironical to say the least when one takes into consideration Gawain's fame as the exemplar of chivalry in matters amorous no less than martial. This reputation, as Thomas Hahn explains, pivots on the character's conventional presentation in the "standard role as the Young

Man, available for both adventure and love, mean that active, competitive masculinity ... is both defined and tested through his exploits" (Hahn, p. 220).

One of the factors to be taken into account when assessing Chrétien's ironical treatment of Gawain's erotic conduct in *Perceval, the Story of the Grail* is the character's propensity, throughout the part of the romance of which he is the protagonist, to function more as a *"persona"* (p. 213), a dramatic type, than an actual *person*. This dubious existential choice does not always prove advantageous to Arthur's perfect knight. In fact, it may blind him to the actual nature of the quest before him, and even lead him to act in comical ways as a result of his decision to embark on a task just because a knight *would do so*, not out of lucid judgement and logic.

A telling illustration of this tendency is the episode in which Gawain endeavors to play the role of the gallant champion of a female in distress vis-à-vis the Girl with the Narrow Sleeves (*Pucelle aux Manches Petites*): that is to say, a decidedly unorthodox object of courtly service. Busby corroborates this proposition, stating that the "relationship" between Gawain and the girl is "clearly based on the traditional relationship between knight and damsel whilst at the same time it cannot be taken seriously because of the girl's age" (Busby, p. 57). Chrétien's masterful handling of descriptive details attests to the girl's immaturity, making it obvious that "she is too young for the role" she is brought in to play. For instance, she "grasps" the knight's "leg" to invite "his attention," as any ordinary little girl might be expected to do, and "is small enough to be carried off on the neck of her father's horse" (p. 58).

The irony pervading this state of affairs resides with the conflict between Gawain's ostensible virtue in his unflinching loyalty to the code of courtly love (the apparent meaning delivered by the narrative), and his underlying inadequacy, as a character unable to understand that there are times when such a code is just irrelevant to the reality around him (the latent meaning which Chrétien wishes us to ponder). This discrepancy ultimately serves to make Gawain "as ridiculous as the uncourtly Perceval" (Haidu, pp. 219–220).

It would seem that Chrétien makes Gawain the butt of ironic humor not because he harbors any personal resentment against him an individual. (After all, nobody, in medieval literature, is truly an "individual" in the modern sense—or rather *construction*—of the term.) Rather, Chrétien seems keen on questioning the values of an entire ethos—namely, the chivalric code enshrined in Arthurian society—and finds an apt metonym for that system in the figure of the gallant Gawain. Thus, what is under attack in the Gawain section of *Perceval, the Story of the Grail* is not a specific person, but rather the conventional protocol by which he acts. Ultimately, parodying prescribed courtly love and courtly prowess alike by means of Gawain's formulaic actions can be seen as a means of bringing an entire world to trial, and of finding it wanting—though still precious, for a writer of Chrétien's imagination, as the repository of endless narrative motifs.

Recognizing the extent to which Chrétien emphasizes the more stereotypical facets of Gawain's role is critical to the reader's appreciation of his art. In a sense, Chrétien's Gawain gains individuality, ironical as this may sound, from the author's knack of making him *even more stereotypical* than the already popular stereotype of Gawain as the perfect knight. However, this is not where the French poet's greatness as a character portraitist ends. In fact, one of the most memorable facets of Chrétien's treatment of the Gawain figure lies with his ability to intimate that there are more dimensions to the illustrious knight than his famed martial prowess, and no less renowned savoir faire in amorous matters. Indeed, Chrétien's Gawain evinces a sensitivity which one would not automatically expect of a medieval character. This is borne out by his attitude to nature, and particularly to animals. One example will have to suffice, in the present context, but its affecting tone will hopefully attest to the knight's gentleness. This is the scene following Gawain's crossing of the Perilous Ford, where the knight devotes his full attention to his destrier before addressing any of the pressing chivalric matters in hand: he "removed the saddle-cloth" with great care, we are informed, and then "rubbed / The horse's back and sides / And legs, until it was dry" (Chrétien de Troyes 1999, p. 269).

Chrétien himself shows great sympathy toward animals, and especially, which is not surprising in the context of *chivalric* romances, horses. A good example of the author's disposition, in this matter, is offered by the touching depiction of the famished palfrey in the Perceval-centered section of the romance. Utterly "exhausted" by overexertion, the creature is described as "staggering" and "poorly fed," and "so miserably thin that it trembled." The palfrey's portrait is rendered downright pathetic by two details: "its mane cut off, its ears / Hanging halfway to the ground" (pp. 117–118). At this juncture, Chrétien shows himself even more sympathetic toward the horse's plight than toward the palpable suffering endured by the damsel riding the unfortunate beast—which is conspicuous, when one considers the emphasis laid by the chivalric romance on the crucial importance of any courteous man's sensitivity to women's plight.

The *Lancelot-Grail Cycle*

The work of numerous authors, the *Lancelot-Grail Cycle* is supposed to have been mainly written in the second quarter of the thirteenth century, and amalgamates disparate strands, drawn from both the pseudo-historical chronicles woven around Arthur and his knights, and chivalric romances of purely fictional orientation. Considered as a whole, the *Lancelot-Grail Cycle* chronicles the history of the Arthurian world from the origins of the Grail after the Crucifixion, to Arthur's demise in his battle against Mordred, and the dissolution of the Round Table. Mordred, who had previously been invested with different, ambiguous, roles, is now unequivocally portrayed as the illegitimate son born of Arthur's incestuous liaison with his half-sister Morgause (at times fused with Morgan le Fay in later versions of the Arthurian legend).

Oscillating between apparent history and blatant fiction, between stark facts and elaborate wonders, the *Lancelot-Grail Cycle* evinces a mixed storytelling mode which harks back to Geoffrey of Monmouth, and looks forward to Thomas Malory. It is worth remembering, as Richard Trachsler points out, that "what we tend to see as a 'romance' shares much of its action with what medieval readers probably would not have hesitated to call 'history'" (Trachsler, p. 23). This is not only due to the relative indifference to the fact/fiction divide characteristic of medieval audiences: it is also a corollary of the fact that romance and chronicle authors tended "to turn to the same reservoir of traditional knowledge for material" in their respective records of a past in which real events and marvels merged in mutual suffusion (p. 24).

In Malory's own work, history and fantasy will again collude. As Terence McCarthy explains, "the reality of events ... is one of Malory's great concerns and not only does Merlin ... oversee events in the land, he is also the one in charge of recording great deeds." Malory's historiographical leanings are most evident in "his battle descriptions," replete with "lists of names, victims or participants" (McCarthy, p. 8). However, Malory's historiographical pretensions are suffused with (possibly self-conscious) irony, since a wizard's reliability as an impartial historiographer is dubitable to say the least.

A potentially sprawling galaxy of narratives distinguished by so keen a passion for digression and detour as to seem to defy the notion of structural coherence altogether, the *Lancelot-Grail Cycle* in fact evinces an extraordinary sense of unity. This is a corollary of its organization on the basis of the *entrelacement* technique, which allows the narrative to indulge in frequent shifts of direction, yet ensures the eventual binding of disparate strands into an organic whole of intricate beauty. However, one further factor is responsible for imparting the *Lancelot-Grail Cycle* with a cumulative aura of unity: a factor which holds special appeal in the context of this study by virtue of its eminently ironical character. This consists of the work's espousal of a contradictory agenda, whereby it aims to Christianize the Arthurian myth, on the one hand, yet derives power and zest from its allegiance to the secular romance tradition on the other. This is true of all its parts, but is most striking in the part of the cycle entitled *The Quest for the Holy Grail* for this is allegedly the most spiritually oriented.

According to Derek Pearsall, the *Cycle* is keen to demonstrate that "the failure of the knights of the Round Table in the Grail Quest" is a corollary of "the irredeemably fallen state of secular chivalry. While individual writers might see at times in the story of Lancelot and Guenevere a human meaningfulness, even a tragic conflict of high ideals of love and honour, the Vulgate compilers, inspired by ascetic … ideals, saw principally a lesson to be learnt concerning the nothingness of worldly desires." The extraordinary competence with which it manages to harness a boundless constellation of materials into a consistent web of dramatic episodes linked by countless anticipations and recapitulations bears witness to the lengths to which the authors of the *Lancelot-Grail Cycle* were determined to go in order to enforce their message.

Nonetheless, what is even more remarkable than such compositional legerdemain is the extent to which the worldly ideals which the saga sets out to proscribe keep resurging as inexhaustible fountainheads of creativity and intrigue. Thus, much as the *Lancelot-Grail Cycle* seeks to purge the romance of its secular passions, it "cannot change its essential nature as the record of the whole life of adventure taken up in the cause of love and chivalry" (Pearsall, pp. 45–46). The *Lancelot-Grail Cycle* can therefore be seen to yield a tantalizing irony: despite its efforts to transcend the "fallen" code of non-spiritual chivalry, if it were deprived of the ethical and aesthetic underpinnings supplied by that code, its textual power would vanish.

All in all, it is undeniable that the *Lancelot-Grail Cycle* is responsible for imparting Arthurian lore with moral messages to be later exploited to variable effect down to the present day. Even so, by interweaving its three narrative threads—the quest for the Grail, the love of Lancelot and Guinevere, and King Arthur's death—the work complicates and enlarges the adventures found in earlier chivalric romances, by adopting with gusto the penchant for meandering, episodic, and multiclimactic narration which has become synonymous with the chivalric romance as a form.

The *Lancelot-Grail Cycle* comprises five prose books. The *Lancelot* (a.k.a. *Lancelot* Proper or Prose *Lancelot*), *The Quest for the Holy Grail*, and *The Death of Arthur* constitute its main body. As Richard Barber explains in the analysis of the collection released online by Boydell and Brewer upon the publication of the ten-volume edition, "the first two romances, *The History of the Holy Grail* and *The Story of Merlin*, were added after the events described in *Lancelot* and *The Quest of the Holy Grail*." This entails that "in Hollywood terms, these are 'prequels'" (Barber 2010).

The ensuing pages examines some of each volume's salient features, devoting special attention to *The Quest for the Holy Grail* for the reason that it is in this romance that the spirit of irony, the topic central to the present study, finds its most intriguing expression. In addition, this text is thematically related to Chrétien de Troyes' *Perceval, the Story of the Grail*, and is therefore of particular relevance to the materials covered in this chapter.

As a linear chronological account of the Grail saga from the Crucifixion, *The History of the Holy Grail* anticipates *The Quest for the Holy Grail*. It is by no means unusual for romance narrators to claim to have drawn their materials from external sources—e.g., another storyteller, named or anonymous as the case may be; a recognized body of tales known to have already gained popularity among courtly audiences; or a book given them by their current patrons. This strategy serves to impart the romance with an aura of authority, and exonerate the teller from direct moral responsibility for the tale's content. No less importantly, it instills into the story a modicum of veracity, despite its obviously imaginary import, to the extent that in grounding it in a preexisting narrative, it also anchors it to an established bedrock of accepted "truths"—i.e., the "realities" embodied in that narrative. No matter how *un*true, and how *un*real, once an idea has attained textual incarnation, it has de facto acquired a degree of authority it did not enjoy before. This status, in turn, is enough to pave the way to its eventual admission to the Olympus of *truth*.

Even the authors of Arthurian works which predate the romance proper often claim to be relying on dependable sources in order to lend credence to their words. Geoffrey of Monmouth's *Historia Regum Brittaniae* is a paradigmatic case in point. Though blatantly fictitious, the work is eager to present itself as an objective piece of historiography. This kind of distortion feels almost natural in the context of a secular work emanating from a culture as yet unconcerned with the distinction between fiction and reality. However, the use of distortion in a text governed by spiritual priorities, such as the *Lancelot-Grail Cycle*, carries quite different connotations. One would expect the use of pure fantasy as a means of investing the text with authority to be somewhat incompatible with Christian ethics. After all, it is only a short step from mendacity.

Yet, there is hardly any doubt that the vision recounted in the prologue to *The History of the Holy Grail* is no less fictitious than any of Chrétien's wackiest chivalric adventures. "Hardly had I begun to doze when I heard a voice that called me three times by name," intones the narrator in his relived transport. "I awoke and looked around me and saw such brightness that nothing so great could issue from any earthly light.... When I opened my mouth to answer, I saw a fiery brand leap from my body, just like burning flames" (*The History of the Holy Grail*, p. 5). Formulated in notes so rapturous as to recall the ecstasies of many martyrs and saints, the piece conveys an ironical stance. On the one hand, it asks to be taken as the honest account of a true and self-validating fact, though one beyond the remit of ordinary human existence. On the other hand, by couching its inaugural passage in transparently visionary terms, the prologue invites the reader to question not merely its own content, but also the bearing of the ensuing narrative.

The ecstatic tone pervading the text's preamble goes on to inform the main body of *The History of the Holy Grail*, imbuing each of its key moments with the status of a mystical revelation. It is in this visionary-revelatory mood that the text discloses the history of the Grail from the Crucifixion to its placement by the Fisher King in the castle of Corbenic. As Barber explains, "many points in the narrative are designed to foreshadow or to explain the later adventures connected with the Grail." At the same time, the text "also draws on the stories in the apocryphal gospels and other legends of the crucifixion such as the story of Veronica, as well as unrelated material such as the story of Hippocrates" (Barber 2010).

In welcoming otherworldly agencies to the textual reservoir, *The History of the Holy Grail* posits a supposedly holy entity as the bearer of an inspirational text. However, the bearer's holiness does not make the information contained in the text unproblematically *true*. After all, the angelic being presented in the prologue to *The History of the Holy Grail* is redolent of one of the many visitors from Faërie who infiltrate the human world at will in countless secular romances. Thus, there is no logical justification for attributing a higher truth-value to "his" words than one would grant to those of Tryamour, Morgan le Fay (or Merlin himself for that matter).

The text's invention of its putatively divine sources is a bold enough move unto itself. Even more audacious is its rewriting of biblical mythology. Firstly, *The History of the Holy Grail* revises the Old Testament's version of the events following the Fall. Secondly, it expands Joseph of Arimathea's deeds from his deposition of Christ from the Cross to the Grail's voyage into Britain. As Carol J. Chase explains, in *The History of the Holy Grail*, "after the Crucifixion, Joseph of Arimathea goes to the house where the last Supper had been held, to seek an object that belonged to Christ. There he finds the bowl from which Christ ate. He uses the bowl to collect blood from Christ's body after taking it down from the Cross." It then chronicles "Joseph's imprisonment and liberation," and "his departure for Britain on an evangelical mission," where he takes the object—now known as the Grail—at God's own behest (Chase, pp. 68–69).

In its reconceptualization of the scriptures for its own purposes, *The History of the Holy Grail* could be deemed irreverent or even heretical by orthodox Christians. These reservations notwithstanding, few readers could deny its enthusiastic espousal of the art of storytelling. The message shining through the text's layered narrative and rhetorical twists is above all a celebration of fiction qua fiction: of the text's right to make things up, even if this means rescripting the Word. Hence, despite its apparent departure from the worldly ethos associated with the chivalric romance, *The History of the Holy Grail* is in fact quite loyal to the latter's philosophy in its implied glorification of fictionality, and related elevation of the fictional text to the status of the *supreme* form of textuality.

In emphasizing the received nature of its *facts*, the *Lancelot-Grail Cycle* as a whole opens up a vista of endless deferral, reminding us that in the romance tradition, any one text is, in principle, both a derivative of other texts, and a source of inspiration for yet more texts to come. At the same time, the cycle alerts us to the inevitably mediated character of all knowledge, and attendant inaccessibility of any pure, immediate, and innocent truth.

Often redolent of a fairy tale for adults with a soupçon of the grotesque and the macabre, *The Story of Merlin* recounts the wizard's role in Arthur's adulterous conception and illegitimate birth. It then traces the king's ascent to fame through his legendary martial triumphs, his marriage to Guinevere, and his acquisition of the Round Table.

One of the most remarkable aspects of *The Story of Merlin* lies with its status in the history of narrative experimentation. Its handling of the narratorial voice, in particular, dislodges the concept of authorial control in ways Roland Barthes would have been proud of. As Annie Combes points out, "we start with an omniscient narrator who oversees the fiction ... but ... as soon as [Merlin] is old enough to speak, he is the one who directs events and analyses them.... Merlin takes over" (Combes, p. 82). With this bold approach to narratorial authority, the text enables the protagonist to usurp the author's place—a move which is quite consonant with Merlin's standing as not only one of the greatest magicians of all times, but also a canny trickster. Running the show in accordance with the erratic flow of his memories and prophecies, Merlin releases the narrative to the great current of the chivalric romance at its most astutely worldly.

In spite of its professed transcendence of the secular thrust of Arthurian society, the *Lancelot-Grail Cycle* often draws attention to the materiality of the human body. *The Story of Merlin* attests to this trend in its detailed account of the wizard's conception as a result of a mortal woman's pollution by a demonic agency: "this one devil had the power to lie with a woman and get her with child.... He lay with her carnally as she slept, and she conceived" (*The Story of Merlin*, p. 51). Merlin himself develops this theme in graphic terms, declaring that he "the son of a devil," an incubus to be precise, and disclosing the powers he has inherited from his father (p. 55). The brute reality of he human body at its least attractive is underlined by the description of the baby's physiognomy in terms which echo the secular romance's passion for monsters. Merlin's hairiness, in particular, appears to be an object of perverse fascination for his biography's anonymous author(s): "when the women had received him, they were all deeply frightened, for they saw that he was hairier than they had ever seen any other child."

To accentuate the newborn's monstrosity, the text declares that Merlin's very mother is deeply troubled by his presence, as though the creature were no less alien and noxious than his demonic father: "after they had shown him to his mother she crossed herself and said: 'This child frightens me very much.'" The dramatic effectiveness of this scene owes much to the sheer simplicity of the language it employs. Moreover, the text announces its imbrication with the corporeal dimension by evoking a visceral sense of sadness through its insistence on the women's avoidance of the baby on the pretext that they are so scared of him, they can "scarcely hold him" (p. 54). After all, aberrant though the baby and the circumstances of his conception might be, he is *only* a baby at this stage.

The most extensive volume in the *Lancelot-Grail Cycle* is the *Lancelot* proper: a full-fledged chivalric romance where courtly love receives at once its greatest paean and its severest indictment. While Lancelot's love for

Guenevere confirms his standing as the best knight in the world, this very love precludes his triumph in the Grail Quest.

The *Lancelot* is the part of the *Lancelot-Grail Cycle* in which the chivalric elements of the Arthurian world are most prominent. Inspired by Chrétien's *Lancelot, or, the Knight of the Cart*, alongside other popular romances, the saga records the knight's personal history from his early childhood and rearing by the Lady of the Lake (a.k.a. Viviane, Niniane, or Nimue), who is supposed to have learned the magical arts from Merlin himself; through his introduction to Arthur's court, where he instantly falls in love with Guinevere; to subsequent adventures leading to Lancelot's admission to the Round Table. A prominent role is accorded to the character of Galehaut: the knight who engineers Lancelot's first tryst with Guinevere, thus sowing the seeds for the downfall of the Round Table.

The romance also dramatizes an event which could be regarded as the dawn of the quest for the Grail: when Lancelot reaches the Grail castle, he is deceived into lying with Elaine under the impression that she is in fact Guinevere, and their union results in the birth of Galahad, the only knight destined for success in the Grail Quest. When Guinevere discovers that her lover has slept with Elaine, she banishes him from Arthur's court, thereby driving him to lunacy. The romance culminates, in a notably open-ended fashion, with Lancelot's recovery of his reason, and Galahad's advent at court.

The technique of *entrelacement* reaches its fullest articulation in the *Lancelot* Proper, allowing the exploits of legion Arthurian knights to unfold concurrently, at times overlapping with one another, and at others branching off in disparate directions. As we have seen, *The History of the Holy Grail* seeks to establish the reliability of the events it relates by defining their source with graphic intensity. In *The Story of Merlin*, as also noted, narrative authority shifts from the storyteller per se to the hero. One may doubt Merlin's trustworthiness as a source, given his personal involvement in the "facts" he recounts. However, his own supernatural origins serve to sustain his authority—albeit in a potentially irreligious fashion, given the nature of the seer's father. As Frank Brandsma explains, in the *Lancelot*, "the text itself explains that [its] ultimate source ... is the narration of the events by the protagonists. The knights are reliable spokesmen according to the medieval ideas on narrative veracity, because they are eyewitnesses" (Brandsma, p. 24).

This facet of the narrative deserves consideration insofar as it underscores the specificity of the literary/philosophical context in which the *Lancelot* was produced. In so doing, it discourages us from assessing the text by the yardstick of modern notions of authenticity or modern audience expectations. Nowadays, not very many critics would consider a character's own account of events as the most dependable source of information for the sheer reason that he or she has witnessed and experienced them. In fact, a character's involvement in a certain event would be deemed most likely to engender a biased report. This does not seem to bother medieval readers, for whom direct involvement and objectivity do not constitute contradictory ideas, and for whom reality and fantasy do not occupy neatly demarcated, and antithetical, territories.

Bearing this critical divergence in mind, it is worth noting that the *Lancelot*'s stance on textual credibility redoubles the ironical disposition revealed by the text on the thematic plane. Indeed, at the same time as the *Lancelot* reflects the chivalric romance's propensity for irony by both upholding and condemning courtly love, it also evinces an ironic temperament by implying that characters who have experienced the narrated events are the most reliable of reporters, and concurrently hinting at their inexorable partiality. This discursive puzzle invites the modern reader to ponder the ultimate tenability of *any* critical criterion on the basis of which textual veracity may be ascertained.

The Quest for the Holy Grail chronicles in detail the exploits surrounding a number of knights committed to the quest, culminating with Galahad's triumph. As Norris J. Lacy points out in his introduction to *The Lancelot-Grail Reader*, the king himself is "far from enthusiastic about the quest; instead, he is angry and depressed about the prospect, for he immediately understands that, although the quest may unite his knights in a common purpose, that purpose does not—except negatively—involve Camelot and the Round Table society itself" (Lacy 2000b, p. ix). Arthur's chagrin is not immediately evident. On the contrary, when a young woman announces the Grail's imminent arrival at his court, where it will "feed the knights of the Round Table," the king decides to hold a tournament in the fields around Camelot to celebrate the portentous news. Yet, it soon becomes clear that he is innerly distressed. Having "now been assured" that his knights will "undertake the Quest for the Holy Grail," he is aware that he "will never again see [them] gathered together" (*The Quest for the Holy Grail*, p. 314). His words are tinged with a melancholy tone which foreshadows the atmosphere to become prevalent in the *Lancelot-Grail Cycle*'s closing romance, *The Death of Arthur*.

When Gawain swears to undertake the quest, and all his fellow knights follow his example, Arthur's mood descends into downright despondency. As the king gives vent to his agitation, mixing genuine despair with juvenile self-pity, Gawain becomes the object of his most stern reprimand. "'Gawain, Gawain,'" he mournfully intones, "how you have betrayed me. All the good you have done for my court does not offset the harm you bring upon it today. Never again will this court be honored by knights as noble and valiant as those whom you have spirited away by your initiative.'" The assertion that Gawain has "spirited" his fellows away is rather amusing, as it places the knight on a par with the enchanters often encountered in secular romances, implying that there is something preternaturally evil about his espousal of a quest which is in fact designed to test its undertakers' moral distinction in explicitly Christian terms.

Having uttered his lamentation, "the king fell into a deep and thoughtful silence. As he thought, tears began to roll down his face.... He remained in this state for a long time and finally said, 'God, I never thought I would be separated from this company of men whom good fortune has sent to me'" (p. 316). Arthur's sadness, the text implies, is intensified by the smarting knowledge that he is being left out, the messenger having made it patent that while he is to "experience the greatest honor ever to befall a knight in Brittany," the Grail "will not be for [him], but for another" (p. 314).

It is interesting, incidentally, that Arthur should address his grievance to "God," as though the latter were to be directly blamed for his knight's forthcoming departure, but posit "fortune" as the benevolent force responsible for delivering the fellowship into his care. This detail suggests that even though *The Quest for the Holy Grail* cultivates a Christian agenda, it does not embrace that ethos in an unambiguous fashion. This idea will be developed later in the discussion.

What must be stressed at this stage is that the launching of the quest inaugurates the gradual disintegration of the entire Arthurian venture as such. The king's resolve to call a tournament in response to the messenger's news is in itself telling. A tournament is *not*, in itself, an adventure, either martial or amorous, though it may bear the semblance of one. In fact, it is *only* a semblance: a simulacrum of a real chivalric exploit—a pageant, a charade, a travesty. Its announcement just before the knights swear to undertake the Grail Quest suggests that the advent of the Grail has robbed Arthur's kingdom of its former power to accommodate the greatest adventures ever recorded by chroniclers and romancers alike. All it can aspire to is the *staging* of toylike replicas of the real thing.

Arthur understands that the quest connotes the enthronement of a radical alternative to the Camelot milieu in the guise of an ideal court governed not by secular chivalric ideals of the Arthurian ilk, but rather by "an ideal of 'celestial chivalry,' which is both a religious ideal and an extraordinarily rigorous moral standard" (Lacy 2000b, p. ix). His anxiety at the prospect of losing his precious knights to the quest attests to the incompatibility of a world predicated on a fundamentally secular definition of knightly brilliance, and the spiritual ideal embodied by the Grail.

In upholding the ideal of a celestial chivalry, *The Quest for the Holy Grail* fosters an austere ethical code. According to Lacy, the text is "uncompromising in its ideological rigor. The narrator explains that only those knights who are morally superior can have even remote hope of success.... The text establishes two degrees of sexual propriety, known as *pucelage* and *virginité*, often translated as 'maidenhood' and 'virginity.' The former is a matter of physical fact: it refers to a person who has never experienced sexual intercourse. But the highest state is virginity, which defines a person who has never had even the *desire* for carnal relations. As that state is attained only by Galahad, the completely pure knight, only he is privileged to witness all the Grail secrets and succeed the Grail King" (Lacy 2000a, p. 171). The text can therefore be seen as a sustained, indeed zealous, effort to "establish a moral, religious, and especially sexual standard that can be met only by one human"—and indeed, not just *any* one human: quite the opposite, it takes a "Christ figure" (Lacy 2000a, p. 172), Galahad, to meet the standard put in place by *The Quest for the Holy Grail*'s Cistercian composer.

This is why Lancelot, in spite of his stature as Arthur's most valiant knight, fails in the Grail Quest: his soul and body alike are irremediably tainted by forbidden desire. Not even Gawain, who in so many ways stands out as the *perfect* knight, is allowed to achieve the Grail. In fact, it could be argued that Gawain is *too* perfect a knight by the standards of secular chivalry to excel at a task which demands the transcendence of all worldly drives, and transition to a spiritual level of being. The extent to which Gawain's identity as a paradigm of courtly secularity is de facto inseparable from his engagement in amorous dalliance whenever opportune is attested to by several scenes in Chrétien's *Perceval, the Story of the Grail*, where the knight takes it for granted—and *rightly* so, we are emphatically told—that playing the courtship game the moment he sits down with a pretty damsel is practically his *duty*, not a self-indulgent move. When he is not engaged in flirtatious repartee, Gawain proclaims his chivalric excellence through diplomatic and martial exploits.

According to Thomas Hahn, in *The Quest for the Holy Grail*, Gawain fulfills his customary role as "the outstanding instance of relentless devotion to physical exertion and worldly honor," but the text's "fervently ascetic underpinnings ... represent such activity as debased and iniquitous.... A nameless, holy hermit eventually banishes him from the narrative, pronouncing that this great champion, like all who live their lives 'astride the powerful war-horse' ... will always live in mortal sin, a prey to pride and envy and many other vices."

The Quest for the Holy Grail functions as something of a Christian manifesto within the galaxy of romance literature, and its emphasis therefore lies with the spiritual dimension—so much so, in fact, that it deserves the title of an "anti-romance" of sorts (Hahn, p. 220). If one thinks back on the adventures recounted in Chrétien's romances, it will be instantly evident that their energy and exuberance result from their protagonists' uncalculated, even haphazard, movement from one goal to another, one Otherworld to another. The rules they follow on the way—assuming they follow *any* rules instead of just improvising—are the very opposite of rigorous. Hence, the ethical system put in place by *The Quest for the Holy Grail* is in a sense inimical to the romance qua romance. Yet, the text deserves designation as a romance in its own right, insofar as its religious messages often belie a secret fascination with the spirit of adventure upheld by the secular chivalric tradition.

The text's insistent opposition to the romance ethos is fraught with aporias. Indeed, *The Quest for the Holy Grail* is intimately embroiled with the very ideology—the ethos of courtly love—which it ostensibly seeks to subvert. It is worth noting, on this point, that the text was in all probability expected to be read in relation to the whole cycle to which it belonged, not as a free-standing narrative, and particularly to the most substantial part of the cycle, the *Lancelot* Proper: i.e., the one where eroticism plays its most crucial role.

As Simon Gaunt maintains, this factor deserves special recognition. If *The Quest for the Holy Grail* "is read in isolation, Galahad is undoubtedly the hero," states the scholar. "However, if [it] is read in the context of the prose cycle to which it belongs, it becomes part of a longer narrative, the hero of which is Lancelot, in many respects the incarnation of the romance ideal because of the link in his career between love and chivalric exploits." It is in relation to a tale of passion and earthly desire, therefore, that its contemporary readership was bound to savor *The Quest for the Holy Grail*— despite its *holiness*. This entails, as Gaunt emphasizes, that even "if it contests the values of romance," *The Quest for the Holy Grail* "does so from within the framework of romance" (Gaunt, p. 55).

A latent sense of guilt courses through the text's abhorrence of worldly passions, hinting at the composers' (and prospective readers') own repressed fascination with erotic matters. This proclivity makes itself felt as a morbid concern with sexuality, whereby Lancelot becomes a victim of obloquy, in spite of his many virtues, due to his lack of the one asset to which the moral hierarchy promulgated by *The Quest for the Holy Grail* accords the highest rank: virginity. The insistence with which the knight's supposed impiety is underscored has the effect of making both the character and his sins more central to the text than would have been the case if his sexuality had not been such a pressing concern for the text's authors. The undercurrent of steamy yearning perceptible throughout *The Quest for the Holy Grail* inscribes it firmly within the tradition of secular romance, even though its creators might have planned it as the ultimate sublimation of romantic principles to a Christian matrix.

Having commented on Lancelot and Guinevere's first torrid night of passion in Gorre, Jeff Rider notes: "another sort of troubling eroticism finds expression in the 'penetrative' divine punishment meted out in [*The Quest for the Holy Grail*]: an angelic knight thrusts a lance through Bademagus's shoulder in punishment for his having borne away a shield intended for Galahad" (Rider, p. 126). On the matter of sexuality, also notable is "the ecclesiastical tendency," manifest throughout *The Quest for the Holy Grail*, "to diabolize sexual desire." This strategy, at once textual and ideological, is presumably meant to engender "a constant anxiety about the moral status of the otherworldly lovers called forth to satisfy it" (p. 127). A perfect example is offered by the episode in which Perceval is stranded on an island, and is soon joined by a satanic damsel who reaches him by means of a black-sailed boat, which in itself would be enough of a giveaway of her status for audiences well versed in romance rhetoric. Perceval sinks into a drunken stupor after a lavish meal provided by his visitor, and the lady seduces him without effort, proclaiming that she has always passionately desired him.

Galahad stands for the end of the Arthurian era to the extent that he singlehandedly severs chivalry from playful fantasy, delivering it instead into the hands of a stern religious doctrine. Ironically, however, the knight also encapsulates the endless perpetuation of that world insofar as he is Lancelot's descendant. He thus acts as an implicit reminder of the undying charisma of the forever wandering knight whose interminable errantry stems from the unfulfillable nature of his desire. Thus, Lancelot's fame survives intact despite his displacement by Galahad. In fact, it is likely that "Lancelot" is more familiar a name than "Galahad" among modern readers, even those who are regular romance aficionados.

It is with the revelation of Galahad's lineage that *The Quest for the Holy Grail* pulls off the ultimate feat of irony. Emmanuèle Baumgartner's exegesis points in this direction: "only the best knight in the earthly (*terrien*) world ... could engender the best knight in the *celestiel* world. Just as the prose *Lancelot* and its hero 'engender' the *Queste* and its Elect, so the conjugated resources of human love and chivalric prowess can alone 'engender' a sublime form of prowess consecrated entirely to the service of God" (Baumgartner, p. 111). Thus, while *The Quest for the Holy Grail* strives to banish secular romance by replacing it with a Christianized version of knightly excellence, the vision of moral perfection it reveals cannot finally occlude its dependence on the reality of carnal passion, in the same way as Galahad's heroic persona is inextricable from a genetic/textual inheritance synonymous with overpowering, unsublimated, desire.

Hence, while Galahad emblematizes the triumph of spiritual chivalry over secular chivalry on the superficial level of the narrative, a contradictory message lies beneath the surface, there inserted by the crafty *eiron* at work in the interstices of *The Quest for the Holy Grail*. In this alternate perspective, Galahad's achievement of the Grail is not a victory for spiritual chivalry but a denial of its relevance to life on earth. Spiritual chivalry is a transcendental concept which may hold value in an afterlife domain, a celestial Otherworld forged as the Christian adaptation of the magical Otherworlds of Celtic lore and fairy tale. In *this* life, the life of the living body, spiritual chivalry has no place, no role to play.

This proposition is confirmed by the suicidal declaration with which Lancelot's son seals his attainment: "raising his hands toward heaven, Galahad said: 'I worship You and I give thanks that You have granted my desire. Now I see clearly what no tongue could describe and no heart could imagine.... I see mysteries that surpass all other mysteries! And since, dear Lord, You have allowed me to see what I have always hoped to see, I ask that You now permit me, in this state of bliss, to pass from earthly life into eternal life.'" The Grail defies the powers of both the tongue and the heart—namely, the instruments whereby human beings give shape to their thoughts and their longings. The mystical reality it epitomizes is therefore alien to the tangible reality from which the chivalric romance draws its life force. The only quester who may fathom the Grail's secrets is the one who, like the Grail itself, is able to transcend the material reality of the chivalric romance.

Ironically, this capacity is also a failure, insofar as it signals the successful quester's inability to go on functioning within the world of the chivalric romance once he has achieved the sought-for prize. To inhabit a reality compatible with the Grail's own, he must cut himself off from the tongue and the heart, the spheres of language and desire supplying the classic knight errant with afflatus. Therefore, after receiving the Eucharist from none other than Josephus, Joseph of Arimathea's very sibling, Galahad dies, and his spirit is borne away by "jubilant angels" (*The Quest for the Holy Grail*, p. 362).

In the secular romance as conceived by Chrétien de Troyes, insanity constitutes an escape from the self: a desperate attempt to insulate both mind and body from an unbearable reality. In this context, self-destructive tendencies constitute the ultimate form of madness, and hence a final effort at escape. The madness incurred by the protagonist of *Yvain, or, the Knight with a Lion*, like the death wish experienced by the eponymous hero in *Lancelot, or, the Knight of the Cart*, marks an absolute shutting down of the knight's emotional life, sensorium, and bodily functioning. Typically, a knight is rescued from so deep a state of dejection either by magical means or by a sudden turn in his fate whose abruptness, though not necessarily induced by a supernatural force, nonetheless carries portentous connotations redolent of Faërie's eccentric laws. The return to sanity signals not only the knight's reinsertion into civil society, but also a jubilant reassertion of his material existence.

In *The Quest for the Holy Grail*, Galahad's yearning for self-annihilation—and its satisfaction by the divine agencies he invokes—denotes *a point of no return*. He has accomplished what no other Arthurian champion could achieve, or even hope to achieve, but this triumph must be taken away into an inscrutable elsewhere. His coup, therefore, is also the most unrescindable and saddest of losses: the negation of the energy which makes all life possible, and ought to be the defining trait of knightly life above all.

The Quest for the Holy Grail also declares its anti-romance leanings by imparting the form immortalized by Chrétien with a teleological thrust alien to the original format. As anticipated in Chapter Two, the chivalric romance's meandering and all-deferring rhythm implies an aversion to the principle of teleology. In *The Quest for the Holy Grail*, this trend is radically revised, as the romance mode is adapted to the delivery of an eschatological construct with a clear end point: the achievement of the Grail. Humanity needs the Holy Grail: its conquest, therefore, will constitute humanity's supreme triumph. At the same time, the Holy Grail needs humanity for its significance to be valued: without an ample entourage of cultish devotees, the Grail means very little indeed. Thus, humanity and the Grail are locked into a bond of mutual dependence. Insofar as the arrival at the preordained quest's target must coincide with a tragic farewell to the human world, Galahad's triumph voids that bond by banishing the human element. Since, in a symbiotic relationship, the removal of one party de facto annuls the role of the other, Galahad's renunciation of his tie to humanity upon conquering the Holy Grail also empties the object itself with a function worthy or recognition: it can no longer command unconditional respect, let alone expect unquestioned worship.

If the authors of *The Quest for the Holy Grail* set out to denounce secular romance's vapid fictions, they did not ultimately succeed in doing so. However, it could be surmised that the text's authors did not in fact *wish* to succeed in affirming their moral agenda, since the real—albeit disavowed—desire pervading the narrative's subtextual terrain moves in the opposite direction, by exposing the irrelevance of spiritual fineness to the human world.

In this regard, *The Quest for the Holy Grail* offers not an indictment of the Arthurian world, but rather a gateway to a reassessment of its essential significance. This lies with that world's status as a symbol for the human condition itself, as an inevitably flawed reality which, though it certainly does not deserve undiluted praise, nonetheless asks to be recognized and accepted for *what it is*, no more and no less. *The Quest for the Holy Grail* understands only too well, deep down, that a moralizing text resolved to slam the door on the last vestige of a secular code may deliver lofty lessons, but can hardly claim to be an honest portrayal of the human condition. Such a claim would, ironically, render it deceptive, mendacious, and hence *immoral*. The text dismantles itself, and falls by its own criteria, by harboring ideological leanings which contradict its apparent, official, message. In a sense, it is a paradigmatic case of deconstruction at work.

As argued in Chapter Two, the idealization of chivalry often encountered in literature belies its imbrication in a history of violence and strife. Real-life chivalry, to put it bluntly, is neither pretty nor truly *chivalric*. Arthur can just about efface this stark reality as long as he can contain his knights within the fold of the Round Table, and monitor the progress of their adventures outside Camelot's walls in the belief that these will abet his society's consolidation. However, as soon as the Grail Quest proposes itself as an alternative to chivalric exploits harnessed to the Arthurian code, things begin to fall apart. Here is the prospect of a commitment which does not fit in with Camelot's agenda, insofar as its thrust is essentially spiritual rather than secular. In other words, it contradicts the consummately earthly leanings of Arthurian culture.

According to Brigitte Cazelles, the conflict between Arthurian culture and the Holy Grail is already evident in Chrétien's *Perceval, the Story of the Grail*. Both of the romance's protagonists contribute to this reorientation. At climactic junctures in their respective quests, both Perceval and Gawain resolve to focus on the search for the Bleeding Lance associated with the Grail myth. They thus choose to pursue a goal alien to the Round Table's expectations: an aim, moreover, tinged with metaphysical connotations at odds with Arthurian secularism. "Taken together," states the critic, Perceval's and Gawain's exploits "jeopardize the principles of Arthurian leadership," and therefore "predict the collapse of the king's rule as he finds himself successively deprived of his formerly most faithful deputy and of his newly acquired champion" (Cazelles, p. 115).

Cazelles is also keen to emphasize that both Perceval's and Gawain's adventures attest to chivalry's embroilment with a reality of "violence and aggression" (p. 8) by exposing the inherently martial nature of Arthurian chivalry. In this respect, *Perceval, the Story of the Grail* as a whole could be read as a "demystification of the chivalric ideal as a mendacious glorification of what is, in reality, an order essentially occupied in warlike activities" (p. 127). An aura of ruthless belligerence surrounds Perceval's first experience of Arthurian society. Indeed, though tempered by the youth's disarming naivety, his slaying of the Red Knight on Arthur's behalf is nothing short of brutal. Gawain himself, according to Cazelles, "is rarely seen in action and is more often occupied by travel and talk than by actual feats of arms" (p. 71). As we have seen, the sequence in which Gawain refrains from joining the Tintagel tournament typifies this disposition: the Arthurian champion's conduct is so *un*martial at this point in the narrative as to induce impertinent misreadings of his true intent among the female spectators. On the other hand, the accusations leveled against Gawain by Guinganbresil and Grinomalant point to vicious, albeit unproven, acts of violence. Thus, the gallant knight's biography is as steeped in bloodshed as his real-life medieval counterparts.

Bringing the cycle to a heart-rending close, *The Death of Arthur* "opens with the aftermath of the Grail Quest, and the king's attempts to revive the much depleted Round Table. But at this point the affair between Lancelot and Guinevere intensifies, and comes into the open when Agravain succeeds in catching them in the act. Lancelot saves the queen from the stake, and flees with her to his castle of Joyous Gard, which is besieged by Arthur. The final pages recount Arthur's death at the hands of his illegitimate son Mordred, and the deaths of Lancelot and Guinevere" (Barber 2010).

By contrast with the preceding romance, the closing book of the *Lancelot-Grail Cycle* is "solidly grounded in the material reality of the Arthurian world" (Lacy 2000a, p. 171). A gloomy and mournful narrative, *The Death of Arthur* "turns almost immediately to Lancelot, who, having earlier renounced Guinevere, quickly lapses again into sin with her." As anticipated, it is to "this adulterous relationship" that the demise of the Arthurian world can ultimately be ascribed. Where in its secular incarnation the chivalric romance has scarce concern for causality, Christianized romance—or *inverted* romance, as it were—is quite unequivocal in its definition of causal links between events. In a sense, its strictness is comparable to Greek tragedy's rigorous handling of the law of nemesis. The catastrophe in which Camelot's dazzling world collapses as though it had never consisted of anything other than a flimsy house of cards, indicates that "Arthurian chivalry and the Grail ideal" are ultimately "incompatible" (p. 172).

The Death of Arthur contrasts starkly with the preceding romance in its metaphysical frame of reference. While in *The Quest for the Holy Grail* every stage in the story is justified with reference to God's will as the ultimate shaping force in human history, *The Death of Arthur* ascribes all turns in the rise and fall of the Arthurian world to the capricious rhythms of fortune. As indicated, *The Quest for the Holy Grail* itself hinted at the Arthurian world's association with fortune in the scene depicting Arthur's reactions to the launching of the Grail Quest. The implication, in both the penultimate and the final volumes of the *Lancelot-Grail Cycle*, is that the secular ethos incarnated by Arthurian society is ultimately *bound* to be governed by a non–Christian, indeed pagan, "goddess," in that it cannot participate in the unfolding of a divine plan.

On the whole, however, *The Quest for the Holy Grail* endeavors to promulgate a fundamentally Christian message. *The Death of Arthur*, conversely, emphasizes the role played by fortune in the shaping of chivalric affairs in and around Camelot. It thus imparts the story with a powerful sense of ineluctability, intimating that its personae are powerless to steer the flow of the action. In this perspective, the fatal incident leading to the climactic confrontation and Arthur's death appears inexorable. Likewise, Lancelot and Guinevere, having been motivated by the holy atmosphere of the Grail Quest to put an end to their illicit liaison in *The Quest for the Holy Grail*, seem to have no choice but to descend again into sin in the final romance.

This suggests that the Grail's blessings are ambiguous. As we have seen, Galahad's triumph can only take place at the expense of his life, which shows that the Grail is not all-powerful: it only grants something by taking something else away. Lancelot and Guinevere's resuming of their affair calls the Grail's authority further into question, to the extent that it suggests that the pious standpoint signified by the sacred icon is ephemeral. This serves to reinforce the hypothesis that *The Quest for the Holy Grail*, despite its moralizing intent, does not stand for the demise of the secular code, but rather alludes to its perpetuation, by exposing the spiritual world view's intrinsic precariousness.

As noted earlier, the *Lancelot-Grail* Cycle foregrounds the concept of textual mediation by claiming to be based on a holy source delivered to the narrator in person by none other than God's emissary. *The Death of Arthur* allows the process of textual mediation to go even further by invoking visual language as the vehicle by which "truth" discloses itself. Having taken lodging in the castle of his sister Morgan, Arthur examines a series of paintings exposing Lancelot and Guinevere's adulterous liaison. "King Arthur could read well enough to decipher a text," we are informed, "and when he saw the letters and images that explained the meaning of the paintings, he began to read them and he realized that they depicted Lancelot's deeds and the exploits he had performed since the time he first became a knight.... When he saw the images depicting the meeting arranged by Galehaut, he was astonished and became pensive. He began to look at that and said quietly to himself, 'My word, if these letters are telling the truth, Lancelot has dishonored me with the Queen."' In this manner, Arthur discovers that Lancelot "has loved Queen Guenevere from the day he first became a knight," that "it was for love of the queen that he did all the feats of prowess he performed as a new knight," and that he loved her "more than any man could love a lady," though he never revealed his feelings to her until Galehaut offered to intercede on his behalf (*The Death of Arthur*, p. 368–369).

The text's emphasis on the king's analytical skills as—one surmises—both an art connoisseur and a refined critic is quite amusing, in the context. However, its main purpose is not—or, at least, not only—comical. Rather, it is to underline the purely *textual* nature of the experiences whereby knowledge is both divulged and received, constructed and interpreted. Had the emphasis fallen solely on Arthur's emotional response to his discovery, the reader might have been led to focus on the *content* of the experience per se. As things stand, we are invited to reflect instead on the *form* in which the experience is couched, and extrapolate its repercussions for the dissemination of knowledge at large. Accordingly, the king's interjection is made to sound rather cheap and formulaic, as though to marginalize the scene's content in the service of form.

In this case, the information gleaned by Arthur *is* true to the extent that Lancelot and Guinevere have *really* indulged in an all-consuming sexual relationship. Yet, it is vital to forget that this "fact" is itself a product of fiction, not history: a fiction, moreover, which has proved itself amenable to endless telling and retelling over many centuries. In other words, the "truth" discovered by the king is inexorably entangled with the fluctuations, quandaries, and quirks of the fictional brain. It is also notable that insofar as the substance of pictorial language is more corporeal than that of its verbal counterpart, the episode serves to accentuate the material dimension of the text as a whole.

The ending of *The Death of Arthur* is pervaded by a pointedly secular tone, as the text lays emphasis not so much on the religious implications of the Arthurian era—and its demise—as on the magical dimension. "Now I tell you to go," says Arthur at the end of the closing romance, addressing the audience no less than the loyal Girflet. "I don't want you to stay with me after this, for my end is approaching, and it isn't fitting that anyone know the truth of my end, for just as I became king here by adventure, so shall I pass from this kingdom by adventure, and after this, no one will be able to boast that he knows for certain what has become of me. For this reason, I want you to go, and after you've left me, if they ask you for news of me, answer them that King Arthur came through God's adventure, and by God's adventure he departed, and he alone was the King of Adventures" (p. 430).

Arthur maintains that his rise to mythical fame has been enabled by "God," which could be read as indicative of a shift from the secular to the spiritual. In fact, the "God" in question is coupled with the quintessentially secular concept of "adventure," which suggests that the supreme being granted a climactic presence in the text's closing words is not a Christian concept, but a consummately pagan "King of Adventures." The general spirit of the scene is one of all-enveloping enchantment, and the quasi incantatory rhythm of the departing king's words have the effect of drawing the reader into the magic circle, bound by the same spell which has lured so many errant knights into their meandering quests.

The Death of Arthur offers a somber reinscription of Arthurian chivalry which, ironically, both plants the final nail in the coffin of that secular ethos, and paves the way to its endless return. The last text's immortal resonance owes much to its style: a lyrical prose in which multiple echoes of things gone and premonitions of things to come fluidly interlace. In this fashion, the texts glories not in the all-revealing light of the *Cycle*'s moralizing intent, but in the stupendously layered darkness wherein all genuine romance is born, and goes on renewing its vigor, unscathed by dogma or ideology. Thus, the *Cycle* ultimately preserves intact the sense of mystery essential to the romance as an art form, and, crucially for this study, as a frank embodiment of the essence of fiction qua fiction.

Therefore, while the *Lancelot-Grail Cycle* may in some ways mark the twilight of the chivalric romance as conceived by Chrétien de Troyes, the atmosphere embracing its final moments serves to reinforce, not attenuate, the romance's spirit as a form inextricable from magic, adventure, and an insatiable desire for yet more magic—and yet more adventure. Indeed, implicit in the king's dying request for solitude is a wish to let the narrative continue beyond the final full stop *in silence*: to leave the page open to an incalculable number of other potential stories, as yet *untold*, perhaps *untellable*, yet always *imaginable*.

As suggested earlier, *The Quest for the Holy Grail* affords no final revelations since, following Galahad's triumph, we see him take the mysteries he has fathomed with him to the grave (and possibly beyond). The text does not, therefore, deliver any final truth despite its posing as a truth-telling venture. It is in keeping with the cycle's overall inconclusiveness that *The Death of Arthur*, the last romance in the *Lancelot-Grail Cycle*, imparts the culmination of its events with a palpable aura of mystery. Arthur's destination remains an enigma. All we can know for certain is that his myth survives the romance's last word in a realm of perpetual, textual and intertextual, dissemination: a phenomenon still evident today in the proliferation of chivalric fiction, and, as Carol Dover observes, in the popularity of "films either inspired by Arthurian themes" or based on "Arthurian works of literature." These movies attest to "the continuing power of Arthurian legends to fascinate and inspire, in the true spirit of the medieval tradition of continuation" (Dover, p. 237).

Central to the *Lancelot-Grail Cycle* as a whole is an ironic tension between the text's quest for exhaustiveness, and the recognition that no work, not even one as gigantic as this, can ever enclose the realm of the tellable in its entirety. Though ostensibly comprehensive, the narrative world mapped out by the five romances is so saturated with allusions to *other* hypothetical stories, which its texts are just powerless to include, as to admit to its inevitable selectivity. It thus reminds us that *any* structure, however inclusive, is always relativized by legion rejected possibilities. This entails that the *Lancelot-Grail Cycle*'s own story is defined by what it does *not* contain as much as by what it manages to contain—that its extensive, visible, tapestry of adventures intersects with another, invisible, quilt of alternate possibilities.

Pearsall reinforces this line of argument, averring that "the vast expanses of the cycle, encompassing the exploits of scores of named knights, have a complexity, an irresolution, that make them resistant to a single interpretation. Characters appear, disappear, and reappear, story-lines cross, run parallel, loop around each other, and are sometimes suspended for long periods.... Characters are typically entwined in endless repetitions—Lancelot is always in love with Guenevere, always going away, always coming back; Tristan is always in love with Isolde (one or the other), always going away, always coming back.... There are endless single combats, conducted according to a set patter as strict as the steps of a dance" (Pearsall, p. 46).

In addition, the *Lancelot-Grail Cycle* shows that the selectivity characteristic of any text, regardless of its scope, goes hand in hand with partiality. No matter how objective a narrative might strive to be, its incapacity to capture all of the material potentially at its disposal makes it arbitrary. The cycle's own specific brand of arbitrariness, as noted, stems from its religious slant, which de facto amounts to the abortive imposition of a Christian template on a body of pagan legends which stubbornly defies domestication.

FOUR

Medieval Masters: Chaucer, Malory, the Lay and the Gawain Poet

Chaucer

Given Geoffrey Chaucer's reputation as the greatest of medieval writers, it is impossible not to consider what he made of the chivalric romance. As Corinne Saunders proposes, "in many ways, Chaucer's use of romance illuminates the complexity of the genre. Because the term originally referred simply to writing in a *romanz* language, it developed only loosely into a literary genre." Even though in Chaucer's times, "there does seem to have been an awareness ... of romance as a distinctive mode," the concept of "genre" was still "much more fluid than our own—a work might be at once tragedy, history, and romance, as is Chaucer's *Troilus and Criseyde*, or saint's life and romance, as are the *Clerk's Tale* and the *Man of Law's Tale*, or comedy and romance, as is the *Merchant's Tale*."

Since this study concentrates specifically on the *chivalric* romance, and, in addition, is most concerned with the latter's imbrication with *irony*, the component of Chaucer's extensive oeuvre deemed of direct relevance to the present context is his introduction of the character of the Knight in the *General Prologue* to *The Canterbury Tales* (late fourteenth century). Before assessing Chaucer's use of irony in this text, however, it is worth paying heed to Saunders' reflections on the author's legacy. "It is possible to see Chaucer's mixed genre," argues the critic, "as looking forward to that of Shakespeare: both poets exploit the dramatic possibilities of shifts in genre and hence in tone, language, and subject matter" (Saunders 2004).

Chaucer's portrait of his Knight opens with the announcement that

"From the time that he first began To ride out," the character "loved chivalry." Renowned for his "Fidelity and good reputation, generosity and courtesy," as well as his prowess "in his lord's war," the Knight is not only "brave": he is also "prudent" and "meek." In short, he appears to tick all the boxes to qualify as "a truly perfect, noble knight." In spite of this, the character contravenes the chivalric code by evincing a problematic attitude to war. This is implied by Chaucer's hint at the Knight's refusal to take part in the Hundred Years War (1337–1453) even though "He had been at many a noble expedition" ("The General Prologue"). Through a deft ironical twist, the text presents the Knight as *both* an exemplary incarnation of his caste's ideals, *and* a nonconformist outsider.

As Jordi Sánchez Martí suggests, the Knight's decision emanates from his conviction that the Hundred Years War "is an immoral war among Christians which is mainly motivated by the lucrative desires of the so-called nobles" (p. 161). The Knight's previous campaigns were consonant with his ethics insofar as they were triggered by spiritual goals, but the Hundred Years War is a conflict of a different breed: one sustained by fundamentally economic interests. Indeed, at the time the *General Prologue* was composed, supposedly *holy* warfare represented a relatively peripheral phenomenon in the context of European, and specifically English, politics. "Although enrollment for crusades occurred in late fourteenth-century England," states Sánchez Martí, "the participation in religious campaigns was insignificant if compared with other more lucrative military expeditions, such as the Hundred Years War. This kind of war had become a source of livelihood for a military class increasingly numerous" (Sánchez Martí, p. 162).

Chaucer's Knight embodies a tantalizing irony. Anchored to an idealized conception of courtesy of the feudal variety, yet inscribed in the modern reality of warfare governed by mercenary goals, the character straddles two incompatible ideologies. The General Prologue uses this irony to intimate that chivalry of the Arthurian ilk no longer has a place in its author's society.

Malory

Responding to a general demand for a unified version of the available stories surrounding the legendary court of Camelot, Sir Thomas Malory's *Le Morte d'Arthur* (1485) offers the first narration in the English language of the adventures revolving around that court, from the early events in the

Holy Grail's history to the Round Table's disbanding—as well as the first notable work of secular fiction in English literature. *Le Morte d'Arthur* comprises three, occasionally overlapping, narrative sequences. These cover Arthur's biography from his birth to his marriage to Guinevere, and Lancelot's momentous introduction to the Round Table; the Round Table knights' miscellaneous adventures, and contributions to the Grail Quest; the Round Table's downfall, and attendant evaporation of the Arthurian myth.

While these sequentially ordered events impart the Arthurian legend with a degree of unity and continuity not found in earlier romances, it would be erroneous to assume that *Le Morte d'Arthur* offers an entirely coherent narrative. On the contrary, as Norris J. Lacy explains, "there are internal contradictions that cannot easily be explained away"—and, one could add, give rise to some distinctive, albeit accidental, humor. "For example, Tristram's birth and youth are related in a tale that *follows* the account of his adult adventures. Elsewhere a character may die only to reappear later" (Lacy 1997, p. 129).

Le Morte d'Arthur was composed during the time of the Wars of the Roses (1455–1487, with connected fighting before and after this period). This is an era, as Helen Cooper reminds us, marked not only by "a simple struggle between Yorkists and Lancastrians," but by "a series of faction-fights in which participants might on occasion change sides, not just over the question of which king they supported, but according to baronial enmities and local disputes that could in turn draw members of rival magnate affinities into larger feuds" (Cooper 1998, p. xii).

The historical significance of Malory's work as the product of a distinctive socio-political milieu cannot be overestimated. It is in fact crucial, as Terence McCarthy emphasizes, to bear in mind that "the periods immediately preceding the completion and (fifteen years later) the publication of *Le Morte d'Arthur* were both turbulent times in which the notions of rightful and stable kingship were burning issues." As a result, the meaning which Malory's work is likely to have carried for both its author and "for Caxton's noble patrons" is one which it "cannot have for us" today (McCarthy, p. 157).

The text's topical relevance does not, however, entail that it offers a realistic or documentary chronicle of a specific era. In fact, *Le Morte d'Arthur* is a consummately *fictional* work, and its adhesion to the realm of fiction qua fiction buttresses its affiliation with the chivalric romance, despite this form's relatively outmoded status in Malory's age. Christine Poulson underscores the text's fantastic dimension, arguing that the fictional era in which the work is set is "a time when magical events are taken for granted." This is patently borne out by many of the key events dramatized by Malory, including Arthur's outrageous conception, his assertion of his caliber as a rightful leader through the extraction of the Sword in the Stone, his reception of Excalibur from the Lady of the Lake, and this formidable weapon's return to the water at the end of the saga. The text makes no effort to rationalize these portentous occurrences with reference to either natural laws or fictional conventions dictated by tradition. On the contrary, it delivers them as *quasi-factual events*, leaving it to its readers to pass judgment—if they *must*—on their veracity. In *Le Morte Darthur* itself, "the significance of these events is never fully explained" (Poulson, pp. 5–6).

Malory's text harks back to Geoffrey of Monmouth's *Historia Regum Brittaniae* in intimating that it deserves serious consideration as a chronicle of—*potentially*—real events. This suggestion, as Cooper observes, is buttressed by the author's insistence "on the fact that the Arthurian adventures were a matter of record: that first Merlin, then Arthur, had written accounts made to document the deeds of the Round Table for posterity." In his effort to play the role of a modern historiographer, and hence invest his text with the aura of a reliable account, Malory intersperses the narrative with "details of names and places" of his own conception, while also abiding punctiliously to "the protocol of giving all his characters titles" (Cooper 1998, p. xii).

The fictive nature of such details and titles is manifest, and Malory does not go out of his way to conceal their fictiveness, even as he advertises his text's semi-historical accuracy. Indeed, even the most selective sampling of *Le Morte d'Arthur* makes it clear that its creator harbors a lusty appetite for invention, and is prepared to give it free rein in his writing irrespective of his supposed commitment to truth. His society's sensitivity to the difference between fact and fiction does not prevent Malory from exploiting to the utmost the paradoxical coexistence of putative authenticity and blatant fictionality with unsurpassed verve. To this extent, *Le Morte d'Arthur* revels in irony, erecting its multi-faceted world on the unresolved rivalry between a simulation of historiographical veracity, and a self-conscious delight in the freedom to invent.

Emphasizing the centrality of the chivalric code to Malory's work, McCarthy avers that in *Le Morte d'Arthur* "chivalry is, first of all, an attitude to war. A knight may have amorous conquests and fight spiritual battles, but his proper occupation, for Malory, is adventure, combat, and war"

(McCarthy, p. 72). Furthermore, "the ideal of knighthood" promulgated by Malory "is not some vague code of gallant patriotism, but a social system with a clear financial and political bond" (p. 73). In the light of the text's commitment to this ethos, one might assume that *Le Morte d'Arthur* marginalizes Lancelot and Guinevere's love as a secondary theme, given the affair's emphasis on fundamentally private sentiments. In fact, this strand of Arthurian lore plays a key role in Malory's opus. The text's emphatic treatment of a subject which its ethical priorities ought, in principle, to marginalize gives rise to a trenchant irony.

Malory engineers a smart way of smoothing over this aporia, proposing that "Lancelot's devotion to the queen is an aspect of his loyalty to Arthur and the realm," and that "the private side of the affair" (p. 95) does not therefore warrant gratuitous consideration as an autonomous matter. Thus, while Lancelot performs many heroic deeds in the queen's name, he is not first and foremost portrayed as a courtly lover. On the contrary, he is a *warrior* whose devotion to Guinevere serves as a source of inspiration, thereby securing the consolidation of the Round Table's fame, and the reinforcement of Camelot's political power.

Reinforcing the irony centered on the discrepancy between the private and the public, Malory intimates that even though as it *destroys* the Round Table, Lancelot and Guinevere's adulterous liaison also gives the system a pretext for *consolidating* its power by giving it the opportunity to administer its punishment in no uncertain terms. An analogy with contemporary Renaissance politics seems apposite, in this context. In the new worlds disclosed by geographical expansion, the dominant culture constructs the Other as a wild presence in need of continual curbing, so as to give itself an excuse to reaffirm ad infinitum a spurious notion of excellence. The adulterous relationship binding Arthur's spouse and his most valiant champion serves a comparable function: its demonization as the ultimate transgression of Camelot's power base enables the system to declare its impregnability through the imposition of a stringent code of law.

However, the irony surrounding the relationship is finally unresolved. While the illicit affair may, indirectly, serve a crucial role in strengthening Arthur's authority, it cannot sustain the public sphere's prime objectives and abstract rules. This is because it remains inseparable to the end from a skein of intensely human emotions, and a commitment to the materiality of the body so intractable as to verge on a mania. Hence, it can only precipitate the fellowship's disintegration to the extent that it is irreconcilable with the ideal of purity commended by the "Pentecostal Oath." As Dorsey Armstrong explains, this concept is Malory's own creation, and designates "a code of conduct" created by Arthur himself "for the members of his knightly community to follow" (Armstrong, p. 28).

Confirming Malory's entanglement with a specific cultural context, the Pentecostal Oath reflects contemporary concerns: far from being concerned exclusively with ethics, it is in fact a potent means of forging social obligations and feudal bonds. The following passage illustrates this proposition to exemplary effect: "then the king established all his knights, and them that were of lands not rich he gave them lands, and charged them never to do outrage, nor murder, and always to flee treason. Also, by no mean to be cruel, but to give mercy unto him that asketh mercy, upon pain of forfeiture of their worship and lordship of king Arthur for evermore; and alway to do ladies, damsels, and gentlewomen succour upon pain of death" (Malory, p. 24).

It is significant that the punishment incurred by a knight if he fails to abide by the etiquette of courtly love should be harsher than the penalty exacted for failure on the battlefield. This points to a further level of irony: while Malory appears to give precedence to the public/political sphere, his Pentecostal Oath implicitly accords priority to the private/emotional dimension of a knight's performance. It is also noteworthy that Malory pays homage to the original doctrine of courtly love by keeping "love and marriage" quite "separate," as Poulson points out. This is demonstrated by the author's treatment of the story of Tristan and Isolde, which encourages the reader to sympathize not with "the cuckolded husband," but rather with "the lovers, who are seen as wholly admirable." King Mark, accordingly, is portrayed as a hindrance to the fulfillment of true love in the purest courtly understanding of the sentiment. This negative interpretation of King Mark's role in the romance is reinforced by Malory's intimation that the lady "has no say at all in the marriage. Her father treats her as a piece of property" (Poulson, p. 34). After all, as C. S. Lewis reminds us, in feudal society, "marriages had nothing to do with love.... All matches were matches of interest." Therefore, "far from being a natural channel" for the realization of the kind of love promoted by the chivalric code, "marriage was the rather drab background against which that love stood out" as the epitome of "tenderness and delicacy" (Lewis, p. 13).

Despite Malory's insistence on the precepts governing both martial and amatory conduct, the overall impression evoked by his masterwork is that precepts exist chiefly to be violated. As Elizabeth Edwards points out, "despite the oath, ... chivalry in Malory is not the result of following the rules; it is more a matter of generating and regenerating the code" (Edwards 2001, p. 72). Hence, the text repeatedly emphasizes the *unfinished* nature of Arthur's code, and the attendant need to go on reassessing and reconfiguring it from one adventure to the next. The code's putative completeness, and reliability, as law is thus called into question. This is because Malory, with his keen eye for irony, is well aware of Arthurian society's failure to respect the rules it so keenly wishes not only to honor, but also to *embody*.

Essential to Malory's attitude to the relationship between history and fiction, to the tension between the public and the private, and to the discrepancy between the ideal and the real, irony further asserts its influence in the writer's handling of gender relations. "Knights in Malory," notes Armstrong "always read women as vulnerable, helpless, and ever in need of the services of a knight—in short, the object through and against which a knight affirms his masculine identity" (Armstrong, p. 36). Malory's women thus come to constitute the nub of a tantalizing irony. On the one hand, they are pushed to the periphery of the Arthurian realm by their ideological construction as passive pawns in a hyper-male system. On the other, they constitute an indispensable part of that social structure insofar as they are necessary to the testing and assertion of their protectors' chivalric mettle.

In addition, as prime recipients of the Pentecostal Oath's positive intent, they are instrumental in inspiring the code's continual redefinition through its many adjustments and fluctuations. This implies that in spite their ostensibly peripheral standing, they play a pivotal role in Arthurian society. Malory's treatment of the formidable Morgan le Fay deserves special attention. On the surface, she appears to retain her customarily transgressive and disruptive role. Yet, "in the danger she poses to the masculine chivalric community," even the legendary sorceress "ironically provides that community with tests which, when successfully passed by the knight in question, serve to strengthen the institution of knighthood" (p. 99). As we shall see, this motif is echoed in *Sir Gawain and the Green Knight*.

Women are often demonized as causes of unchaste conduct, a knight's supreme virtue, but also lauded as nurturing presences. As Edwards observes, even as they stand for "malevolence," "ill-will," and "a threatening sexual voracity," epitomized by Morgan le Fay, Malory's female personae concomitantly evince constructive faculties, such as "mediation and guiding," or even "healing." The positive side of femininity "apparently prevails among the ladies on the barge, surprisingly including Morgan le Fay herself, who mysteriously arrive to take the grievously wounded Arthur.... The arts of medicine and healing have been female activities all along: Elaine of

Astolat nurses and heals the wounded Lancelot; both Isoldes are first sought out by Tristram because of their ability to heal; and Elaine (Galahad's mother) is responsible for the healing of Lancelot by the Grail" (Edwards 2000, p. 43).

Le Morte d'Arthur culminates in a trenchant irony. As Armstrong explains, at the end of the saga, "Lancelot and Guenevere enter into religious life," and "both die in an undeniable aura of sanctity and goodness" (Armstrong, p. 26). When Guenevere chooses to do penance by entering a convent, rather than set up a new chivalric circle with Lancelot as an alternative to Camelot, her lover resolves "to follow her example and leave the courtly secular world for the spiritual" (p. 200). On the one hand, this ending signals the lovers' transcendence of the secular world to which their carnal appetites have kept them bonded. The shift from the secular to the spiritual is not absolute, however. In fact, the *eiron* surreptitiously at work throughout Malory's text manages to worm its way into its climax, by intimating that the worldly code of Arthurian romance ultimately resists sublimation to the tenets of religious life.

This is borne out by the fact that the erstwhile Arthurian champion does not relinquish the secular sphere altogether. In fact, he establishes a "knightly monastic subcommunity" (p. 205) with the "fellows-in-arms" (p. 203) who have chosen to follow him down the religious path. The irony of this situation is that the Lancelot squad within the monastery in a sense replicates the Round Table ethos within the spiritual realm. The same sense of fellowship which underpinned Arthur's milieu can be seen to animate this grouping. In addition, Lancelot is still venerated as the supreme *exemplum* every knight should aspire to embody. This idea carries latently impious connotations, in that it implies that the knight-monks' objective is to emulate not Christ and his disciples, but another (legendarily sinful) human being.

Just as Guinevere has thus far been the source of Lancelot's inspiration in the performance of his chivalric deeds, so now she motivates and sustains his commitment to monastic life and priesthood. Although the emphasis has moved from the material to the spiritual domain, the essence of the relationship, from Lancelot's point of view, remains the same. The intrinsic nature of his attachment does not alter in the wake of the Round Table's downfall. This means that without Guinevere, Lancelot could not function as either a knight or a man of God. This is demonstrated by his conduct following the former queen's demise: "he sickened more and more, and dried and dwined away; for the bishop nor none of his fellows might not make him to eat, and little he drank, that he was waxen by a cubit shorter than he was, that the people could not know him; for evermore day and night he prayed, but sometime he slumbered a broken sleep, and ever he was lying groveling on the tomb of king Arthur and queen Guenever" (Malory, p. 183).

The death which brings Lancelot's formidable career to a close is pitiable more than tragic, pathetic more than heroic. Nevertheless, the eulogy Malory grants the knight via the character of Ector emphasizes his more-than-human stature. As a farewell to the knight's career in which any fan of his exploits would be ready to join, Ector's tribute deserves exhaustive citation: "Ah, Lancelot ... thou were head of all Christian knights; ... thou were never matched of earthly knight's hand; and thou were the courtiest knight that ever bare shield; and thou were the truest friend to thy lover that ever bestrode horse; and thou were the truest lover of a sinful man that ever loved woman; and thou were the kindest man that ever strake with sword; and thou were the goodliest person ever came among press of knights; and thou was the meekest man and the gentlest that ever ate in hall among ladies; and thou were the sternest knight to thy mortal foe that ever put spear in the rest" (pp. 185–186).

According to Armstrong, the words with which Ector "describes alternately Lancelot's behavior toward ladies and toward his fellow knight seems interestingly—even dangerously—interchangeable." The speech indeed suggests "the inextricability of Lancelot's identities as both valiant warrior and courteous gentleman" (Armstrong, p. 207), rendering martial prowess and amorous excellence inextricably intertwined. What is most intriguing about this scene is its effort to emphasize Lancelot's standing as a secular knight—as both fighter and *fin amant*—despite the holy context in which the knight has drawn his final breath. This suggests that at the close of *Le Morte d'Arthur*, the secular ethos still reigns supreme even though its responsibility for the Round Table's annihilation is frankly acknowledged.

Malory is not simply unable to let go of the Arthurian era: he is in fact *unwilling* to do so. While he does not fail to recognize the knightly code's shortcomings, and Arthurian culture's failure to live up to its own principles, he still wishes to celebrate chivalry as an ideal. *Le Morte d'Arthur* as a whole can be read as an homage to that irretrievably lost world: a realm only ever revisitable in reverie or dream. The incantational rhythm of Ector's speech immerses Lancelot's departure in the ambience of such a vision, suspending its meaning in a liminal domain between the human and the otherworldly.

Malory's text departs in a radical fashion from *The Quest for the Holy Grail*. As Jill Mann emphasizes, "what for the French author is a story of chivalric success acquires in Malory a note of nostalgia and longing. In the French *Queste*, Galahad's role is to 'put an end to' the adventures of Logres, as if they were an unpleasant interruption to normal life. In Malory, the ending of adventures brings sadness as well as a sense of fulfilment. The dominant mood of his work—particularly towards its end—is elegiac" (Mann, p. 220). Most importantly, the loss lamented by *Le Morte d'Arthur* is not only the demise of the fictional universe centered on Arthur and his court. What Malory's work seeks to mourn, in its multi-dimensional reconceptualization of the chivalric romance, is the unattainable state of plenitude to which all human beings vainly aspire, time and again believing they have conquered this ideal state, time and again witnessing the dissolution of their illusions.

In keeping with this melancholy world picture, Malory's text does not regard the Grail Quest as the adventure of adventures, so to speak, but as just *one* adventure out of many: an adventure, moreover, undertaken *not* by supernatural beings guided by wholly spiritual ends, but by humans within a palpably human, albeit fantastical, reality. This reorientation creates a textual terrain rife with opportunities for irony to flourish. This is because transferring the focus of the legendary pursuit from the mystical sphere to the human world inevitably gives rise to a disturbing uncertainty. Chivalric principles, for Malory, belong to the material human world, not to an ineffable celestial domain. This renders them real, almost tangible, according them the quality of a Weltanschauung to which any human being should, in principle, be able to relate. On the other hand, their firm anchoring to the actual world also throws into relief their status as *abstract* tenets: the likelihood of their goals ever being accomplished is disastrously undercut by the fallible humanity of their pursuers.

In other words, the humanist stance denotes an ironical double blind, whereby being human represents the measure of all things, yet constitutes an inevitably flawed and misguided state. Malory's humanism ultimately reveals that all the elements which ought to secure the ongoing glory of Arthur's realm cannot but work in concert to hasten its destruction. This vital aspect of *Le Morte d'Arthur* functions as a metaphor for a widespread human condition: for Malory, humans are free to *aspire* to a perfect world in their earthly life, but not to realize it within its boundaries. They can fantasize about an afterworld, but only *fantasize* without any guarantees other than religion's vaporous (and politically biased) promises.

It is worth recalling, in this perspective, that Renaissance humanism is itself fraught with ironies. On the surface, it stands out as a glorious affirmation of the human. At the same time, however, its agenda suggests that this gesture is not an unproblematic outcome of a belief in human supremacy: in the human animal's ability to withstand all conceivable challenges, and achieve any objective he might set his eyes upon. Quite the opposite, it points to deep cultural anxieties, engendered by a troubling perception of humanity's precarious status. On the microcosmic level, this was exacerbated by the displacement of feudal hierarchies by more unstable social structures, marked by the emergence of new classes. As Armstrong points out, in this matter, "traditional medieval concepts of class structure and social order were undergoing transformation" in Malory's days, making England "a time and place of social fluidity" (Armstrong, p. 5). On the macrocosmic level, the Copernican Revolution had the effect of dislodging the Earth from its erstwhile privileged position in the universe. Moreover, cosmology's exposure of the planet's mobile nature showed that like the chivalric romance's protagonist, the Earth has a propensity to *err*. Its human inhabitants, by analogy, are prone both to wander ad infinitum and to blunder.

Territorial and colonial expansion, another major trait of Renaissance humanism, gave rise to further anxieties. While providing the invading nations with perfect excuses for asserting their cultural, moral, and spiritual superiority, the West's infiltrations into as yet unimagined worlds entailed as many encounters with a dark and disquieting Other. This baffling presence could only be kept at bay through the endless renewal of the threat it posed to a specious notion of civilization. The wild spaces depicted in the chivalric romance, such as the forest and the barren waste, can be read as foreshadowings of such encounters.

Even though for many English-speaking readers, Malory's work is practically synonymous with Arthurian chivalry, compared with its twelfth- and thirteenth-century predecessors, it evinces features which could be described as quite *uncharacteristic*. As Eugène Vinaver points out, Malory "was determined *not* to lose his way" in the potentially infinite maze of Arthurian lore. Rather, he sought to condense "the bulk of the material" at his disposal, while "treating each sequence of events as a single unit," and rendering "some of the themes complete within their respective limits." Pursuing this objective, "he discovered the meeting point between traditional material and a form suited to the sensibilities and tastes of modern readers. The choice for him was between interlace and straightforward narrative, between stories which adhered to each other in an infinite series of echoes and anticipations, and those which fell apart, clearly and dramatically marked off at each end; and because he chose the latter method he rescued Arthurian romance ... from the fate which befell all cyclic romances" (Vinaver, p. 22).

In this fashion, Malory was able to ensure the survival of the chivalric romance in the modern era by finding a way of meeting modern requirements. Appreciating that his culture tended to deride or ignore the medieval romance not so much because it objected to its content, but rather felt uncomfortable with its meandering and inconclusive narrative, he endeavored to impart the Arthurian adventures in his hands with a novel sense of coherence and unity. Lovers of the typical chivalric romance of old might find this redefinition of its form somewhat unsavory. Nevertheless, it would be hard to deny that it is to Malory that we owe the perpetuation of Arthurian lore into modernity, and for this, if nothing else, we should be grateful to both the author and his monumental literary accomplishment.

It is also of note that the formal and structural traits of Malory's work which distinguish him from earlier romances can be attributed to its author's ideological priorities, which Pearsall persuasively explains as follows: "for him the story of Arthur is more than a romance. Chivalry he regards as a serious political and moral ideal, a temporal expression of timeless virtues, and the destruction of that chivalry, and the downfall of the Round Table, are the matter of tragedy." This gives *Le Morte d'Arthur* a teleological thrust, despite its multi-branching adventures. Indeed, the entire work can be viewed, retrospectively, as the orchestrated elaboration of a coherent narrative building towards the collapse of a "whole system" as a result of the "tragic division of loyalties" plaguing its central character, Lancelot, between service to his king, and service to his loved one (Pearsall, p. 103).

The Lay

As a short romance, or perhaps a subgenre of the chivalric romance proper, the lay adds to the kaleidoscopic range of its parent genre as a compressed and highly refined work, which can be regarded as the narrative equivalent of an illuminated miniature. Central to the lay's narrative development is the ironical interpenetration of this world and one or more Otherworlds. This is dramatized by means of plots which tend to involve the protagonist's quest for a loved one: a creature who might originate in the supernatural realm, such as a fairy, or else have been abducted thereto by an otherworldly agency. The quest tends to be resolved in the end, often by magical means. However, this is not before the protagonist has been subjected to trials which require extreme self-denial—a tough test for a character of noble extraction, which such a character would normally be— or even the prospect of execution. Thus, at the same time as it deploys its magical motifs in order to secure a felicitous resolution, the lay capitalizes on a tantalizing ironical tension between the weakness of humans, and the seeming omnipotence of their Faërie counterparts.

The lay represents a fairy tale of sorts, closely reflecting the conception of this popular form proposed by J. R. R. Tolkien. "Fairy-stories are not in normal English usage stories about fairies or elves," argues the author, "but stories about Fairy, that is Faërie, the realm or state in which fairies have their being. Faërie contains many things besides elves and fays, and besides dwarfs, witches, trolls, giants, or dragons: it holds the seas, the sun, the moon, the sky; and the earth, and all things that are in it: tree and bird, water and stone, wine and bread, and ourselves, mortal men, when we are enchanted." By severing Faërie from the fabulous creatures reputed to inhabit it, Tolkien is in a position to propose that any cogent "definition of a fairy-story—what it is, or what it should be—does not, then, depend on any definition or historical account of elf or fairy, but upon the nature of Faërie: the Perilous Realm itself, and the air that blows in that country."

Most crucially, where the lay is concerned, Faërie eludes definition in terms of familiar human criteria, insofar as it resolutely resists capture "in a net of words." As a result, "it is one of its qualities to be indescribable, though not imperceptible." At the same time, while "it has many ingredients," rational "analysis will not necessarily discover the secret of the whole. Faërie itself may perhaps most nearly be translated by Magic—but it is magic of a peculiar mood and power, at the furthest pole from the vulgar devices of the laborious, scientific, magician. There is one proviso: if there is any satire present in the tale, one thing must not be made fun of, the magic itself. That must in that story be taken seriously, neither laughed at nor explained away" (Tolkien, J. R. R. 1965).

Faërie's defiant rejection of neat labels does not only expose humanity's inadequacy in the face of worlds that evade its comprehension. In other words, it does not merely tell us that we are powerless to name it. In fact, and more crucially, it emphasizes that we should not even attempt to name it. Were we to do so, we would be disregarding its principal attribute and, ironically, would end up further away from any prospect of grasping its reality than we were when we first embarked upon our vain quest for definitions.

According to Yejung Choi, Thomas Chestre's *Sir Launfal* (late fourteenth century) is one of "the only two Middle English Breton Lays that can be traced directly back to the lais by Marie de France," the other one being *La Freine*. "Extant translations or adaptations of *Lanval* are found in Old French, Middle English and Old Norse.... In England alone, we have *Sir Landevale*, *Sir Launfal*, and the Percy Folio *Lambewell*.... There is no compelling evidence to suggest that Thomas Chestre consulted Marie's *Lanval*, when he composed *Sir Launfal*. Instead, he appears to have three other sources. The immediate and primary source is *Sir Landevale*, a rather close translation of Marie's poem. Another known source is *Graelent*, an Old French lay" (Choi, pp. 1–2).

Like Chaucer's portrait of his Knight in the "General Prologue," and Malory's adaptation of Arthurian lore in *Morte d'Arthur*, Chestre's *Sir Launfal* bears the influence of the historical context in which it was composed. Thus, whereas Marie de France's *Lanval* "is born of French soil in the twelfth century," the English *Sir Launfal* "is born in England approximately in the same period as the Peasants' Revolt [1381], an age brimming with radical socio-economic changes" (p. 3).

Marie's *Lanval* highlights its protagonist's social and psychological isolation: a state to which he is condemned when Arthur, having apportioned land and titles to all his followers, decides to leave him out. The king's gratuitous meanness stigmatizes Lanval as the only knight unrewarded by royal largesse. His extravagant spending habits and ensuing penury are presented as corollaries of his isolation: Lanval wastes money to compensate for his unjust exclusion from royal favor, and because he does not feel able to confide in anyone.

In the English *Sir Landevale*, by contrast, it is the knight's reputation that is posited as paramount: the eponymous hero's profligacy is presented as the result of a desperate effort to ensure that the chivalric community goes on holding him in high esteem. The poem can therefore be read as an implicit commentary on a society where material criteria prevail over spiritual and ethical ones. Nevertheless, *Sir Landevale* does not bear any explicit connection with any definite historical setting, being concerned instead with transhistorical chivalric principles.

Chestre's *Sir Launfal* provides an innovative interpretation of the familiar tale by bringing to the foreground a very particular world and its mores. In the process, the lay marginalizes its protagonist's status as a member of a dignified chivalric circle by divesting him of any heroic qualities, and indeed calling into question the excellence of the knightly caste at large. Furthermore, at the same time as he debunks the chivalric ideal, Chestre "de-idealizes romantic love and discloses the cohesiveness of wealth and knighthood" (p. 27).

The paramount importance of the social dimension is underscored by Chestre's early portrayal of the Arthurian court. As Choi points out, "differing both from *Lanval* where Arthur's distribution of lands is nothing more than a scaffold to explain Lanval's socio-economic status, and from *Sir Landevale* where the hero's socio-economic background is totally omitted, in Chestre's poem the detailed information about the society accumulates" (p. 7). As indicated in the preceding segment of the discussion, Malory posits Arthur's apportioning of land to the knights of the Round Table as a key part of the ceremony by which he binds them to the Pentecostal Oath. He makes it clear that the act should be read not so much as a manifestation of royal generosity per se, but rather as a social ritual laden with economic and political significance. The gift-giving scene in *Sir Launfal* ushers in an analogous state of affairs, presenting this practice as "a kind of a trade between the interested parties"—a cultural procedure for which the knightly ideal of magnanimity serves as no more than a convenient façade. Hence, the portrait of fourteenth-century England delivered by *Sir Launfal* is that of a "society in which courtliness and economy are indistinguishably compounded" (p. 9).

According to A. C. Spearing, "it is in his evocation of the social dimension of a materialistic way of life" that Chestre indeed "shows his greatest strength " (Spearing 1990, p. 154). Kate Mertes pursues a related argument, maintaining that "giving gifts—usually in the form of food, sometimes of cloth or jewels—was an important social function, sometime with political implications" (Mertes, p. 93). The fact that Arthur's two nephews, who accompany Launfal on his journey at the king's behest, do not hesitate to forsake him when he becomes indigent demonstrates that "economic conditions seem to weigh heavier than loyalty " (Choi, p. 9).

In Chrétien, it goes without saying that inner worth is matched by outer beauty. In Chestre's *Sir Launfal*, the opposite obtains: if outer appearances are unsatisfying by conventional social standards, one cannot hope for one's worth ever to be recognized. This is explicitly borne out by the scenes in which Launfal is unable to go to church or out to dine due to his lack of adequate raiments. This reflects a stark legal reality, insofar as "the first and second sumptuary laws, respectively in 1337 and 1363, substantiated the idea that a dress should correspond to his/her social status"

(Choi, p. 11). Various commentators corroborate this idea: according to Mertes, for instance, "people evaluated others by their clothing" (Mertes, p. 103). Relatedly, Frédérique Lachaud states that "the idea of a strict hierarchical view of society expressed by the means of dress" stands out as a distinctively "fourteenth-century phenomenon" (Lachaud, p. 119).

In Choi's view, the original *Lanval* distinguishes "the private from the public" in unequivocal terms, choosing to focus on the former as the lay unfolds (Choi, p. 12). In this perspective, the protagonist's fairy mistress epitomizes a pure and uncorrupted world of love which contrasts starkly, as Myra Seaman observes, with "the flawed, earthly world of the court" (Seaman, p. 110). *Sir Launfal* offers a radically different scenario: as Choi explains, Chestre concentrates on "the public display of the 'benefits' accompanied with the love: economic prosperity and personal advancement.... The gift package and the gift-giving process arranged by Tryamour herself inevitably entails his exposure to the public view." Relatedly, while Lanval's fairy lover dispenses her bounties unseen by anyone other than her mortal lover, "*Sir Launfal*'s lady provides her gifts ostentatiously," which leaves no doubt about Chestre's determination to prioritize "public relations" over any romantic notion of "a private paradise of love" (Choi, p. 13).

It is no coincidence, given Chestre's focus on the dispassionate portrayal of a world where material advantages reign supreme, that the moment Launfal betrays Tryamour, the ever-refilling purse he has received from the fairy lover reveals itself empty. At the same time, both the horse and the attendant he has been granted by Tryamour just vanish into thin air— as sprites themselves are wont to do in both Celtic lore and many popular fairy tales. In other words, the loss of love is rendered synonymous with the loss of financial gains—and vice versa. Chestre's emphasis on the material dimension is reinforced by an important departure from his sources: the omission of the scene in which the knight entreats his mistress to absolve him, in seemingly frank acknowledgment of the gravity of his trespass. With Chestre, one gets the feeling that the poet's priority is to *get on with it*, so to speak, and focus on the restoration of the hero's material status as soon as the action makes this feasible.

It is also worth mentioning, with regard to the lay's connection with a particular socio-historical context, that the renewal of Launfal's knightly status courtesy of Tryamour alludes to an actual state of affairs. Indeed, the "acquisition of knightly status through marriage" is "specifically reminiscent of the remarkable increase of inheritance through daughters in England in the wake of Black Death.... The new demographic conditions after the plague affected the rearrangement of lands. Absence of male heirs in many households redirected the line of descent. Merging of estates through marriage was frequently found" (p. 16).

By means of irony, *Sir Launfal* provides a subtle critique of Arthurian culture and its mores. On the surface, the lay depicts this society as harmonious and impervious to disruption by external agencies. The latent message coursing beneath this jolly façade conveys quite a different scenario: that of a world which fails to live up to the ideals it purports to uphold—justice, gallantry, and benevolence in particular—and whose camaraderie and impregnability to discord are, therefore, quite hollow. It is as a result of Arthur's foolish susceptibility to his wife's advice, not his judgment, that the king accuses Sir Launfal of treason. Not for a second does it occur to the putatively wise monarch to examine the reasons for Guinevere's vitriolic abhorrence of the gentle knight. Spiteful, vindictive, selfish, and wanton, Chestre's Guinevere actually offers one of the least sympathetic portrayals of the queen to be found in the romance tradition at large.

When Launfal's magical lover materializes—notably, *despite* the knight's breach of his oath of secrecy—and takes him away into Faërie, she does not level any explicit accusations at Arthur and his supporters. Nonetheless, the tale's climax makes its underlying message clear. Through her spectacular intervention, Launfal's lady makes the king the object of public disgrace, albeit temporarily, thus alluding to his inadequacy as the prime champion of the ideals which his court ought to profess and embody without fail.

Yielding an intriguing variation on the chivalric romance, a well-wrought lay like *Sir Launfal* reminds us that "medieval romance," as Claire Delacroix emphasizes, "is a natural outgrowth from fairy tales—just as the paintings of the Pre-Raphaelites are the natural extension of those illustrations. Fairy tales are the seed from which medieval romance is sprung, perhaps even the seed that gave birth to all of the romance genre. The themes and expectations of fairy tales have shaped romance as nothing else—and it could be argued that the most satisfying romances echo a familiar fairy tale in some way," even though the best of them "will still manage to surprise us along the way" (Delacroix).

These reflections bring to mind Vladimir Propp's assertion that "of all the various literary genres ... the fairy tale is the most likely to absorb elements from legend and epic." "The chivalric romance" is clearly one of the major contributors to the shaping of fairy tales over time. Yet, at the same time as the fairy tale may seem to borrow from the chivalric romance, the latter "is frequently a product of the fairy tale. The process occurs in stages: fairy tale—> romance—> fairy tale" (Propp, p. 64).

The world of Faërie transcends the boundary between good and evil, rendering the conventional barrier between the infernal and the paradisal quite irrelevant. Faërie is a universe that operates according to its own idiosyncratic laws: ordinary mortals should not attempt to measure it by their own standards. Such a move is both misguided and presumptuous since fairies neither can nor should be assimilated to the mortal world.

As Corinne Saunders suggests, the chief part played by an "otherworldly encounter" in the context of the medieval romance is "structural." This entails that "the magic of the otherworld never needs to be explained, excused or enacted through studied practices. Rather, faery enchantment shapes, mis-shapes and transforms human lives, sometimes promoting but most often challenging the social order that romance tends to uphold" (Saunders 2010, p. 204). The same could be said of fairy tales, at least in their more pristine versions, as yet unadulterated by latter-day moralistic concerns of the kind rife in Europe since at least the eighteenth century.

Moreover, the magic witnessed time and again in the chivalric tradition is essentially ironical in its defiance of strict categories. Indeed, it is simultaneously "appealing and troubling," as Saunders states. "It offers the possibility of fulfilment of desire in love, and promises the ideal, beautiful lover," as *Sir Launfal* bears out. It may also provide means of "healing and perfection of the body" unavailable to common mortals, as seen in *Yvain, or, the Knight with the Lion*, among many others tales of chivalric wonder. "These are the aims too of human magical practices, but faery magic requires no complex and suspicious rituals" of the kind associated with necromancy and witchcraft.

In fact, otherworldly magic knows no impediments to the realization of the most astonishing metamorphoses, and hence involves no byzantine formulae and no shady conjurings. This signals Faërie's distance and ineradicable *difference* from the human world in unequivocal terms, though it does not imply that this alternate reality's magic is necessarily benevolent. On the contrary, its occasional penchant for brutality and callous indifference to human suffering indicates that "the wish-fulfilment" it promises "remains uncertain," and full of "danger as well as delight" (p. 206).

Sir Orfeo attests to this proposition, insofar as its otherworld is "infernal, connected with violence, suffering and death," especially in the handling of Herodis' abduction, and the depiction of the dismal state in which many of Faërie's human denizens seem condemned to live. On the other hand, it stands out as "a brighter, more powerful reflection of the human world, a rival kingdom" of glorious beauty, "glittering, sophisticated, full of artifice" (p. 204). *Sir Launfal* likewise posits Faërie as a perilous world, insofar as it is the protagonist's injunction not to reveal its secrets that brings him close to execution; yet, it is also a world of boundless beauty and freedom, offering the knight solace and wealth when his fortunes reach their nadir, and ultimately rewarding his faithfulness by admitting him to its privileged lifestyle, its pleasures, and, one assumes, never-ending peace.

The anonymous lay *Sir Orfeo* (c. 1300) relocates the classical myth of Orpheus and Eurydice in Celtic fairyland, thereby yielding a perfect example of what Jeff Rider terms the "irruption of another world in the central social world" (Rider, p. 117). Comparable events in Chrétien de Troyes are signaled by the protagonists' transitions to the realm of Gorre in *Lancelot, the Knight of the Cart*, and to the Fisher King's castle in *Perceval, the Story of the Grail*. As Blythe Hsing-wen Tsai explains, *Sir Orfeo*'s unknown author "makes use of romance elements to relocate the Underworld/Otherworld in a context blended with Celtic folklore and chivalric conventions," thereby evoking "a world full of natural and artistic spectacle": a dimension which, in contrast with the classical conception of Hades, does not swarm with "mournful shadows," but actually asserts itself as "a domain of light and hope where mortals encounter adventures, undergo trials, and return to the corporeal world in bliss and good faith" (Tsai).

It is vital to appreciate, on this point, that the Fairies are never negatively portrayed in incontrovertible terms in *Sir Orfeo*. In fact, as Sarah Läseke observes, "the description of the outward appearance of the fairies and their kingdom is surprisingly positive considering Heurodis is threatened and subsequently abducted" (Läseke). This has led Bruce Mitchell to propose that Heurodis' suffering is not triggered by the fairies per se, but rather by her prospective and definitive separation from her beloved husband (Mitchell, p. 157). Relatedly, "the fairy world" portrayed by *Sir Orfeo* "resembles paradise rather than hell" (Läseke)—a paradise, to be more specific, akin to the idealized meta-worlds of Celtic legend rather than the heaven enshrined in Christian doctrine.

To grasp the full bearing of *Sir Orfeo*'s Celtic substratum, it is necessary to reflect on the *royal* stats of the fairies depicted in the poem. Its representation of magical Otherness indeed focuses on a particular social stratum, and this specificity must be acknowledged in order to appreciate the mythical significance of Herodis' captors. Mika Loponen regards the nobility of medieval fairies in general as their most salient attribute. "While the bogies, boggarts and brownies were seen as ugly, simple and often quite stupid household helpers with little magical abilities," argues the critic, "these 'noble' faeries were seen [as] the picture of everything high, and respected, envied and even feared."

Given the centrality of Celtic lore to the romance ethos in general, and to the lay's portrayal of Faërie in particular, it is striking that the first reference to the nobility of fairies should appear in "Irish-Celtic mythology," in specific connection with the "Tuatha de Danann (the children of Dana, mother goddess of Eire)." The fairy aristocracy's mythical origins deserves special notice. "In time the Tuatha de Danann diminished in size and power," argues Loponen, gradually evolving into Sidhe: namely, "the most beautiful, noble and humanlike kind of faeries." The Sidhe are the creatures most intimately connected with the romance tradition, being often painted as "heroic faeries who enjoyed the pleasures of the medieval chivalric life. "Human-sized," they were typically portrayed as "unbelievably beautiful beings, who, depending on the tale, could become invisible whenever necessary, or could only become visible when in the presence of humans" (Loponen, p.11).

Lady Jane F. S. Wilde's description of the Sidhe invites close attention, in the present context, due to its implicit emphasis on the irony underlying the creatures' outlook. The Sidhe's dwelling offers a close matrix for *Sir Orfeo*'s Faërie kingdom, being depicted by Wilde as a "fairy palace of gold and crystal." The Sidhe are endowed with just about every attribute any mortal could wish for, having "been given youth, beauty, joy, and the power over music." Mysteriously, however, "they are often sad." The reason adduced by Wilde for this seemingly incongruous state of affairs is that the Sidhe "remember that they were once angels in heaven though now cast down to earth, and though they have power over all the mysteries of Nature, yet they must die without hope of regaining heaven, while mortals are certain of immortality" (Wilde, p. 132).

Not everybody would readily subscribe to Lady Wilde's proposition that human beings are fundamentally "immortal," whereas the Faërie folk are "doomed to annihilation" (Wilde, p. 132). Moreover, not all readers would be prepared to accept that the Otherworldly beings found in the romance—including creatures like the ones encountered by the longsuffering Orfeo and his loving spouse—are intrinsically gloomy. It is, however, possible that the reason for which *Sir Orfeo*'s fairies deem it so vital to emerge periodically into the mortal domain to purloin one or more of its inhabitants is that they *lack* something—or at any rate *feel* they do. If this were the case, it could be argued that fairies and humans are more alike than one might at first be inclined to believe, insofar as they are brought together by a common fate of unavoidable unfulfillment.

Of course, it could also be argued that the fays, in their uninhibited Otherness, do not perform any actions in accordance with human criteria, and that their abductions are a game, the elvish equivalent of knightly tournaments, say. It is towards this interpretation that the present study tends to lean, this tendency proceeding from the conviction that the Other's *genuine* Otherness, so to speak, may only be duly recognized when it is not measured and contained with reference to everyday norms. It is after all worth remembering, as Katherine Briggs enjoins us to do, that "the morality of even the most ordinary, decent, well-wishing fairy is of a brand of its own" (Briggs, p. 111).

A germane body of legends to the one invoked in *Sir Orfeo* consists of tales in which humans are spirited away in the night to stately mansions, where they are waited upon by courteous servants of peerless charm, garbed in gorgeous raiments of brilliantly colored silk, satin or velvet, and regaled with exquisite refreshments, only to discover, in the clear light of day, that these settings and their denizens are quite delusive. As noted in *The Fairy Tale and Anime*, "when mortals are able to perceive the reality ensconced behind the sortilege, they are likely to face a blood-curdling truth. What is more, those who partake of a fairy feast may well remain spellbound forever. It is also worth noting, in this regard, that fairies are often renowned for the radiant and even riotous beauty of their attire, where hues overtly derived from the natural realm reign supreme and an opulent feel of silken fluidity or velvet plushness is ubiquitous.... Particularly sumptuous costumes regale the periodic Fairy Cavalcades, during which sinuous lines of riding fairies on their white steeds may be fleetingly glimpsed. Flowing gowns adorned with silver and gold patterns, satin slippers, fur-lined or thistle-lined capes, embroidered vests and doublets, leather gauntlets, multicolored breeches and feather-decked wide-brimmed hats, alongside glorious jewels of all conceivable shapes, are among the most conspicuous items one could hope to behold on such occasions" (Cavallaro 2011, pp. 35–36).

One such event is captured by Sir Joseph Noël Paton's "The Fairy Rade Carrying off a Changeling, Midsummer Eve" (1867): a work replete with motifs drawn from Arthurian lore, Renaissance and Pre-Raphaelite painting, and Classical mythology. As Iain Zaczek observes, "accounts of these rades were commonplace in ballads.... Some folk claimed to have witnessed one of these events, drawn by the eerie sound of jingling bridles, clattering hooves and low chanting, though it was highly dangerous for mortals to spy on a rade" (Zaczek, p. 32).

Sir Orfeo attaches considerable significance to fairy fashion, as does *Sir Launfal* along numerous Breton lays. It is noteworthy, on this matter, that Faërie apparel tends to mirror the wearer's temperament and lifestyle. As D. J. Conway explains, it is not unusual, for instance, for "solitary fairies" to favor "long robes or loose trousers and tunics, the colors of which blend in perfectly with their surroundings," in preference to the more ostentatious clothing typically donned by paraders, revelers, hound and falcon handlers, or dancers (Conway, p. 111). It must also be stressed, however, that just as fairies' manor houses, ballrooms, pavilions, and banqueting halls have a distressing propensity to evaporate in daylight, so their weeds' brilliant hues dissolve in proportion to one's proximity to the wearer.

A further situation in which a human being may experience a life-altering exposure to elven magic consists of his or her accidental sighting of a ring of dancing sprites. According to Susannah Marriott, the enchanted circle is "a means of drawing mortals into the warped time and space of fairyland.... Join the circling dancers at your peril: once entranced, few make it home. Because a ring has neither beginning nor end, it is all but impossible to break from" (Marriott, p. 240). The circle's Otherness is magnified by its knack of saturating the grass on which its intricate patterns unfurl with mysterious energies.

Ultimately, Faërie's Otherness thrives on an uncanny specularity: its beings are able to awe us into submission because they know how to exploit our *fear* of their hidden powers. It is from our own sinister fantasies that the Gentry draws its enduring strength, and, no less importantly, its puckish sense of humor. Herodis has good reason to fear her uninvited noontide visitors, but it is likely that the most horrifying part of the experience does not lies with the fays themselves but with her own dark fantasies: the day-nightmares which induce her to tear her lovely visage and clothes apart, and turn in the space of mere hours into a specter of her former self.

Ruth Evans offers a political interpretation of *Sir Orfeo*, viewing the titular monarch himself as the epitome of the *rex inutilis*. As the *Wikipedia* explains, this topos "links Orfeo with several late thirteenth- and early fourteenth-century sovereigns, including Edward II," while Orfeo's "role as a harpist" posits him "as a type of David, the royal figure upon whom many medieval kings modeled themselves" ("*Sir Orfeo*"). According to Evans, Orfeo's decision to leave his realm in the hands of a steward while he cuts himself off from society to nurse alone his private grief attests to his inadequacy as a ruler.

Another political interpretation of the lay is advanced by Cathy Cupitt with the evaluation of the image of the humans peopling the castle's courtyard, who are all depicted in the—often dire—states in which they were captured by the Fairies. "All of these 'taken' people are being mysteriously kept alive, and on display by faerie magic," notes the critic, surmising that the depiction constitutes an implicit commentary on "political power relations between a King and his subjects." This reading leads Cupitt to conclude that "the faerie kingdom seems to be representative of the worst of the Middle Ages" (Cupitt). This appraisal echoes Johan Huizinga's conception of "the feudal age" as one in which "the private wars between two families have no other discernible reason than rivalry of rank and covetousness of possessions" (Huizinga, p. 21). To emphasize the Faerie King's arbitrary power, Cupitt points out that "Heurodis was stolen for no given reason, other than that the Faerie King wanted to" (Cupitt).

John Block Friedman supplies a likewise damning assessment of Faërie's ethics, claiming that the people seen by Orfeo in the courtyard were dismembered by the fairies themselves (Friedman, p. 194). This reading of Faërie's mores is reinforced by Friedman's comparison of the Fairy King himself to Satan (p. 190). This contention is grounded in a topos ingrained in several time-honored folk tales: Satan's habit of turning up at noon—just the time picked by *Sir Orfeo*'s formidable fay cortege to catch Herodis unawares.

However, this perspective does not quite tally with the fairies' general conduct, and especially their king's supreme sense of honor. More congruous is Curtis Jirsa's suggestion that Faërie's denizens do not abduct humans randomly, but in fact rescue—or *relieve*—those about to suffer an abrupt and painful death (Jirsa, p. 148). It is indeed feasible that the taken people were actually removed from their thrall to horror, pain and strife. It could further be suggested that the creatures one sees in the courtyard are only simulacra, or theatrical doubles, and that the real humans they replicate lead lives of peace and pleasure in Faërie's serene woods and meadows, just like Heurodis. This reading is substantiated by the presence, amongst the seemingly suffering people, of a person bearing Heurodis' semblance at the time she was taken. This is clearly not her permanent state—either in Faërie or anywhere else—since we have already seen her happily engaged in riding and falconry in the company of other pretty ladies.

The Gawain Poet

As noted in the previous chapter, the chivalric romance often presents the character of Gawain as the epitome of chivalric excellence. The Gawain Poet's portrayal of his hero, and related dramatization of one of his key knightly exploits, strikes an original note when compared to his treatment in other romances. His Gawain comes across as a rather inexperienced youth, a sapling in the resplendent orchard of Arthur's court, whose principles are as yet untested, and hence vulnerable to temptation. This depiction of the illustrious knight may seem to depart from Gawain's classic representation as the definitive embodiment of chivalric brilliance, as described in Chapter Three.

The Gawain Poet foreshadows the reputation which Gawain is destined to gain, particularly in the temptation scenes: to lure him into unchaste conduct, Bertilak's wife indeed appeals to the chivalric virtue, courtesy, in which the knight will one day excel. The kisses received by the lady in exchange for her erotic advances suggest that Gawain already harbors in embryonic form the qualities of the perfect courtly lover he is destined to become. On the whole, however, the Gawain Poet's protagonist is portrayed as something of a hero in the making, not the exemplar of chivalric distinction he is shown to be in Chrétien's works, and in other contemporary romances. This is arguably what renders the titular hero of the late fourteenth-century Middle English poem *Sir Gawain and the Green Knight* all the more endearing to many modern readers.

It is worth recalling that in Chrétien, whenever Gawain can sort out thorny situations through civil argumentation and rhetoric (amorous or political depending on the circumstances), he refrains from fighting. In other words, he is the arch-diplomat of the Round table. However, when combat is inevitable, the knight's martial prowess does not fail to assert its caliber with both energy and style. In *Sir Gawain and the Green Knight*, Gawain fails on both the rhetorical and the martial fronts. The former defeat occurs within the intimate setting of the boudoir, whereas the latter takes place on the open stage of the Green Chapel. Ironically, Gawain proves deficient precisely in the handling of the codes, and attendant modes of conduct, he is known to master with aplomb in other popular romances.

As A. C. Spearing observes, when the Green Knight "explains that the three strokes" he deals in the ultimate testing scene "represent the three days' temptation in the castle," Gawain explodes into a paroxysm of shame-ridden ire: "he throws down the girdle, and, a little later, raves uncontrollably against the wiles of women, his *cortaysye* quite abandoned" (Spearing 1968, p. 104). In the climactic Green Chapel episode, the hero's exasperation is such as to reach absurd self-dramatizing extremes. At this point, as Christopher Tolkien observes, "the honour he has gained in the great test [i.e., the Beheading Challenge] is of small comfort to him." There is something almost robotic about Gawain's sudden switch from one role to another, as though the suave and judicious knight we have known so far were no more than a cardboard persona, ready to give way at a moment's notice to its impetuous, strident and irrational counterpart.

The impression is reinforced by the somewhat automatic rashness with which Gawain "accuses himself of Greed, Cowardice, and Treachery," even though, strictly speaking, "of the first two he is guiltless, except by a casuistry of shame," and of the third, one may add, he is guilt merely through a sin of omission which only the harshest of judges would deem a capital offence. Yet, it is the sheer *excess* of the knight's emotions that makes his portrayal so "true to life," and so persuasive "a picture of a perhaps not very reflective man of honour, in his shame at being found out" (Tolkien, C., pp. 4–5).

Some commentators have argued that the Gawain Poet was keen to rewrite the Gawain character by Christianizing his assets. This is suggested by the poem's emphasis on the knight's allegiance to St. Mary. (Some critics have seen this element as evidence for the author's identity as a member of the clergy or of a monastic establishment.) Nevertheless, by accepting his hostess' amulet, the knight, having thus far been powerless to affirm either his amatory gallantry or his martial valor, also fails to incarnate the religious ideal. Indeed, as E. Talbot Donaldson remarks, "when the pressures increase, St. Mary's Knight, no longer able to rely on himself, relies not on St. Mary but on a belt of supposed magical powers" (Talbot Donaldson, p. 99). The knight's acceptance of the green girdle and agreement to keep it hidden from his host signals an ironical u-turn in the direction of paganism at its least Christian precisely at the point when orthodox Christianity would expect its followers to trust most keenly in God's support.

The poem's overall allegiance to Christian ideals is further quizzed by its connection with a palpably pagan body of beliefs and rituals. As John Speirs observes, the romance appears to be, "near the surface, a Christian poem," but it is in fact rooted in a much older substratum of stories and beliefs. Thus, "it is Christian rather as some of the mediaeval Christmas carols are Christian, as Christmas itself is Christian; Christian in harmony with pre–Christian nature belief and ritual, a Christian re-interpretation of these" (Speirs, p. 85). The testing of Gawain's chastity itself can be interpreted in line with the romance's take on a regeneration theme grounded in pagan culture rather than in terms of its Christianized significance: "chastity has here nothing very particular to do with monastic asceticism. Chastity has immemorially been a requirement in fertility—or nature—ceremonies and initiations. The chastity theme—chastity as a pre-condition of fertility—is here complementary to the fertility theme" hinging on the character of the Green Knight (p. 93). The Gawain Poet's depiction of the so-called "Chapel" itself casts doubt on the authority of the Christian dimension, since the venue is nothing like a chapel in the ordinary sense of the term. In fact, as Mother Angela Carson avers, it is essentially "a burial mound' (Carson, p. 246).

According to Jessie Weston, the romance tradition associates the figure of Gawain himself with the pre–Christian/pagan concept of regeneration. A good example is the scene in Chrétien's *Perceval, the Story of the Grail* "where Gawain, finding a wounded knight by the roadside, proceeds to treat him." Further "reference to Gawain's possession of medical knowledge" can be found in "the poem entitled *Lancelot et le cerf au pied blanc*," where "Gawain, finding his friend desperately wounded, carries him to a physician whom he instructs as to the proper treatment" (Weston, pp. 106–107).

Most importantly, in the light of the Welsh connection established by the Gawain Poet in *Sir Gawain and the Green Knight* through the description of the hero's journey, it is in the "Welsh *Triads*" (a medieval compendium of ancient Welsh myths and legends), that the knight's healing powers are most emphatically underlined. In this context, "we find Gwalchmai, the Welsh Gawain, cited as one of the three men 'To whom the nature of every object was known,' an accomplishment exceedingly necessary for a 'Medicine man'"—though not, at least "at first sight," an obviously essential component of "the equipment of a knight" (p. 107). This would seem to indicate that Gawain, at least in his original configuration as a persona shaped by a tradition of druidic orientation, is a more multi-dimensional figure than his somewhat stereotypical portrayal as the paragon of secular knighthood might suggest. It is in fact ironical that the perfect embodiment of chivalry should harbor capacities which have precious little to do with chivalry per se, in either the soldierly or the sensual interpretations of the concept.

Several of the structural and thematic mainstays of *Sir Gawain and the Green Knight* are rooted in pre–Christian Celtic lore, the Beheading

Game and the Temptation Game prime among them. Gawain's voyage resembles the archetypical journey to the Otherworld: a major topos in pagan mythology since at least Classical times. Furthermore, the Pentangle emblazoned on Gawain's shield, though linked with the knight's dedication to the Virgin Mary, predates Christianity as a pagan symbol of crucial significance to many mystical and esoteric traditions the world over. According to Donald R. Howard, "the symbolism of shield and girdle suggests an essential and inescapable conflict between chivalry and Christianity."

What is most striking about the Gawain Poet's treatment of this tension is his tendency to view it "in a spirit of amused and ironic detachment," as though to intimate that "these contrarieties of mediaeval thought, being irreconcilable, should be taken in good humor as a condition of life in an imperfect world" (Howard, p. 56). The writer's use of irony puts forward this stance as the only available—indeed, peculiarly *logical*—response to a world of insoluble ambiguities, tensions, contradictions, and disruptions defying the strictures of any rule-bound social existence.

On the matter of the poem's allegiance to paganism, it is also worth noting that the Green Knight himself bears salient affinities with the pagan figures of the Green Man and the Wild Man of the Woods, both of whom emblematize the concepts of fertility and renewal. The holly, which the Green Knight carries into Camelot's festive hall at the start of the poem alongside his formidable axe, is redolent of the popular pagan character of the Holly King. As Jennifer Cole explains, the Holly King, garbed entirely in green, presides over the winter season, overruling the Oak King at the Winter Solstice (Cole). According to Laura I. Kenny, the "Christian tradition" itself accommodates a figure akin to "the pagan personification of nature: Father Christmas who has his origins in St. Nicholas. This saint is usually depicted, just like the pagan king, all dressed in green" (Kenny). The Christian saint is obviously a descendant of a much more ancient pagan personage, thus bearing witness to Christianity's tendency to weave its own mythology out of preexisting traditions and motifs. This adaptive move resembles the Christian appropriation of the pagan Grail, examined earlier in this study: one of the most blatant examples of Christianity's co-opting of established pagan traditions, and of their recasting in a spiritual light.

It is in keeping with the poem's ironical disposition that "the decorous, calm, and aristocratic world" presented in the opening lines should, as Morton W. Bloomfield puts it, be "menaced by the indecorous, wondrous, and mysterious, but only for a while. Order and decorum reestablish themselves with a laugh after we have both been held in thrall and amused" (Bloomfield, p. 55). It is also ironical that stability should be restored through what Mikhail Bakhtin persuasively portrays as the *disruptive* force par excellence, especially in the medieval context: laughter. "Having on the one hand forbidden laughter in every official sphere of life and ideology," argues Bakhtin, "the Middle Ages on the other hand bestowed exceptional privileges of license and lawlessness outside these spheres: in the marketplace, on feast days, in festive recreational literature" (Bakhtin, p. 72).

This means that in medieval culture, laughter "remained outside all official spheres of ideology and outside all official strict forms of social relations," being methodically extirpated "from religious cult, from feudal and state ceremonials, etiquette, and from all the genres of high speculation" (p. 73), and yet was capable of sneaking back into the picture with unhampered zest to rupture the putative solidity and gravity of authority. Therefore, "every feast" possessed, beside its "official, ecclesiastical part," quite a different "folk carnival part whose organizing principles were laughter and the material bodily lower stratum" (p. 82).

The fact that even clerics would participate in such events, and hence in their transgressive humor, suggests that an author like the Gawain Poet, regardless of his religious affiliations, would not have been indifferent to the glorious power of laughter. It is in this perspective that one may do full justice to his ability to frame a sophisticated and challenging narrative by recourse to exuberant revelries, at one end, and mirthful glee, at the other. His outlook validates, albeit indirectly, Bakhtin's assertion that "festive folk laughter presents an element of victory not only over supernatural awe, over the sacred, over death; it also means the defeat of power, of earthly kings, of the earthly upper classes, of all that oppresses and restricts" (p. 92).

Through an ironical twist of logic, the Gawain Poet inverts the social paradigm implied by Bakhtin's opposition between a supposedly humorless official culture and a laughter-rich folk culture. In fact, in *Sir Gawain and the Green Knight*, laughter is located with courtly society. This is not totally surprising, however, if we consider that by time the romance was composed, courtly society was no longer regarded as the epitome of high culture but rather as an increasingly marginal social stratum. It was therefore becoming less "official," as it were, than either the burgeoning mercantile classes or the ranks of career politicians.

R. H. Bowers' reflections on the Gawain Poet's handling of laughter are worthy of attention, in this context. *Sir Gawain and the Green Knight* evinces a propensity for "constant laughter," argues the scholar. This is borne out by the fact that "the Green Knight and his wife are constantly laughing, he in the loud merriment of a practical joker, she in sophisticated amusement." Moreover, following "the decapitation scene" triggering the entire romance, both "Arthur and Gawain burst into laughter as if they had just witnessed a merry interlude" (Bowers, p. 82). Most importantly, laughter is the collective response with which the Round Table meets Gawain's mortified revelation of the outcome of his quest upon returning to Camelot. According to the critic, the Gawain Poet's use of laughter is central to his perception of "the idea of chivalry whole": a concept he approaches "with affection and good-natured understanding" by portraying "good-natured aristocrats, free from bourgeois envy and wrangling" (p. 83), yet also refraining from glorifying its representatives. In fact, Arthur's entire court comes across as a community of young, immature, and not terribly *heroic*, people with a keener appetite for fun that for either martial or doctrinal priorities.

The Gawain Poet's approach to the Arthurian ethos—of which the chivalric romance is the prototypal repository—exhibits neither the somber nostalgia pervading Malory's *Le Morte d'Arthur*, nor Chaucer's redefinition of chivalric priorities in his portrait of the Knight. However, he is keen to emphasize, with verve and tactful wit in equal measures, that chivalric culture is not perfect—and certainly not as perfect as earlier idealizations of its representatives and customs might have suggested. Hence, *Sir Gawain and the Green Knight* is able to look with compassion—and without, mercifully, lapsing into sanctimoniousness—at the romance tradition and its underpinning values. However, its aim is not to deliver an undiluted paean to the chivalric world, but rather to allude to its limitations by underscoring the imperfection of even the courtliest of the Round Table's members. The poet's unique penchant for irony enables him to keep his sympathetic and his critical perceptions of the chivalric world in a delicate balance. Humor is key to his achievement: the means whereby neither pole of his purview is allowed to gain undiluted supremacy over the other as the narrative unfolds by its own splendid momentum.

According to L. D. Benson, *Sir Gawain and the Green Knight* can be read as *both* an attempt to perpetuate the loftiness of chivalric values *and* an indictment on their spuriousness; as *both* a romance *and* an anti-romance: "what Gawain really learns from his adventure is that chivalry takes itself a bit too seriously, that men become ridiculous and foolish when they attempt to live up to so superhuman an ideal. Yet it would be a failure of tact for Gawain to make light of his own actions, and it would be almost impossible for him to do this without rejecting chivalry itself, and that is not the poet's purpose. Therefore, Gawain remains a knight." In other words, he cannot erase his *Gawain-ness*.

Nonetheless, "the court to which he returns can and does change, and it is amused rather than discomfited by the adventure" (Benson, p. 28). Gawain's potential as a chivalric paragon persists, insofar as "the touch of villainy" has not destroyed his reputation irreparably—if at all, in fact—amongst his companions. It has, rather, redefined its parameters. This redefinition is sanctioned by the Round Table's implementation of a novel vestimentary motif pregnant with symbolic import: a green girdle akin to the one received by Gawain in Bertilak's household. "As the laughter shows," comments Benson, "the fame of the Round table and the ideal it represents is now modified by the bend of bright green and the tolerant acknowledgment of human limitations that it implies" (p. 29).

There is even a hint at the possibility that the Arthurian circle wishes to appropriate the green girdle as a *fashion symbol*. After all, the medieval equivalent of fashionability would have been considered a prime asset for any knight worth his mettle, and especially for a member of the Round Table. This contention is eloquently substantiated by the sheer amount of lines devoted to the description of the protagonist's, and his destrier's, accoutrements in *Sir Gawain and the Green Knight*—and, more generally, by the attention accorded by the chivalric romance at large to clothes and accessories through the meticulous depiction of fabrics, patterns, and ornaments.

Sir Gawain and the Green Knight's consummate realism makes it possible to identify some of its geography with very specific locations, which also makes it possible to guess at its author's provenance. Indeed, as Laura Hibbard Loomis explains, "the realistic references ... to North Wales, Anglesey, and the wilderness of Wirral in Cheshire (697–701) are unusual. The scenic descriptions, the extensive use of words of Scandinavian origin, the dialect, all place the author's home in the Northwest Midland area" (Hibbard Loomis, pp. 5–6).

Despite the geographical specificity of the poem's setting, it is crucial to appreciate, as Denton Fox points out, that it would be quite inappropriate to ideate its author as "a backwoodsman, a gifted but secluded provincial who followed the ways of his fathers because they were all he knew. He certainly lived far from London, probably in southeast Cheshire or in northeast Staffordshire, near north Wales. But his audience was presumably drawn from the wealthy and cosmopolitan Lancastrian nobility, and it has been suggested several times that he may, like Chaucer, have been in the service of John of Gaunt, the duke of Lancaster. There is no reason to suppose that he was at all isolated from the European intellectual or literary currents of his times" (Fox, p. 5).

The author's association with Northern lands and climes is confirmed by his realistic depiction of the forbidding season in which the hero travels to his rendezvous. Depicting "winter with all its harsh rigors," as Hibbard Loomis notes, and dwelling with special immediacy on "its freezing rain and snows" as well as "its howling winds," the Gawain Poet is able to evoke the overwhelming "cold with an intensity hardly matched till Keats wrote *The Eve of St. Agnes*," enhancing the text's climatic impact by means of a vivid portrait of "the English north country," its "heath and crag and ... tangled forests of hoar oaks, hazel, and hawthorn" (Hibbard Loomis, p. 19). The climate's severity appears to be a greater source of affliction, for the lonely traveler, that any of the wild beasts, dragons, and unnamed monsters he encounters along the way. (The description of the harsh winter landscape proffered by John Keats, to which Hibbard Loomis in her analysis, reads as follows: "St. Agnes' Eve—Ah, bitter chill it was! / The owl, for all his feathers, was a-cold; / The hare limp'd trembling through the frozen grass, / And silent was the flock in woolly fold" [Keats 1884].)

The Gawain Poet's mastery of the descriptive arts can hardly be overemphasized: his knack of bringing even the most marginal scene or setting to life through a welter of evocative details is indeed quite unique. It should, however, be noted that his lexicon exhibits a special sensitivity to the cumulative sensory impact of scenes, not only to their visual connotations. His handling of the interplay of the optical and auditory dimensions is particularly notable—which is, after all, quite congruous with the romance's alliterative style.

As Dorothy Everett contends, "this writer, like other alliterative poets, is lavish with his details. The three hunts, Gawain's armor, the clothes he was given at the castle, and even the cushions placed on his chair—all these, and much more, are minutely described. For the most part, the things the poet chooses to describe are those elaborated by other romance writers; but he had a mind stored with *unusually vivid memories of sight and sound*" (Everett, p. 18; italics added). In addition, the luxurious proliferation of descriptive minutiae used in the depiction of items such as furnishings, trappings, and garments enables the romance to evoke haptic impressions of palpable immediacy.

The capsulated account of Gawain's adventures on his way from Arthur's court to the Green Chapel provides *in nuce* an eloquent testimony to the entire romance's narrative flair. Indeed, its concise rendition of the many challenges faced by the hero on his perilous journey reflects the poem's pervasive penchant for narrative condensation, its impeccable structural coherence, and its knack of capturing a whole scene's distinctive atmosphere by means of a few well-chosen descriptive details. Those who have experienced *Sir Gawain and the Green Knight* in their student days will perhaps recall with a certain amusement, or even fondness, their first encounter with the lines, "Sumwhyle wyth wormez he werrez"—a line bound to raise questions about the real magnitude of the knight's exploits among those not yet familiar with Middle English, who might have legitimately wondered what could possibly be so life-threatening about creatures like "wormez." Intriguingly, J. R. R. Tolkien has chosen to translate the word as "worms" (Tolkien, J. R. R., II.31.8) in the interests of alliterative coherence, though most students will have been instructed to opt for the rather more *chivalric* "dragons."

As anticipated, the Gawain Poet is endowed with a unique sense of irony. It is in his exercise of this capacity that the real essence of the poem's narrative identity resides. In *Sir Gawain and the Green Knight*, irony operates to a significant degree by means of the strategy of displacement—or, to be more precise, through the repeated displacement of responsibility. This ruse is already at work in the poem's opening segment. On the one hand, the Green Knight is implicitly equated to the terrifying giants of legend, at the same time as the figure's hue links him, as noted earlier, to the figures of the Green Man and the Wild Man of the Woods, and to pagan fertility rites. These associations emphasize the Green Knight's supernatural stature, minimizing his ties with humanity. In the face of such a representative of the awesome realm of magic, it is suggested, Arthur and his court do not have any real choice but to bow to his peremptory request for an Exchange of Blows, and participation in the ceremonial of the Beheading Challenge, in terms sanctioned by an unwritten but unbending law etched in ancient lore. In this respect, the human characters are exonerated from the moral duty to exercise their own free will.

On the other hand, the Green Knight is portrayed as a genteel scion of chivalry whose language and manners bespeak rare proficiency in the code of courtesy. As his speech resounds through Camelot's festive hall, the character's supernatural attributes fade into insignificance. In this regard, the Arthurian court cannot be regarded as the victim of an otherworldly ruse which it is beyond its power to control. Accordingly, its participation in the Exchange of Blows and Beheading Challenge can be seen as a pact which the human characters embrace of their own free will. This makes them, by implication, morally responsible for what is to come.

Moral responsibility is hence displaced from the inscrutable Beyond signified by the Green Knight as a likely denizen of Faërie upon his dramatic appearance, to the human sphere of which the Green Knight seems, after all, to be a respectable specimen. The effect of this displacement is a mood of undecidability. The foreclosure of conclusive solutions to the conundrum posed by the poem's indigenous ethics as presented in the opening scenes makes the whole situation profoundly ironic.

The poem's play with displacement reaches a new level of sophistication as the Green Knight metamorphoses into Sir Bertilak: a figure who inherits all of his double's more urbane and courteous features, while also showing himself capable of engineering a highly refined game, meant to enhance his guest's pleasure during his sojourn at the castle of Hautdesert—or, at any rate, *claiming* to be so intended. The ritual exchange of winnings proposed by Bertilak involves a double irony. Firstly, while Bertilak is portrayed as both the mastermind and the stage manager behind the game into which he inveigles Gawain, he is actually operating in accordance with a script outside his control. This consists of a time-honored set of conventions embedded in both orally transmitted stories, and earlier texts in the chivalric tradition. Secondly, the recreation initiated by Bertilak for his guest's supposed solace is not a game at all. On the contrary, it turns out to be a dead serious test of the knight's moral fiber—a test whose gravity within the story's overall fabric turns out to exceed by far the significance of the conventions in which it is couched.

The double irony involved in Bertilak and Gawain's courtly exchange at the end of each day consists of an exquisite charade in which manifest and latent meanings slide in and out of the action so stealthily that their ploy goes undetected until the end. In the process, Gawain's predicament lends itself to multiple, and often contradictory, readings. The displacement of responsibility inherent in Bertilak's pseudo-game—and its double irony—involves an ongoing shift of emphasis, during Gawain's stay at Hautdesert, from the image of Bertilak the impish deceiver to that of Bertilak the wise agent of truth. The former makes Gawain's host the sole carrier of moral responsibility, casting Gawain himself as the green (so to speak) knight with insufficient experience and maturity to have any say in how the test is conducted—let alone the capacity to penetrate through the mock-ludic façade of Bertilak's pantomime. The latter presents Bertilak as a benevolent father figure intent on facilitating Gawain's moral growth, and resting the moral responsibility for the game's outcome squarely on the young knight's shoulders *for his own good*, as it were.

The scenes in which Bertilak's wife visits Gawain in his chamber with the intention of seducing him, redoubling her seductress skills with each successive attempt, offer some of the most sophisticated instances of amatory dalliance to be found not only within the formal boundaries of the chivalric romance, but in Western literature at large. In Chrétien's romances, one encounters many an episode in which the hero is said to engage in amorous discourse with the lady of the mansion. However, the French romancer does not, on the whole, regale the reader with anything like the volume of rhetoric delivered by the Gawain Poet.

Within the earlier writer's corpus, it is sufficient for the narrator to inform the audience that a knight and a lady are engaged in the exchange of romantic lines to guarantee the automatic evocation of a specific kind of repartee—a discourse replete with certain stylistic devices, a particular lexicon, and attendant non-verbal language, in which most members of Chrétien's contemporary audience would themselves be well-versed. In *Sir Gawain and the Green Knight*, the sheer amount of richly variegated language which the poet devotes to romantic colloquies makes the relevant scenes inimitable.

No less distinctive, and no less remarkable, is the poet's insistent incorporation of religious references into the temptation scenes: the Lord, Mary and Christ are brought into play throughout without compunction despite the worldly nature of the situation. Without wanting to doubt the authenticity of the writer's belief, it could hardly be denied that the religious invocations peppering the dialogue come across as rather formulaic compared with the vitality of the erotic banter itself. This ironical disjunction serves to imbue the poem with a decidedly secular feel regardless of its professed spiritual moral.

The full caliber of the Gawain Poet's penchant for irony becomes truly patent in the poem's climactic scenes, where it is disclosed that neither the Green Knight/Bertilak nor his beguiling lady have been directly responsible for subjecting Gawain to his trial, but rather played out their roles at the behest of Morgan le Fay. The *Lancelot-Grail* Cycle contains an interesting antecedent for the use of this multi-faceted Arthurian character. In the French romance, Morgan herself attempts to seduce Lancelot three times, each time being rejected. This time around, she appears to have sent her younger avatar as a woman more likely to triumph over the young knight around whom she wishes to weave her portentous wiles.

By positing Morgan le Fay as "the prime mover in the plot," as Hibbard Loomis puts it, *Sir Gawain and the Green Knight* makes Bercilak and his spouse "helpless in the power of a malignant goddess" (Hibbard Loomis, p. 14). This shift of responsibility renders the couple innocent in the protagonist's own eyes, despite what he has suffered at their (ostensible) behest. Ethical responsibility becomes again the nub of an ironical ambiguity, as the ultimate authority of Morgan le Fay herself is questioned. This coincides with Bercilak's assertion that the sorceress owes her expertise in the magical arts to Merlin (with whom the character is traditionally reputed to have had a torrid love affair).

Moreover, Morgan le Fay's role is only disclosed at the end of the poem, which in itself serves to relativize her significance in the plot as a whole. The figure's downgrading is congruous with a tendency identified by Sheila Fisher as characteristic of the poem as a whole: namely, its emphasis on male bonds at the expense of women, who are thereby pushed to the action's periphery. Morgan le Fay's power is further belittled by the revelation that her aim has been to test Camelot's reputation (and, by implication, its code of conduct), and to scare Guinevere out of her wits. While the trial of the knightly community's credentials could be regarded as a lofty goal serving a public interest, the enchanter's adversarial stance to Arthur's spouse is merely the result of private hatred. As such, it "trivializes Morgan's power. The threat of the woman as a free agent who can construct her own exchanges with men is undermined and marginalized by being projected onto Morgan's jealousy of Arthur's wife" (Fisher, p. 154).

The tale's ironical moving of goalposts involves that what seems at first a test of courage turns out to be a test of another virtue—but *which* virtue exactly, courtesy or loyalty? The key moment in which this conundrum makes itself evident with glaring irony is the moment at which Bertilak's wife offers Gawain the girdle supposed to guard him from harm. Derek Pearsall addresses the ethical implications of Gawain's response to the offer of the magic girdle with witty incisiveness. "Is he entitled to take it?" he wonders, arriving at two clashing, yet equally plausible, answers, namely: "yes, because romance-heroes are always accepting talismans of this kind"—and are *expected* to do so if the donor is a lady, whom the laws of courtly love enjoin them to honor practically without reservations. "No, because if he takes it, intending to make use of it, he will have to keep it and not give it back to Bercilak [*sic*] under the exchange of winnings agreement. But surely he has an obligation to try to save his life…. It is an impossible conundrum, and nothing is solved by Gawain's confession to the priest immediately after accepting the girdle.... One wonders, indeed, what any priest in his senses might have made of a 'confession' about a game of exchanges and a magic girdle" (Pearsall, p. 78).

This amusing question is well worth pondering, but we must remember that we are in a world where standard notions of sense and nonsense do not apply, any more than they ever did in *Sir Launfal* or *Sir Orfeo*, for the sheer reason that the authority of this world's human laws is time and again voided by their intersection with Faërie's own rules. *Sir Gawain and the Green Knight* is more realistic than many other chivalric romances or lays. Yet, it is a chivalric romance nonetheless, and one tinged with the magical hues of the Breton lay and its fay-ruled world view.

Notwithstanding their otherworldly aura, the ritual games central to the poem's diegesis may also be interpreted by recourse to a sociological frame of reference: the one supplied by Marcel Mauss' analysis of gift exchange (*The Gift*, 1925): a crucial aspect of the political, economic, and ritual operations of many societies. The term "potlatch," in particular, is used to describe the custom of competitive gift exchange whereby gift-givers strive to out-give their opponents in order to augment their power (Mauss). Embedded in this practice is a strident irony, since the logical conclusion of potlatch is a situation in which a society depletes itself completely in its effort to assert its superiority, thereby achieving not a final victory but a total self-defeat. Mauss is concerned with collective, as opposed to individual, gift exchange. Nevertheless, his analysis is relevant to the textual economy of *Sir Gawain and the Green Knight*.

In the poem's handling of the convention of the Exchange of Winnings, it is suggested that the protagonist has the choice of whether or not to surrender all his gains. In the warped logic of potlatch, triumph is conditional on the willingness to strip oneself of all possessions. Gawain does not choose this route when he decides to keep the girdle and hide it from his host. Failing to embrace the ethos of potlatch to the full, he *loses*—not material possessions but his reputation as a knight of spotless virtue: a treasure deemed infinitely more important than any tangible entity by the code to which he adheres. This makes Gawain the butt of a supernatural joke—one which, alas, he does not have enough of a sense of humor to share (perhaps due to his immaturity or self-importance) even at the end. It is plausible that this is just what triggers the sparkling laughter which crowns his contrite return to Camelot.

All things considered, the poem can be seen to articulate with flawless formal elegance what Pearsall describes as "a new art of the interior self."

Shame and guilt cause Gawain to engage in tortured self-introspection. He does not, therefore, indulge in the kind of conduct one would have expected from the knights of older romance narratives: "Yvain, faced with the shame and humiliation of having forgotten his promise to Laudine ... can only run mad in the woods. Lancelot behaves similarly when accused by Guenevere of disloyalty. This is the customary response to extreme embarrassment in medieval romance." This is not to say, however, that Chrétien's or Malory's worlds are *simplistic* on the psychological level— this is far from true, since the kind of conduct evinced by Yvain and Lancelot bears witness to a refined sensitivity to the subtlest nuances of the errant knight's psyche. Thus, running mad into the woods can be regarded as "a kind of mental suicide, a revulsion against the pain inflicted on the inner self so violent that mental life must be suspended, blocked off, until some form of redemption becomes available" (Pearsall, p. 80).

Notably, even though Arthur and his knights do their best to reintegrate Gawain into their society, and minimize his guilt by agreeing to wear a girdle like the one he has received from Bercilak's wife as a sign of solidarity, Gawain is not consoled. "Is Gawain's persistence in self-accusation and self-mortification," wonders Pearsall, "a sign of pride and refusal to recognize the inevitability of human imperfection?" (Pearsall, p. 79). This is a question, at once ethical and aesthetic, which readers are invited to take away with them as the Gawain Poet's special freebie as they leave the poem's fictional world behind.

The issue of ethical failure, as we have seen, plays an important part in the evolution of the chivalric romance as both a form and a world view. In the *Lancelot-Grail Cycle*, Arthurian culture's espousal of a secular ethos incompatible with the ideals enshrined in the Grail Quest is deemed responsible for its ultimate downfall. Although the work is profoundly ironical in the declaration and maintenance of its Christian stance, there can be little doubt about the official explanation for Camelot's tragic failure. For Chaucer's Knight, chivalry fails by discarding the principles fostered by the Arthurian world, for all its flaws, in the name of a materialistic ideology bereft not only of morality but also, it is implied, of literary charisma. The Knight's attitude renders him, ironically, *both* a champion of chivalry *and* a renegade at one and the same time.

Malory's approach to Arthurian chivalry is likewise ironical: he is well aware that its ideals are no more than ideals: vacuous signifiers whose objectives are unlikely to reach fruition due to their upholders' pathetic fallibility. This attitude suggests that ideals exist, and that it is commendable to pursue them insofar as the principles they promote are noble; yet, to expect anything other than failure is both unrealistic and pernicious. *Sir Gawain and the Green Knight* reflects a comparable world view. As Helen Cooper argues, the poem "does not question the worth of the ethical system by which its hero tries to live, but ... it does question whether such ideals are achievable in a fallen world."

Perfection is incompatible with the Gawain Poet's world picture, not because he does not believe in the principle of "perfectibility"—which, in fact, features prominently in the work—but because he does not believe that "it is possible." Aiming for perfection is a worthy endeavor, but assuming that it is realizable is misleading to say the least. In this regard, the romance looks forward to Spenser, who similarly underscores "the centrality of ethics and the need to aim for perfection," but only with the proviso that "perfection is not achievable within this world" (Cooper 2008, p. 370).

FIVE

Renaissance Refashionings: Ariosto, Spenser and Shakespeare

Ariosto

Barbara Fuchs argues that "Ariosto's poem addresses the incompatibility of romance and epic: the conventions of the former, which involve magical journeys and heroes wandering off the field of battle in pursuit of a beautiful maiden or into some treacherously beguiling space, are precisely about evading the latter, while the irreverence of his tone belies the seriousness of heroic poetry. The matter-of-fact marvels of romance are constantly *ironized*: Ruggiero, for example, goes red in the face for shame at the unfair advantage his magic shield confers on him."

As noted, in foregrounding its fictionality, the romance opposes the ethos of myth, whose prime aim is the promotion of official truths. Ludovico Ariosto's work appropriates and reworks the romance for the aesthetic sensibility of his time with the intent to challenge myth's truth-seeking aspirations.

To this end, the poet destabilizes the epic's ideological agenda, and the burgeoning national identities which the epic is required to bolster. Fuchs corroborates this proposition, arguing that Ariosto's treatment of the romance conventions highlights "the contrast between the easy mobility of romance—the mobility of individuals across geographical borders but also between different religious or racial camps—and the obsessive concerns with separation and difference of the emerging early modern states," thus disputing "the political myth-making of epic, and its tight networks of obligation and belonging" (Fuchs, p. 69; italics added).

Five—Renaissance Refashionings

The most salient feature of Ariosto's *Orlando Furioso* (1516) consists of its structure: an inexhaustible reservoir of sophisticated and surprising techniques. As a result, this aspect of the poem will punctuate the ensuing discussion as something of a leitmotif. In *Orlando Furioso di Ludovico Ariosto raccontato da Italo Calvino*, the latter compares the space of the poem to "an immense game of chess played on the geographic map of the world, a boundless game which branches out into several simultaneous games" (Calvino, p. 87). Ariosto's romance game, like the game of chess for Ferdinand de Saussure, is comparable to language at large, as a system in which the rules governing the game (*langue*) remain unaltered even if the individual player's moves (*parole*) vary from one contest to another. Saussure's analogy between language and the game of chess, proposed in his *Course in General Linguistics*, is meant to bolster the idea that language abides by fundamental rules inherent in its underlying structures (Saussure). Ariosto's poem, according to Calvino, reflects a similar outlook insofar as its randomness is only apparent: "the world's map is much more varied than a chessboard, but upon it, each character's moves follow one another according to fixed rules like chess pieces" (Calvino, p. 87).

In fact, Ariosto's chessboard is ultimately unable, or unwilling, to *contain* the romance's exuberant diversity—or better, it is not truly *designed* to contain it. The poet is far more interested in the unruly elements which escape language's fixed structures, and indeed in intimating that *no* linguistic structure is conclusively stable and reliable. This does not, of course, entail that *Orlando Furioso* is shapeless: *center*less it surely is, but *structure*less it is not. Rather, it deploys its form to show that structures in general are not a dependable means of keeping a challenging reality at bay. On the contrary, they exist to remind us of their precariousness, and thus urge us to acknowledge life's vagaries and intricacies. At the same time, they aim neither at dispelling the fear of entrapment in reality nor at offering the key which might offer a flight therefrom viable.

Thus, Calvino resorts to an image other than the chessboard to describe *Orlando Furioso*'s distinctive space: "a labyrinth," giving rise at every turn to "other labyrinths," at whose center Ariosto's unflustered irony locates "a trap." This occurs in Canto XII in the guise of the second of Atlantes' magical castles (the first having featured prominently in Cantos II-IV): "a vortex of nothingness in which all of the poem's images are reflected" (p. 167). On the one hand, in mimicking the architectural and psychological workings of a labyrinth, *Orlando Furioso* suggests that in order to face up to the baffling uncertainty of the real, it is necessary to trace the most detailed of all possible maps of the labyrinth. On the other hand, the romance invites us to experience the sheer pleasure intrinsic in getting lost in the labyrinth. As the mind and senses travel from one potential map to the next, they encounter one complex image after another. The task is strenuous but titillating at the same time: it is laden with logical riddles, yet also bathed in the glorious illogic of *jouissance*.

Ariosto plays this double game with consummate irony throughout his monumental work, cherishing each twist of the narrative. The deliberate rhythm of his descriptive scenes would seem to indicate that the romancer feels he has all the time in the world to tell his tale, to launch on endless digressions, embark on preposterous detours and, in so doing, postpone ad infinitum the poem's conclusion. At the same time, however, the breakneck speed at which many a paladin pursues both his enemies and the objects of his acutest longings, racing through the romance's labyrinthine map like a crazed beast haunted by thunder, conveys an impression of almost intimidating urgency.

As a mixture of feelings of imprisonment and liberation, the labyrinth stands out as an image impelled by the yearning to generate order in a universe given over to escalating chaos. Concurrently, it provides a metaphor for writing and reading which evokes both the sense of an enclosed ludic space, and the open-ended play likely to unfold within it. As Allen Thiher observes, "labyrinthine constructs" offer contexts in which "symmetries are created by the infinite possibilities of choice that allow the indefinite proliferation of possible order" (Thiher, p. 162). The symmetries yielded by labyrinthine structures, therefore, are illusory symmetries in which the beauty of regularity and harmony on which the principle of symmetry depends is continually challenged by the opposite pull toward entropy.

The repetitive impulse which gives rise to Ariosto's lyrical maze often produces anxiety, uncertainty, and confusion among *Orlando Furioso*'s copious cast. Readers themselves would experience these harrowing emotions were it not for the poet's ironical voice: the voice which, in seeming to celebrate with authentic reverence the "goodly truth in cavaliers of old" (Ariosto, Canto I, 22), alerts us at every available opportunity to the arbitrariness of their goals, and the inanity of their pursuits. Furthermore, the version of the real one encounters in the Ariostesque labyrinth is an aleatory one: repeatedly defying the faith in the existence of a single order which might prevail over all other orders, and hence obliterate the threat of chaos, the knights' quests stretch indefinitely through each segment of the construct, and through each of its innumerable corridors and diversions.

The overall atmosphere of randomness is reinforced by the impression that to begin with, Ariosto is as yet undecided about his plot's future trajectory: an impression which the poem deftly cultivates through tone and diction. What is, however, evident from the start are the "enthusiasm" and "effortlessness" feeding the writer's fabulistic skills. These are the fundamental ingredients of his "poetry's *errant* motion." The poet feels at liberty to "take it easy, if he so wishes, employ several stanzas to say something which others would say in one line, or else condense in one line what could be the subject of a long discourse" (Calvino, 31; my translation; italics in the original).

Orlando Furioso also intimates that although the romance, like any other fictional form, is powerless to reveal the way out of the labyrinth, it is nonetheless able to prompt the reader's awareness of another world—a world Other—to a degree unattainable by other forms. This results from its frank acknowledgement of its fictionality: of the constructedness of its realities, and, beneath them, of the system of signs in which these are couched. In order to intensify the poem's fictionality, Ariosto uses *Orlando Furioso* itself not just as a literary mold in which multiple adventures may be cast for the purposes of entertainment and political eulogy, but also as a metaphor for the individual's encounter with reality *via literature*.

This is paradigmatically typified by Ruggiero's adventures, and his interpretation of Alcina's island in particular. The knight is here positioned not merely as a character in a narrative constellation, but also as a reader, on whom it is incumbent to interpret the situation in which destiny has thrown him in literary terms, with reference to the specific codes and conventions of different forms and genres. The key moment in the episode set on Alcina's island, where Ruggiero has been taken captive, comes with the knight's realization that each of the three witches on the island personifies an abstract concept: Alcina and Morgana, the *bad* sisters, stand for Luxury and Lasciviousness, whereas the *good* sister, Logistilla, represents Reason or Virtue. As Calvino explains, faced with talk of "vices and virtues," Ruggiero begins to grasp "the story's drift." Having set out as a character in a "chivalric poem, packed with adventures and wonders," he suddenly "risks finding himself in the middle of an allegorical poem, in which every appearance carries a moral and pedagogical meaning."

Ruggiero, as a reader of Ariosto's work no less than one of its pivotal heroes, makes an interpretative decision, in detecting the poem's shift from the chivalric to the allegorical mode, which in turn leads to an active reorientation of the narrative. This indicates that he is not only a reader but also, more specifically, the type of reader that takes an active role in the text's construction: a reader straight out of Roland Barthes or Reader Response Theory. Indeed, his immediate reaction is that "it is necessary to get out" of the allegorical framework "as soon as possible" (Calvino, p. 69). Thus, when Ruggiero explores the island, and, upon meeting a variety of monsters which embody the worst vices, strives to overcome them, he is endeavoring to destroy not just a series of foes, nor indeed the sins they signify, but a narrative modality—the allegory—which he deems uncongenial to his temperament (and, by implication, to his creator's ultimate plan).

The idea that Ariosto's heart lies with the chivalric romance rather than allegory is demonstrated by the episode in which Astolfo travels to the Moon astride the loyal hippogriff. The satellite is here portrayed as the apotheosis of the very kind of Otherworld which distinguishes the medieval romance as immortalized by Chrétien's de Troyes. The principle of alterity is foregrounded by a simple, yet highly effective, verbal strategy—the insistent repetition of the word "other":

> Here other river, lake, and rich champaign
> Are seen, than those which are below descried;
> Here other valley, other hill and plain,
> With towns and cities of their own supplied;
> Which mansions of such mighty size contain,
> Such never he before of after spied.
> Here spacious hold and lonely forest lay,
> Where nymphs for ever chased the panting prey.
> [Ariosto, Canto XXIV, 42].

Central to *Orlando Furioso*'s interpretation of errancy is a dispassionate grasp of the unfulfillable nature of human longing—a topos which, as argued in depth in Chapter Two, is one of the chivalric romance's chief preoccupations. Chiara Dini corroborates this contention. Ariosto's poem, according to the critic, deals with "all the themes of the traditional chivalric romance," including martial and amorous exploits alongside all manner of wonders, in order to convey a specific philosophical stance, and thus foreground human fallibility. The characters' "vain search for the object of desire" constitutes the kernel of this existential perspective, expressing a perception of human life as a course "continually exposed to deceptions and illusions," and at all times "threatened" by the onset of "insanity" (Dini, p. 79).

As Deanna Shemek reminds us, the term "errancy" is conventionally used to designate "a wandering away—be it spiritual, moral, or geographical—from the straight path that is thought to be right and good." This common interpretation of errancy is both corroborated and complicated by the tendency to conceive of "errant spirits" as creatures that "both diverge from the norm and stray from the course of truth, rectitude, or purpose."

In this respect, the term echoes "the second meaning recorded in the Oxford English Dictionary for wayward: 'Capriciously wilful; conforming to no fixed rule or principle of conduct; erratic." However, as Shemek emphasizes throughout her study of the position of women in the literature of early modern Italy, the word carries an "additional," and no less significant, sense: namely, "disposed to go counter to the wishes or advice of others, or to what is reasonable; wrong-headed, intractable, self-willed; forward, perverse. Of children: disobedient, refractory" (Shemek, p. 1).

While in the period in which *Orlando Furioso* was composed, wayward female conduct was perceived first and foremost as a threat to male identity—and hence social order and political stability—it is possible to approach errancy as an act of resistance, rather than a culpable form of deviance or deviation from the sanctioned cultural norm. Ariosto's poem bears witness to this contention through the representation of female characters whose errancy serves not so much to reinforce the stereotypical misogynistic equation of femininity to slippery and fickle conduct, as to demonstrate woman's positive struggle for intellectual, emotional, and ethical autonomy in a world affording scarce leeway for the expression of such a capacity.

Shemek evaluates in depth Ariosto's presentation of Angelica and Bradamante as women whose "roles ... appear to offer two very different models for feminine character and conduct. Through each, however, Ariosto manages both to expose and to reinforce the order of patriarchy while at the same time granting each character some leverage against the circumstances women share in this order" (p. 45). Angelica plays a structurally axial part insofar as she "inspires movement and thus sets off the narrative mechanisms of errancy that structure Ariosto's poem." As she repeatedly flees one or the other of the paladins longing for her love, the princess' actions "interrupt the linear progress of specific narrative threads and propel the *Furioso*'s centrifugal, straying story lines outward into the busy tapestry the poem becomes" (p. 45).

In the bulk of the action, "Angelica functions less as a real character than as an abstract value, an endpoint for the desirous gazes of the poem's male knights." To this extent, she serves to reinforce the conventional binary opposition between male activity and female passivity: she can only signify, as a poetic presence, in the guise of a passive object of desire for an active male subject. The situation undergoes radical redefinition as Angelica begins to act "as an autonomous, desiring subject" (p. 47). It is through the frank assertion of her "love for Medoro" that the princess "verifies her own subjecthood and desire" (p. 76).

The titular character's madness, in this perspective, can be read as a response not only to the discovery of Angelica's love for Medoro, and to evidence of the ecstatic consummation thereof, but also to the collapse of a belief system: one which can only grasp gender relations in terms of unconditional principles, the chief of which is woman's duty to function as an ideal devoid of independent desires for a self-determining male subject to seek, and possess. Orlando is only capable of seeing Angelica's assumption of an autonomous identity as an assault on his mores, and hence his very identity. He cannot even begin to conceive of it as a right.

Thus, for Orlando, "the price" of Angelica's achievement of her "humanity" is the loss of "his own. Orlando's fate thus suggests that absolute oppositions are based on a fragile illusion, the sudden shattering of which results in … a pouring out of the subject into madness" (p. 76). It is also worth stressing, however, that Ariosto's articulation of female desire as an independent force does not signal an incontrovertible triumph for womanhood, insofar as just as Angelica "reveals herself to be, *like* the knights who pursue her, a desiring subject … the absolute oppositions that sustain her existence can no longer hold, and she falls out of the narrative" (p. 47).

Bradamante's function is likewise special within the fabric of the poem as a whole. In her case, it "results from her destiny" which is "to found along with the young knight Ruggiero the family line of the poet's patron, Ippolito d'Este." Bradamante's genealogical significance is underscored by the poem's suggestion that "her movements" have the capacity to "carry the poem toward its resolution rather than continuing the multiplication of narratives typical of romance" (p. 77). Hence, Bradamante stands out, as a distinctive female agency, as a result of her ideological function. This effectively enables the character to transcend the boundaries of the fictional plot on the temporal plane, and the poem's rhythm of zigzagging deferment and rampant ramification on the geographical plane. Bradamante comes to represent a specific destiny, requiring her to pursue not the desire for adventure per se, the customary motivator in a chivalric romance, but rather an appointed end. In her fate, therefore, an element of teleology can be seen to infiltrate the classic romance structure of indefinite ramification.

Eleonora Stoppino maintains that "chivalric culture, the dynastic system, and gender relations" are intimately interconnected through out *Orlando Furioso* (Stoppino, p. 2). The character of Bradamante is instrumental in the articulation of this interrelation. Indeed, she "is a woman warrior; one of the protagonists of the *Furioso*; and, with Ruggiero, the destined founder of the Este dynasty, for whose scions (Cardinal Ippolito and Duke Alfonso) the poem was written." Bradamante therefore brings together the three fundamental elements of Ariosto's work by embodying the chivalric ethos through her martial exploits, and by playing a pivotal part in the establishment of dynastic connections between a fictive past and a historical present though her attachment to Ruggiero. Concurrently, her role in *Orlando Furioso* challenges the social subordination of women by according her a unique textual privilege: "she is the sole addressee" of the poem's "prophetic sequences. Prophetic communication, a hallmark of epic from Homer to Virgil to Boiardo, is in the *Furioso* directed for the very first time to female ears and eyes" (p. 5).

Ariosto is clearly challenging the mores of his day in investing women with the kind of centrality he grants Angelica and Bradamante. It could be argued that this move is facilitated by the author's natural attraction to the *freedom* permitted by the romance as opposed to the epic. Appropriating this defining characteristic of the form's thematic and structural preferences, Ariosto feels able to defy convention, and hence make it possible for the male-centered nature of epic prophecy to be displaced by a female orientation. It is worth recalling, on this point, David Lodge's suggestion that the romance's orchestration of multiple plot strands, each with its own climax, bears affinities with the poly-orgasmic nature of the female experience of sexual pleasure.

Moreover, Ariosto's ploy can also be seen as an elliptical commentary on a historical reality, if one considers that within the court of Ferrara, of which the Este were the rulers, women held special importance. "Three important marriages—that of Ercole d'Este to Eleanora d'Aragona (1473), of Isabella d'Este to the Marquis of Mantua Francesco Gonzaga (1490), and of Alfonso d'Este to Lucrezia Borgia (1501)" opened up a new avenue "in the court's history. For the first time, prestige and power were concentrated in the hands of wives: women were acquiring a space within the dynastic structure of power" (p. 1). This makes Ariosto's poem "a work of fiction ... responsive to its historical context in imagining a position for women within the formation of a lineage" (p. 176).

Ariosto's assertion of women's centrality does not imply, however, that his treatment of gender is monolithic. In fact, like so much else in the poem, it is layered with subtle irony. As a result, even as he promulgates what some would call a feminist agenda, the poet simultaneously undercuts his own unconventionality by relegating the female presence to a relatively marginal position. Angelica, as we have seen, vanishes from the scene at the point when she is in a position to declare her autonomy as a desiring subject. Bradamante, for her part, is ultimately marginalized, "despite her central role in the genealogical plot and its poetics," to the extent that she "becomes the less interesting half of the dynastic pair, playing second fiddle to a character as insubstantial as Ruggiero" (p. 178). As it bears witness to its author's divided stance on gender relations, *Orlando Furioso* exudes a genuinely deconstructive energy.

In its treatment of genealogy, a politically sensitive theme, *Orlando Furioso* could be said to enact a daring ironical dismantling of the conventional boundary between fiction and historiography. The poem is not a historical document, so its "truth" is recognized instantly as an invention, yet must also be acknowledged as a reflection of, and on, a real state of affairs. In addition, it implicitly invites us to question the reliability of historiography: if fiction can house historical reality, intimates Ariosto, it is feasible to suspect that historiography, in turn, may harbor fictional elements.

Ruggiero's exploits vis-à-vis the predetermined fate revealed for him and his beloved by Merlin the wizard are also imbued with irony. The idea that the knight's moves are governed by a destiny written for him in advance, and over which he therefore holds no control, may suggest that he advances unerringly towards a clear outcome. In fact, Ariosto seems less interested in the fulfillment of Merlin's prophecies than in the orchestration of a hypnotizing whirl of incidents. These, as Calvino maintains, render Ruggiero's march towards the appointed end "not a straight line but an interminable labyrinth." Although readers may trust that all impediments will be overcome, and all enemies vanquished, they will be left with a lingering "doubt": the sensation that "the distant point of arrival" may matter less than the maze itself, and the countless "obstacles, errors, trials which give it life" (Calvino, p. 61). Atlantes' attitude to Ruggiero's fate is similar to the incredulous reader's. Knowing not only that the knight is destined to convert to Christianity, and marry Bradamante, but also meet a premature end, the magician endeavors to defy fate by keeping Ruggiero imprisoned in a magical castle among beautiful knights and ladies, and thus impede his pursuit of the longed-for amazon, and eventual compliance with Merlin's prophecy.

In his retelling of *Orlando Furioso*, Calvino underlines the poem's political dimension. "*Orlando Furioso* originates in a Ferrara" which regards "military glory" as "the foundation of all other values," declares the author, "yet is aware of being merely a pawn in a much greater diplomatic and military game. The poem splits continually between two temporal planes: that of the chivalric fable, and that of the politico-military present; a current of vital impulses is transferred from the time of the paladins ... to the Italian wars of the fifteenth century" (Calvino, 18; my translation). Undeniably, *Orlando Furioso* is very much a product of its culture, the Italian Renaissance, as is the author himself.

Nevertheless, Ariosto's structural preferences bear witness to his partiality to medieval aesthetics. The centerless proliferation of multifarious adventures delivered by *Orlando Furioso* brings to mind San Bonaventura who, as Eugène Vinaver points out, saw "order and perfection" as "synonymous with the elaboration of the material, with its multiplication and its development, whereas to us," heir as we are to Renaissance and neoclassical aesthetics, "terms such as order and perfection naturally suggest a process of selection and simplification." Those who advocate the latter's preferability posit the notion of a neatly centered and unified form as the apotheosis of formal excellence. Ariosto, like San Bonaventura, shuns "unity" in favor of "multiplicity," and few dedicated readers of *Orlando Furioso* would deny that the imposition of a unifying grid on Ariosto's dizzying plethora of enchained fictions would sap the work of its living energy (Vinaver, p. 11).

The legacy of the medieval tradition outlined above makes itself felt throughout *Orlando Furioso* as a rejection of all stable centers of meaning and truth. Time and again, Ariosto bursts the poem's structure open from within with ludic glee and teasing agility. Its incidents branch off in disparate directions, intersecting in myriad unexpected ways, all the time engendering fresh symmetries and contrasts. As Calvino remarks, the poem evokes "a universe unto itself in which it is possible to journey far and wide, enter, exit, get lost" (Calvino, p. 24).

At the same time, it pivots on a sustained, self-conscious, profession of fictionality, which epitomizes the genius of the chivalric romance at large as the essence of fiction. Viewed from this angle, *Orlando Furioso* can be seen as the culmination of the two trends posited at the start of this study as the chivalric romance's most salient features: its intrinsically *acentered*—or *centerless*—nature, which enables it to interrogate the viability of any shaping agency meant to enforce the authority of preestablished principles; and its knack of approximating fiction at its purest by shunning the notion that it is literature's duty to communicate a given ideology's contingent concept of truth. Key to the advancement of this objective is Ariosto's proverbial irony.

According to Chiara Dini, Ariosto's distinctive irony functions as the poem's "cohesive principle," manifesting itself primarily by means of the strategy of "'estrangement,' which consists of a shift in the perspective from which the object of the narration is viewed." A classic illustration of this procedure is Ariosto's recounting of supposedly "'illustrious' events" not to celebrate genuine chivalric excellence, but rather to shed light on his characters'—and hence human nature's—incurable imperfection. At the same time as it pervades the poem's dominant mood, irony governs *Orlando Furioso*'s structure by choreographing with lucid detachment an "assortment of adventures and situations" which are strikingly "different in quality and register," combining in varying degrees "the heroic, the pathetic, the frivolous, the comic" both within the poem as a whole and each of its discrete episodes (Dini, p. 47). Through this studious modulation of tonal effects, Ariosto ensures that "every sentimental (but also comic) excess" (p. 48) is ironically counterbalanced by the evocation of a contrasting mood. In the process, the chivalric myth itself is unsentimentally de-heroized.

Ariosto's compositional method is itself underpinned by a palpable irony, to the extent that it underscores the fluidity, multiplicity and mutability which pervade human life by recourse not to random narration, but rather to a "highly balanced architecture of profound correspondences and calculated symmetries." Ariosto's ironical handling of the philosophical essence of his poem by means of a technique grounded in its very opposite gives rise to "an open and multidirectional narrative machine" which is "never left to itself" (p. 52)—not even when the accumulation of incidents and complications appears to verge on sheer chaos.

The core of the poet's ironical disposition is encapsulated by his conception of a deliberate discrepancy between the poem's title and its actual events. One would expect the eponymous hero to hold the role of protagonist, and his adventures to constitute the poem's main focus. This is not, however, the case. Both expectations are patently frustrated by Ariosto's buoyant quill. The poem's multiperspectival focus challenges the titular character's supposed centrality, rendering him, in fact, a somewhat ancillary persona, whose significance depends on his inscription within a huge cast, not on his exclusivity.

Ariosto relativizes Orlando's importance from the start by defining him in relation to another character, his colleague Rinaldo. The early parts of the action indeed dramatize Orlando's quarrel with Rinaldo, explaining that the dispute has been triggered by the two paladins' shared infatuation with Angelica, and likewise common determination to marry her at any price. What neither champion knows is that the gorgeous damsel has journeyed west from Cathay for the express purpose of throwing Charlemagne's ranks into disarray through the deployment of her magical skills. Angelica's prime goal is to ensure that the paladins will become so infatuated with her, and so fiercely jealous of one another, as to disregard the war against the Moors, and focus solely on their amorous success. The lady's disappearance—despite the monarch's promise he would keep her safe on the two knights' behalf on condition they put off their contest until the end of the war—results in Orlando and Rinaldo channeling the energies which the emperor would wish to see devoted to the Saracens' defeat into the quest for Angelica instead.

It is when Angelica becomes enamored of the Saracen knight Medoro, and elopes with him to Cathay, that Orlando loses his sanity, hence performing the actions which give the poem its title. Not even at this point, however, does the paladin become the sole center of the poem's attention. Though intensely dramatic, his feats of folly are relatively marginal occurrences, when viewed in the broader context of the poem's tapestry: a vast spread of adventures centered on Rinaldo, his sister Bradamante, the paladin Astolfo, the Saracen knights Rodomont and Ruggiero, and the latter's sister, Marfisa—among legion other characters who must perforce remain unnamed in this context.

It is only in the finale that Ariosto prioritizes the love story of Ruggiero and Bradamante, the putative ancestors of the House of Este, in order to convey the ideological message expected by his patron. While *Orlando Furioso* seems keen to fulfill its political function, Ariosto's heart remains set to the end (and feasibly beyond) on a different goal: the prioritization of the spirit of adventure per se over any specific motives or goals. The poem's very shape bears witness to this proposition, insofar as it resembles an eddy, or vortex, of competing, yet interconnected, characters: the knights who, besotted with the elusive Angelica, forget their martial duties and, in their blinding urgency, merely go round in circles, now chasing, now dueling, now jousting, but never set on a lucid objective. In fact, there comes a point when they appear not even to know clearly what it is that they pursue so frantically.

On one level, Ariosto's conspicuous use of Orlando's name in his title is motivated by the desire to situate the poem within a specific tradition, and a likewise distinctive literary-historical trajectory. This harks back to Matteo Maria Boiardo's *Orlando Innamorato* (1482), and, beyond Boiardo's poem, to *La Chanson de Roland*, composed in the eleventh-twelfth centuries. Boiardo had already subjected the epic image of the famed paladin to radical reimagining, by morphing the stern warrior into a love-smitten chivalric character, and focusing on his pursuit of Angelica. The identity of Boiardo's Orlando is therefore defined by amorous ambitions more than martial valor per se. This reinterpretation of the paladin's role and temperament runs parallel to a shift of emphasis from the communal to the personal.

The medieval *chanson de geste* gave precedence to its hero's part in the Battle of Roncesvalles (778), in which Roland is cast as the intrepid rear guard of Charlemagne's army. The *chanson*'s focus is on the paladin's selfless commitment to a collective cause, which he is prepared to champion to the furthest extremity. In *Orlando Innamorato*, by contrast, at the center of attention are the private feelings of an individual who, despite his unquestionable involvement in a momentous conflict, comes across, first and foremost, as a *lover*.

Ariosto takes the Carolingian hero even further away from the austere world of epic, emphasizing not only his personal situation vis-à-vis the code of courtly love, but also the dangerous, albeit risible, absurdity of that ethos when pushed to its logical extremes. The poet's hearty appetite for irony comes again to the fore—demonstrated, in this instance, by the tension between the work's apparent commitment to the revival of Carolingian epic, and its irreverent adaptation of that tradition to the humorous exposure of humanity's inveterate folly.

As Calvino puts it, Ariosto is tormented by the disparity between "how the world is and how it is not but *could* be, yet depicts it as a multicolored and multifarious spectacle to be contemplated with ironic wisdom" (Calvino, p. 20; my translation; italics added). This is abetted by Ariosto's passion for "*understatement*, that is to say, that special knack of self-irony leading to the minimization of substantial and important things" (p. 24; my translation; italics in the original). It is with his portrayal of the Palace of Atlantes (alluded to earlier in this study) that Ariosto's thought-provoking message reaches its apotheosis. The same ironic spirit enables Ariosto to oscillate freely between the "lyrical," and even the "sublime," on the one hand, and the "prosaic" and the "playful," on the other, all the while pondering the vanity of human desires with knowing eyes.

As argued in Chapter Two, the many monsters which pepper the romance tradition underscore the intrinsic weaknesses and inadequacies of both the knightly heroes they challenge, and the societies which such champions are meant to protect. Monsters, in other words, alert their human antagonists to both their personal vulnerability, and their culture's encroaching fears. *Orlando Furioso* abounds with monsters. In his portrayal and dramatic management of these and other anomalous creatures, Ariosto lends an original twist to the traditional romance's passion for monstrous Others.

According to Cristiana Lardo, Ariosto's monsters represent an ever-present "doubt," by incarnating on the *literal* plane the irrepressible suspicion that the order which the paladins are supposed to defend, and whose values they are held to embody, is neither stable nor inviolable. The anomalies evinced by monsters in a physical guise symbolize the ethical and spiritual aberrations to which society is prone to fall prey from one second to the next, and no champion of justice, regardless of his chivalric credentials, could ever presume to stave off with anything other than a precarious show of puissance.

The monster's chief function, in this perspective, is comparable to that of a "*mirror*," insofar as it constitutes the specular, grotesquely symmetrical, counterpart of the paladins themselves. "The deformed creatures which transgress the *ordo naturalis* stand in men's way to indent them, infect them, pollute them, transmitting upon them certain deformities, to let them then go back to being men," *but*—and this is a crucial *but*—"with the awareness of what the alternatives could be" (Lardo, p. 9; my translation).

This awareness does not rest merely on a detached *observation* of the monster's alterity. In fact, it is not unusual for a knight to be affected so deeply by his encounter with a monstrous Other as to *absorb* some of its monstrosity. At times, his participation in the Other's monstrosity in the role of a *surrogate* monster is what enables the hero to defeat the *real* monster. Yet, Ariosto's handling of monsters, and of the becoming-monster topos in particular, often inaugurates a more intimidating state of affairs, which brings to mind Friedrich Nietzsche's warning: "he who fights with monsters might take care lest he thereby become a monster. And when you gaze long into an abyss the abyss also gazes into you" (Nietzsche 1886, Aphorism 146).

A memorable illustration of the becoming-monster theme is supplied by Canto X with the scene in which Orlando confronts the orc, a sea monster with a hearty appetite for tender female flesh. It should be noted, incidentally, that at this point, Orlando has already partaken of monstrosity by giving vent to his pathological jealousy through terrifying explosions of insanity. Identifying with a monster might therefore be easier for him than for knights unfamiliar with that state. The strategy Orlando adopts to vanquish the formidable sea monster requires the paladin to *become* the orc, albeit temporarily, by "identifying with the monster, merging with it, identifying its vulnerable and soft spot" (p. 107; my translation). Eugenio Refini reinforces this argument, proposing that Orlando, in overpowering "the orc by entering its jaws," performs "a kind of small-scale *katabasis*" (Refini, p. 93; my translation)—namely, a hero's descent to the Underworld in classical epic.

With Astolfo, an alternative interpretation of the knight-monster relationship is explored. When the character is first introduced by Ariosto, he is having to endure a state of monstrosity as a result of his imprisonment, courtesy of the malicious Alcina, in the form of a myrtle tree. It could be suggested that Astolfo is able to interact with the hippogriph—a monster, after all—with natural ease precisely because he knows what it is like to *be* a monster in an intimate and visceral fashion. The significance of this particular aspect of Ariosto's treatment of monstrosity should not be underestimated, considering the axial part played by Astolfo's exploits, and especially his journey to the Moon, in the poem's overall trajectory.

In the circumstances, it is ironical that Astolfo should also be, if one subscribes to Lardo's interpretation of this character, the "hero closest to man." It is as though his very familiarity with monstrosity is what renders him a fit candidate to incarnate the essence of true humanity. Being the outcome of his own "weakness," the entrapment in the myrtle itself bears witness to Astolfo's consummate humanity: his standing as the representative of an inherently flawed species. He is a *real* human being because he is fallible, he recognizes his fallibility, and is able to extrapolate a double lesson from his experience: "no-one is ever safe … and … wisdom is not after all humanity's optimal condition" (Lardo, p. 13; my translation).

Ariosto's animals form a counterpoise to his monsters. While the latter embody human foibles in grotesque form, the former throw human defectiveness into relief by displaying much more sense and wisdom than their knightly colleagues. Commenting on Canto I, Calvino brings this idea into focus, arguing that amidst the "crazy carousel" of pursuing and sparring knights, the only character who acts "sensibly" is "a horse" (Calvino, p. 44): namely, Rinaldo's Baiardo, who has fled his master to seek Angelica of his own accord on the knight's behalf, thus demonstrating his "loyalty and intelligence." Baiardo is complemented by another formidable beast: the hippogriff. Baiardo, argues Calvino, "tends to trespass equine nature" precisely in the effort to become the "ideal horse." The hippogriph, by contrast, evinces "few equine qualities, yet is made to serve as a tame horse, albeit a flying one" (p. 47). In both instances, the coexistence of conflicting character traits bears witness to Ariosto's distinctive irony.

Further instances of Ariosto's passion for interesting animals is supplied by Canto VI. When the hippogriph and Ruggiero land on Alcina's enchanted isle, we encounter an array of beasts, and indeed plants, who move so gracefully as to recall the delicate embroideries of a medieval tapestry. The passage's suave beauty deserves suitable citation:

> Small thickets, with the scented laurel gay,
> Cedar, and orange, full of fruit and flower,
> Myrtle and palm, with interwoven spray,
> Pleached in mixed modes, all lovely, form a bower;
> And, breaking with their shade the scorching ray,
> Make a cool shelter from the noontide hour.
> And nightingales among those branches wing
> Their flight, and safely amorous descants sing.
> Amid red roses and white lilies there,
> Which the soft breezes freshen as they fly,
> Secure the cony haunts, and timid hare,
> And stag, with branching forehead broad and high.
> These, fearless of the hunter's dart or snare,
> Feed at their ease, or ruminating lie;
> While, swarming in those wilds, from tuft or steep
> Dun deer or nimble goat, disporting, leap.
> [Ariosto, Canto VI, 21–22].

Yet more examples of intriguing animals occur later in the same Canto, in the context of Astolfo's narrative. Here the English king's son tells Rinaldo about his capture by Alcina, lingering on the moment when the sorceress conjures up a small island-cum-vessel, which is in fact a whale, to abduct the young man:

> Thither swift dolphins gambol, inly stirred,
> And open-mouthed the cumbrous tunnies leap;
> Thither the seal or porpus' wallowing herd
> Troop at her bidding, roused from lazy sleep;
> Raven-fish, salmon, salpouth, at her word,
> And mullet hurry through the briny deep,
> With monstrous backs above the water, sail
> Ork, physeter, sea-serpent, shark, and whale.
> [Canto VI, 36].

Spenser

Ariosto was writing for his patrons, the House of Este of Ferrara, within an Italy which was not yet a country—and indeed would not be one for three more centuries. In exchange for patronage, the author was required to provide the Este dynasty with a heroic lineage. Quite a different set of political circumstances obtained in England, where the first Tudor king, Henry VII, having overthrown Richard III at the Battle of Bosworth in 1485, put an end to the baronial wars that had been plaguing England throughout the fifteenth century, the Wars of the Roses. He thereby marked the beginning not only of the Tudor dynasty, but also of the English nation-state. (Note that the king also reinforced his position by marrying Elizabeth of York, Edward IV's daughter and the deposed Richard III's niece.)

This political backdrop must be taken into consideration in the appraisal of the overarching objective pursued by Spenser in the composition of the *Faerie Queene* (1590–1596). Announced in his dedicatory Letter to Sir Walter Raleigh, this is to "fashion a gentleman or noble person in vertuous and gentle discipline'" (Spenser, p. 205). Few statements could declare more explicitly than these words the great distance traveled by the chivalric romance since Chrétien de Troyes' times. While the medieval romancer's ideal was a knight embodying martial prowess, valor, honor, lack of concern for material gain, sophistication, conviviality, and, above all, courtesy in amatory matters, the model which Spenser seeks to forge is that of the perfect *courtier*. In considering the possible reasons for the decline of the chivalric romance, it is vital to appreciate the relative incompatibility between the latter's ethos and the figure of the courtier, as a social type spawned by an altered societal set-up.

While the knight was typically a member of a hereditary martial class, the courtier is pretty much a self-made man. His prime virtues are a politic cultivation of discretion, expediency, diplomacy, and the skills necessary to abet self-promotion through apparent self-effacement. Gaining favor with influential government administrators in order to obtain coveted positions in national offices is arguably the courtier's primary goal.

A product of the demise of feudalism, and attendant rise of the nation-state, the courtier had two options at his disposal with regard to Arthurian champions and their code of conduct. On the one hand, he might choose to distinguish himself from medieval knights, viewing them as the representatives of an outmoded system, and hence as inimical to his own search for new models—i.e., ideals which might prove more appropriate to a burgeoning regime, and to the requirements of social climbers like himself. On the other hand, the courtier might choose to perceive himself as the rightful successor of the knights of old, construing Arthur's followers as characters in whom he could catch a prophetic glimmer of his own current status as a member of an alternative elite.

Either way, the courtier had to negotiate a socio-political reality in which every member of his class was desperate to assert his worth in the eyes of a ruler or patron, yet aware of the need to exercise great caution in his tactics of self-promotion and self-ingratiation. The courtier would therefore be chary of parading his abilities in too conspicuous a fashion, lest he should draw to himself the unwanted attention of enemies—with which the courtly milieu would always be rife, in the form of conspirators, spies, and assassins.

There is nothing the courtier would desire more than invisibility as he went about engineering his personal advancement by surreptitious means. In other words, this is a culture dominated by the imperative of dissimulation—a strange virtue, paralleled by the aesthetic concept of *sprezzatura*, a principle central to all major self-fashioning manuals of the Renaissance. Ushered in by Baldassare Castiglione in *The Book of the Courtier* (1528), *sprezzatura* constitutes "a certain nonchalance, so as to conceal all art and make whatever one does or says appear to be without effort and almost without any thought about it" (Castiglione, p. 32). The concept of *sprezzatura* also underlies Niccolò Machiavelli's notorious political treatise, *The Prince* (1532).

In its intention to fashion a perfect courtier, *The Faerie Queene* is heir to the medieval chivalric tradition, incorporating many of the form's techniques, themes and images, as well as the most quintessentially knightly of recorded heroes: Arthur himself. However, Spenser's magnus opus is also the direct child of a more recent mentality, encapsulated precisely by works such as Castiglione's and Machiavelli's tracts.

The cultivation of dissimulation as a socio-political strategy, and of *sprezzatura* as a cognate aesthetic priority, is paralleled by the literary preference for texts distinguished by structural and rhetorical complexity. Spenser's ideation of *The Faerie Queene* in its entirety as a "dark conceit" (Spenser, p. 205) is fully consonant with the Renaissance aesthetic notion that *claritas* is not the product of explicit statement and literalism, but a form of enlightenment to be reached, through meticulous decoding, by readers well-versed in poetic and rhetorical matters. Renaissance poetry is not for the lazy. Clarity, as illumination, is by no means coterminous with plainness. It is deemed immoral for a poet to resort to direct or obvious statements, and no less deplorable for an audience to expect explicitness as integral to the reading experience.

The commitment to textual complexity was determined, to a significant extent, by specific conditions of production dictated by the ascendancy of court and patronage. By placing both explicit and implied constraints on expression, these institutions inevitably encouraged the use of elliptical forms of discourse. This stylistic trend was bound to yield complex and multilayered texts, which effectively assumed the existence of sophisticated audiences. At the same time, it contributed significantly to the sustained use of irony.

While Spenser is renowned as a master allegorist, his irony should not be regarded as interchangeable with, or indistinguishable from, his allegory. In fact, it is important to differentiate between allegory and irony. "Irony and allegory," argues D. H. Green, "both say one thing and mean another. But whereas allegory establishes a correspondence between statement and meaning, irony insinuates a contrast.... Even when the correspondence may be no more than partial it is on this that the allegory concentrates to the exclusion of those features where difference obtains, whilst irony concentrates on points of contrast and grants these a greater importance than any similarities" (Green, p. 7).

Spenser deploys irony, even as he strives to weave a coherent allegorical tapestry encompassing the entire scope of his poem, precisely to the extent that he does not suppress the "points of contrast" which Green describes as pivotal to the ironical disposition. This is demonstrated by the insoluble conflict which *The Faerie Queene* persistently articulates between the yearning for resolution, and the impossibility of ever reaching such an outcome with any degree of finality. In this fashion, Spenser embraces a rhetorical tradition which, as Carol V. Kaske explains, amalgamates irony and allegory as cognate manifestations of *alieniloquium*: a verbal situation in which a statement's apparent content and its latent meaning do not coincide (Kaske 2006a).

Of the three authors studied in this chapter, Spenser might seem to be the one who takes his materials most seriously, and thus allows limited leeway for irony's disruptive intervention. Yet, it is enough to look at Book I of *The Faerie Queene* to realize that the contrast between manifest and underlying meanings is central to his work. While allegory is emplaced from the start as the book's governing trope, therefore, nestled within the allegory dwells the subversive spirit of irony. This is borne out by both the nature and the rhythm of the ordeal undergone by the Redcrosse Knight. An allegorical incarnation of Holiness, this character ought to be endowed with an impregnable morality, and to act as the champion of a likewise unassailable ideology through unrelenting vigilance. It is ironical to say the least, in the circumstances, that it is by falling asleep, and hence relinquishing his chivalric duty, that the knight makes himself vulnerable to Error's tricks, and opens himself to temptation.

Alongside the transition from feudalism to the nation-state, another cultural factor responsible for imparting Spenser's romance with a decidedly Renaissance flavor lies with the expansionist ethos so dominant in his age, and with the exploratory and colonialist enterprise which this underpinned. The poet's decision to dedicate the poem to Sir Walter Raleigh is telling, in this regard, insofar as the famous knight is renowned not only as having been one of the most audacious explorers of all times, but also as having played a key part in the promulgation of a colonialist ideology largely responsible for the demonization of the colonized as a savage Other. It is likely that Spenser felt a natural affinity with the ideological leanings evinced by Elizabeth I's prime voyager on the matter of colonization.

The poet's own stance on English rule in supposedly *wild* lands abets this contention: sent by Queen Elizabeth to Ireland, Spenser endeavored to manage the province with notorious ruthlessness. At the time, Ireland was by and large regarded by the English as an uncivilized region, whose barbarous state rendered the use of violence quite justifiable in the implementation of appropriately repressive measures. In a pamphlet entitled *A View of the Present State of Ireland* (1596), Spenser promoted in incontrovertible terms the draconian obliteration of Irish language and culture by the harshest of means.

Thomas Herron maintains that Raleigh's function in *The Faerie Queene* is not merely that of a dedicatee, insofar as the poem actually "involves" him in other major capacities: namely, "as a reader, as a writer of commendatory sonnets (Raleigh wrote two of them for *The Faerie Queene*, both praising Spenser's work) and as a subject of topical allegory in *The Faerie Queene* (in both the 1590 and 1596 editions).... Spenser famously praises and advertises Raleigh's colonial ambitions in the New World" (Herron). In the Proem to Book II of *The Faerie Queene*, Spenser makes direct reference to "fruitfullest *Virginia*" (II.Proem.2.9). This mention draws the reader's attention to Raleigh's pivotal role in the English colonization of North America, which derived impetus precisely from his receipt of a royal patent to explore this land. At the same time, it can be read as a hint at the possible existence of a connection between the infamous voyager and the Virgin Queen of a not wholly professional nature.

The Faerie Queene bolsters the colonialist ideology advocated by Elizabeth via officers just like Spenser and his mate Raleigh throughout its unfolding to the extent that the exploits dramatized in the various books are not simply chivalric adventures. On the contrary, they are first and foremost *ideological constructs* designed to coach a specific political program in the guise of edifying entertainment. In nuce, this agenda champions the subjugation by supposedly "superior" agencies of challenging presences which are conveniently construed as dark, unruly, and intractably alien.

Profoundly influenced by Neoplatonism, numerical symbolism, Classical sources (above all Virgil's *Aeneid*), and Italian Renaissance literature

(Ariosto's *Orlando Furioso*, Tasso's *Gerusalemme Liberata*), *The Faerie Queene* subjects the romance tradition to radical reconceptualization in order to deliver a vision whose prime function, as Douglas Brooks-Davies reminds us, is eminently "political." This is "to celebrate England under Elizabeth, whose grandfather Henry VII had brought peace to England after civil war as the Emperor Augustus had brought peace to Rome after civil war. Augustus and Elizabeth were both, popular mythology said, restorers of the golden age." It is also worth mentioning, in this context, that both Roman mythology and Arthurian lore trace the origins of the cultures they seek to glorify to the mythical land of Troy. Augustus' self-definition as a direct descendant of Aeneas provides the underpinning of the idealizing propaganda enfolding the emperor's person. As mentioned in Chapter One, "Brutus, Aeneas' great-grandson" (Brooks-Davies, p. 3), is presented as Britain's founder and first ruler by some eminent Arthurian pseudo-historians, such as Nennius and Geoffrey of Monmouth.

As Michael O'Connell explains, Spenser's dedicatory letter to Raleigh explains that his allegorical treatment of the "character of Gloriana" serves "a dual purpose" (O'Connell, pp. 16). The relevant segment reads thus: "in that Faerie Queene I meane glory in my generall intention, but in my particular I conceive the most excellent and glorious person of our soveraine the Queene, and her kingdom in Faery land." Thus, while on the macrocosmic plane, Gloriana signifies glory in the most comprehensive and extra-personal sense, on the microcosmic plane, that name holds a highly individualized referent: England's current ruler. The English nation itself, in this perspective, become synonymous with Faërie—albeit a *very different* conception of Faërie than the one encountered in earlier ample-breadth romances such as *Yvain, or, the Knight with the Lion*, or lays such as *Sir Launfal*.

This duality does not, however, exhaust Spenser's allegorical plan. What he has in mind is a multi-layered and multi-branching map of concurrent allusions, which renders any attempt at a mechanical translation of characters or places into singular symbolic meanings quite risible. "And yet in some places els," continues the dedication to this effect, " I do otherwise shadow her. For considering she beareth two persons, the one of a most royall Queene or Empresse, the other of a most vertuous and beautifull Lady, this latter part in some places I doe express in Belphoebe, fashioning her name according to your [i.e. Raleigh's] owne excellent conceipt of Cynthia, (Phoebe and Cynthia being both names of Diana)" (Spenser, p. 206).

Spenser's use of the word "shadow" deserves close attention. Its Elizabethan connotations are such as to make us wonder what exactly the poet is trying to do *to* and *through* Gloriana. What kind of character does he intend to project onto her? What kind of character does he intend to emblematize via her? Is such a character truly equivalent to a *real* person, historical or fictional as the case may be? Or is it rather of the nature of a performance, of an enacted *role*? This last question is invited by the Elizabethan usage of the word "shadow" as synonymous with "actor": a custom famously enshrined in Macbeth's climactic speech: "Life's but a walking shadow, a poor player / That struts and frets his hour upon the stage / And then is heard no more" (5.5.24–26).

Also worthy of note is Spenser's insistent reiteration of the monarch's greatness. Why be so insistent? Is the poet, by any chance, trying to convince *himself* of the authenticity of such an attribute? After all, the function of repetition as a psychological mechanism meant to create belief by means of ongoing en*act*ments and re-en*act*ments is well documented. If Spenser were indeed using repetition for this purpose, this would render the poet himself an *actor*—or *shadow*—of sorts. At the same time, the repeated assertion of Elizabeth's distinction is also a rhetorical ruse based on the strategy of incremental glorification. This is borne out by the purposeful addition of the title of "Empress" to the one, already used in the previous sentence, of "Queene."

Spenser relies on an ironical disjunction to sustain his allegorical program, since his words make it patent that in conceiving of Elizabeth/Gloriana as a composite creature, he is both amalgamating and differentiating two divergent facets of her identity: her public significance as a mighty leader, and her private role as a virginal maid. Spenser's splitting of his supposedly pivotal character alerts us to one of the poem's chief proclivities: its tendency to shun clear-cut explications of its allusions and symbols in favor of multiple meanings which may coexist harmoniously with one another, but may also clash and conflict. As a result, readers are enjoined never to lower their guard, and rather endeavor to keep their interpretative skills sharp and refined throughout the reading experience.

As O'Connell maintains, the terms in which Spenser phrases his plan represent "a challenge to his reader's powers of perception and judgment." They indeed prompt us, in a nimbly inconspicuous style, to ponder "where else" Elizabeth might be "represented," and "what aspects of her person or rule" Spenser might be alluding to in each depiction (O'Connell, p. 16). Faithful to a rhetorical tradition which prizes understatement even in the delivery of the most involved conceits, Spenser does not offer any clear key to such queries. In fact, "the answer he seems to give in the mention of

Belphoebe is really no more than a hint: 'in some places' he has expressed the queen's private person in a certain character. But the reader is left to wonder whether these two characters are the limit of the poem's portrayal of the queen and in what sense her kingdom is to be understood in the fictional Faeryland" (p. 17).

In the proem to Book I, Spenser addresses the queen as a "Goddesse heavenly bright," which tallies with her idealization as a creature of mythological stature, as well as the "Great Ladie of the greatest Isle," which encapsulates her official role. However, he also describes Elizabeth in more arcane terms as the "true glorious type" at the heart of his poem. As Kaske explains in her notes to Book I, the word "type" is here employed "in the biblical sense" as synonymous with "prototype"" i.e., as a preexistent character "analogous" to her (Kaske 2006b, p. 5).

As an idealized vision of Queen Elizabeth I in the guise of Gloriana, a creature of such unparalleled excellence as to be comparable to a deity, *The Faerie Queene* bears witness to chivalric romance's standing as the epitome of fictional literature. Indeed, Spenser's poetic dream is meant to embody a message with a direct bearing on the political reality of his times; yet, the substance of this message is inextricable from the fiction wherein it is generated. *The Faerie Queene* comes close to being a myth with its implicit claim that it encapsulates an unquestionable truth: i.e., the monarch's moral and physical status as a nonpareil. However, Spenser's contemporaries would have known as well as today's readers do that such a truth is only apparent (the actual monarch bearing no resemblance to Gloriana).

Spenser himself might have wished to assert the veracity of his vision, but his text in fact exposes the fantastic import of the truth it purports to enshrine through its extreme artfulness. Much as the poet might have wished his readers to believe that the virtues of both body and mind encapsulated in the figure of Gloriana were realistic reflections of the queen's own assets, *The Faerie Queene* asserts itself first and foremost as an elaborate fantasy, albeit one prompted, to a significant degree, by a political reality. This is confirmed by the sheer complexity of Spenser's magnus opus—as an intricate allegory, a clever reworking of diverse sources, an ideological manifesto, an exercise in sophisticated rhetoric, and, last but not least, a recreation of the romance conventions for a new era.

The Faerie Queene's artistry demonstrates that in order to construct a "truth" as elaborate as the one embodied in Spenser's glorification of Elizabeth I, and hope to meet with a modicum of success, one cannot rely on anything other than an exceedingly elaborate fictional edifice bound both to invite passionate interpretative efforts (over several generations of readers), and to mock decoding by revealing, beneath each level of meaning, yet more potential levels and sublevels. The poem thus intimates that the less true the "truth" at the core of a fiction, the more solid it must appear to be. Ironically, the only means of creating the impression of a solid reality is to rely on a convoluted web of fictional devices—alongside a panoply of marvels and splendid absurdities—which foreground at every turn the work's dazzling *un*-truth. In other, and cruder, words, it could be argued that to invent a *big* "truth," one needs a *big* fiction.

Just as Ariosto uses *Orlando Furioso* to lend the House of Este an enviable pedigree, Spenser connects Arthur himself with the Tudor lineage. At the same time, as Derek Pearsall points out, he imparts him with "a new identity as the allegorical embodiment of all the virtues that the heroes of the different books of *The Faerie Queene* ... individually personify" (Pearsall, p. 112). As argued in Chapter One, Arthur is a sliding signifier: a name filled with diverse meanings for different purposes over several generations. Spenser's adaptation of the legendary monarch's character to suit his allegorical purpose corroborates Arthur's standing as a versatile vessel.

As an incarnation of Arthur connected with the Tudors, the Redcrosse Knight—Book I's protagonist—plays a pointedly historical part. The character should not, therefore, be approached as an atemporal allegory of virtuousness. This is made clear in the episode where Spenser intimates that "holiness ... is not a mere yearning for otherworldly perfection," as O'Connell points out, "but a commitment to what is most ennobling in human history." The city revealed to the knight by the hermit is "the New Jerusalem." This vision sharpens the Redcrosse Knight's awareness of "spiritual perfection," making him disposed "to abandon the pursuit of merely mortal glory." It is in this context that Spenser's ideological message makes itself felt most keenly in the guise of a positive grounding of the knight's quest in a definite historical reality. Indeed, in response to the knight's disdain for worldly achievements, "the hermit warns against an ascetic scorning of the earthly participant of the heavenly city" (O'Connell, p. 41).

This is because his "gaze is not so firmly fixed upon the eternal and transcendent" as to make him forget his "knowledge" of the knight's "earthly nation" (p. 42), and attendant awareness that he is, specifically, "sprong out from English race" (Spenser, Canto Ten, 60). The Redcrosse Knight's fate, in the grand scheme of things, is to "become a link between the New

Jerusalem and its earthly sharer": namely, England. "The cross of St. George," the nation's patron, is iconographically associated with the knight's persona from the start, presaging this role with emblematic force (O'Connell, p. 42). It is most likely that Spenser also meant "Arthur to discover his British origin at some climactic moment" (p. 43), as part of his overall program of national consolidation.

Brooks-Davies argues that in his capacity as an avatar of England's patron saint, the Redcrosse Knight "stands for England," while his beloved, Una, represents "the true Church, the one faith (Elizabethan Anglicanism); that is, the primitive Catholic Church restored, purged of Roman Catholicism's temporal excesses." As anticipated, the protagonist is severed from Una by the joint agency of two equally nefarious figures, Archimago and Duessa. Both characters function as personifications of "the papal Antichrist." The Redcrosse Knight and Una's eventual betrothal symbolizes "the reunion under Elizabeth, after Mary's Catholic interregnum, of country and true faith" (Brooks-Davies, pp. 8–9).

In seeking to consolidate the myth of national identity by imbuing his latter-day romance with interleaving allegorical messages, one of the poet's chief intentions is therefore to strengthen the body politic's specifically *doctrinal* dimension. "Spenser's most complete adumbration of England's national religious experience," states O'Connell, "comes in the cantos that narrate Redcross's [sic] deception by Duessa and his captivity by Orgoglio." In tandem, these experiences allude to "England's submission to the yoke of papal authority, either during the Middle Ages or during Mary's reign." The connection is reinforced with visual immediacy, since "Duessa is endowed with the iconography of the papal whore of Babylon: she is dressed in scarlet, covered with jewels, and crowned with a '*Persian* mitre,' the tiara" (O'Connell, p. 54). Orgoglio, as the incarnation of hungry pride, refers to the Catholic Church's sinful masquerading as the only true faith. His carnal entanglement with Duessa, in this perspective, could be seen to allude to the papacy's indulgence in unnatural and unholy practices.

It is critical to appreciate that the Redcrosse Knight's equivalence with England's patron saint is potential, rather than fully actualized. For a large part of Book I, the knight's saintliness is by no means unequivocal. In fact, he seems unable to achieve the quest he initially sets out to fulfill—to free Una's parents, the rulers of Eden, from their thrall to a hideous dragon—insofar as he falls prey to the wiles of evil types such as Archimago and Duessa (dubbed "Fidessa" in the majority of the narrative to confuse the poor Redcrosse Knight even further by masking her treacherous duplicity as faithful loyalty). In *The Faerie Queene*, Brooke-Davies reminds us, "even saints are human."

In this context, Archimago can be interpreted as "a metaphor" for the Redcrosse Knight's "own, fallen, spiritual inadequacy" (Brooks-Davies, p. 9). Thus, the magician stands out as a parodic perversion of St George's holiness, just as the whorish Duessa constitutes a gross distortion of the pure, angelic, Una: the object of the Redcrosse Knight's true devotion as preached by the courtly love tradition. Irony presides over Book I as the story's guiding principle, since the proto–Tudor hero's supposed virtue is actually asserted not by means of his undertaking of superhuman deeds, but by proof of his all-too-human vulnerability.

On the matter of *The Faerie Queene*'s religious dimension, also worthy of attention is Spenser's ongoing concern, throughout Book I, with a point of disagreement between the Anglican and the Catholic faiths regarding the place of free will in human life. As Kaske explains, "the Catholic Church said that mankind must earn heaven and must earn day-to-day forgiveness by exerting free will." By contrast, "the original Protestant reformers" accorded no role to this faculty in their scheme (Kaske 2006a, p. x). The vanity of free will is advocated by Spenser in Canto Ten of Book I, where he asserts that "If any strength we have, it is to ill," which entails that "all the good is Gods, both power and eke will" (Spenser, Canto Ten, 1). Nonetheless, even among Protestants there were still those, including Elizabeth herself, who "retained a certain limited trust in human agency—though none dared call it 'free will,' which was a rallying cry of the Catholics—and they always stipulated the help of divine grace." In the latter portion of Book I, Spenser appears to embrace this conservative view, "preaching good deeds as the ticket to heaven" (Kaske, p. xi), and hence suggesting that "free will might play a part in abetting or thwarting the advance of a predestined soul.

Spenser's effort to harmonize free will and predestination is attested to by the fact that the Redcrosse Knight is assured of his eventual salvation, yet at the same time so cruelly tested as to be brought to the verge of suicide. Book I's ninth canto exemplifies this syncretic disposition. At this point, in order to release him from Despair's trap, Una reminds her loyal champion of his predestined triumph. "Ne let vaine words bewitch thy manly hart," urges the heavenly lady, "Ne develish thoughts dismay thy constant spright. / In heavenly mercies hast thou not a part?" (Spenser, Canto Nine, 53.4). Nevertheless, the knight's ordeal intimates that predestination is not unto itself sufficient to guarantee a person's success, and that the advancement of one's fate therefore requires an element of free will. In the Redcrosse Knight's case, this resides with his determination to disentangle himself from the delusions which impede the fulfillment of his quest. Spenser's commitment to a harmonizing agenda is further indicated by his handling of the Redcrosse Knight Knight's defeat of the dragon as dependent at once on divine intercession and human will.

On the whole, Spenser does not propound unequivocally *either* predestination *or* free will as the cause of his hero's achievements. This is borne out by the ambiguity of Una's words at the close of Canto Eleven: "Then God she praysd, and thankt her faithfull knight, / That had atchievde so great a conquest by his might" (Spenser, Canto Eleven, 55). Whether the possessive pronoun *his* is meant to designate *God's might*, or rather *the knight's might* remains a moot point—and does so, arguably, as a result of a deliberate decision on Spenser's part. Book I of *The Faerie Queene* declares its loyalty to the original spirit of the chivalric romance as a form ill-disposed to conclusive answers.

Arthur's semiotic adaptability, central to Spenser's allegorical program, is further confirmed by the fact that claims to a royal dynasty's descent from the legendary king have been advanced by disparate regimes over the centuries. The evidence adduced by different rulers to substantiate such claims varies substantially from one government to the next.

Spenser's poem demonstrates with unique vigor Elizabeth's eagerness to propagate the myth of the Tudors' descent from Arthur. So was "the magician, John Dee," as Christine Poulson explains: "a Merlin-like figure in his own right." When he succeeded to the throne, James I went on to claim "not only to be descended from Arthur," but also to be "fulfilling one of Merlin's prophesies by uniting England and Scotland." However, even though "the Tudor propaganda of Arthurian descent was handed down to the Stuarts," an opposite trend took shape "in the seventeenth century" whose aim was "to stress the Saxon origin of England, in order to counter the royalist appropriation of Arthur" (Poulson, p. 9).

In Pearsall's opinion, this concomitantly anti-royalist and anti–Arthurian trend was abetted by a growing interest in the study of Anglo-Saxon history as "the subject of much antiquarian research and writing, some of it taken up by parliament in order to oppose James I's insistence upon the divine rights of kings by appealing to the witness of ancient Saxon laws. Throughout the century, the focus shifted from Briton to Saxon depending on which political party was in the ascendant" (Pearsall, p. 113). With the transition to the House of Hanover, we witness a radical transfer of emphasis from Arthur's Celtic world to Saxon tradition in the construction of the crown's origin myth. Accordingly, "if Stuart identification with Arthur was strong, then conversely supporters of the Hanoverian dynasty were likely to see the Saxons as more natural and desirable ancestors than Celtic Ancient Britons" (Poulson, p. 9).

So pivotal as to stand out as a character in its own right, or even a protagonist at times, Spenser's key setting calls for special attention. In order to appreciate the precise import of the writer's treatment of the forest in *The Faerie Queene*, it is necessary to situate it in the broader context of the romance as an evolving art form. As Corinne Saunders observes, in this matter, "Malory's wistful retrospective tone as his great Arthurian romance draws to a close and the curtain falls on the *forest avantureuse*"— the forest of adventure, a place in which marvels are ubiquitous—can be read as a metaphorical correlative for the impending marginalization of the chivalric romance by the literary establishment. "The forest is, however, to undergo yet more metamorphosis, becoming a construct which plays consciously upon the romance landscape of the Middle Ages to create in the poetry of Spenser and Shakespeare a new and literary otherworld" (Saunders 1993, p. 186).

Saunders argues that Spenser's magnus opus is intimately indebted to Malory in its narration of "a tale of quest and adventure whose protagonist is Arthur himself, and whose forest may well appear to be, if not the *forest avantureuse*, then at least the highly symbolic landscape of the Grail Quest" (pp. 186–187). However, Spenser strives to redefine the conventional setting bequeathed to him by the romance tradition, configuring the forest as the embodiment of a parallel reality in which humanity's aspirations and limitations may be explored in an allegorical fashion.

At the same time, "the forest of *The Faerie Queene*" also "plays on the range of philosophical and allegorical meanings for *silva* or *hyle*" (p. 189)— its Latin and Greek equivalents. "The Latin *silva* stands not solely for "the physical world of the forest, but also for an allegorical world of untamed emotion and passion. The link between the forest and chaos, disorder or primordial matter stems from classical usage of the Greek word ... to represent these philosophical concepts" (p. 19). Spenser's debt to such ideas is a result of the fact that "in the Renaissance, this classical tradition was far more widely known than in the Middle Ages." Thus, he would be well aware of the forest's metaphorical association with the notions of "passion, savagery," and "chaos" (p. 189).

Spenser's forest "maintains the potential for transformation, as does the forest of medieval romance. The world is not wholly unredeemable, for it is possible after all to vanquish Error, to reach the temple of Holiness and to catch sight of the Heavenly City." Una's moral and spiritual excellence, and the Salvage man's natural gentility play vital roles in facilitating the forest's purging of its more inchoate and wild passions. However, even these virtues are powerless to impose a lasting sense of stability and safety on the *Faerie Queene*'s bewildering forest. Any hope of a more durable order lies in an unspecified future, symbolized by "the uniting of Arthur and Elizabeth" (p. 193).

Given that Arthur never achieves his goal, it is doubtful whether the poem gives any tangible evidence of this lasting achievement being anything other than an ideal. In fact, throughout Spenser's work as a whole, we find frequent intimations that "the order of this world, although a beautiful and necessary ideal, can … only be fleeting and impermanent." It may, on rare and precious occasions, find expression in poetry, but is scarcely likely to permeate tangible human society. "Spenser's creation of a faery land rests upon this tension between the vividness of his ideals and the threat of reality" (p. 195). As anticipated earlier in this discussion, it is at this level of the narrative that the poet's irony, manifests itself most poignantly.

As Helen Cooper comments with specific attention to Book I, the unresolved nature of the poem's quest is confirmed by the fact that "moments of closing equilibrium are never more than temporary, if they are achieved at all." Time and again, in keeping with the traditional romance's passion for deferral and open-endedness, *The Faerie Queene* frustrates the desire for closure by intensifying from within the potential for complication, and attendant narrative expansion. For example, one may be tempted to assume that the protagonist's defeat of the dragon will pave a safe course to the achievement of his quest. In fact, "his old enemies Duessa and Archimago promptly reappear. Instead of settling down with his bride Una, he is recalled to the world of questing against continuing evil: Holiness and Truth will not achieve lasting union this side of the Apocalypse, even in Elizabeth's Anglican England" (Cooper 2008, p. 371).

Shakespeare

Saunders centers her analysis of Shakespeare's treatment of the forest of romance on two comedies, *A Midsummer Night's Dream* and *As You Like It*. Therefore, the critic does not deal explicitly with either *The Winter's*

Tale (1610) or *Cymbeline* (1609). However, in both of these late plays, as in the earlier comedies addressed by Saunders, sylvan locations rise to the status of "an essential part of the dramatic structure." This applies to both wooded and pastoral settings. As such, they abet the construction of "an alternative and literary world of the imagination." Shakespeare makes use of forests and pastoral locales as more than mere settings, capitalizing on their metaphorical potentialities as catalysts, capable of initiating both emotional and material metamorphoses of great consequence.

At the same time, Shakespeare's penchant for self-reflexivity, whereby no opportunity is lost to comment on, or, at any rate, allude to, the art of fiction-making means that sylvan settings also become, in his hands, "the world of the poet" (Saunders 1993, p. 197): a space designed to accommodate artistic creation, and symbolize its essence. This proposition is substantiated by the scenes featuring the famous song "Fear no more the heat o' the sun" (*Cymbeline*, 4.2), and Perdita's speech on her floral preferences (*The Winter's Tale*, 4.4). In both instances, the rural environment is first and foremost a stage for the composition and performance of a special kind of poetry, designed to stand out from other aspects of the dialogue. This is characterized by a conscious orchestration of a *specifically poetic* reality.

The settings employed for the two scenes consist of untamed, or only partially tamed, versions of nature. In *Cymbeline*, this is conveyed by the suggestion that the forest has not been interfered with by its inhabitants, who are so keen to keep their whereabouts hidden as to have no desire to leave any obvious traces of their presence in the rustic environment. In *The Winter's Tale*, Perdita and her folk have, to some extent, tampered with the natural environment insofar as they do not live by hunting, like Arviragus, Belarius and Guiderius, but through shepherding and agriculture. Nevertheless, the primacy of undomesticated nature is still ensured by Perdita's firm reluctance to grow flowers other than those favored by the season without human intrusion.

By orchestrating two notable pieces of carefully crafted poetry in the context of unadulterated surroundings, Shakespeare revels in irony, intimating that the world at its most *natural* may also function as the receptacle of the most refined *artifice*, and that the celebration of ostensibly natural beauty calls for rhetorically sophisticated compositional strategies. The explicitness with which this move is performed anticipates Brecht's *Verfremdungseffekt*.

It is also worth noting that both *Cymbeline* and *The Winter's Tale* refrain from any facile idealization of their arboreal and bucolic settings. The forest introduced in Act 3, scene 3, of *The Winter's Tale* is beset by adverse climate and wild beasts, and even in countrified scenes, reminders abound that not all seasons are congenial. In *Cymbeline*, the forest is depicted as the locus of some of the play's most serious deceptions and confusions. Thus, Shakespeare yields a subversive interpretation of the concept of the sylvan scene as a utopia, or the incarnation of a golden age, found in texts of a less ironical disposition.

The closest sources behind Shakespeare's romances were the prose narratives of the late Greek writers Heliodorus (2nd century BC), Chariton (1st century AD), Longus (2nd century AD), and Xenophon of Ephesus (2nd/3rd century AD). Cedric Watts argues that the romance, as a distinctive genre, originates in these authors, and has since been used as a blanket label for "literary works which ... depict the far-fetched, strange and exotic (sometimes invoking the supernatural): their plots usually involve dramatic or even melodramatic events, coincidental meetings, and reunions of long-separated people" (Watts, p. 9). Bruce R. Smith elaborates this idea, remarking that "these tales transport us into a world of the imagination where anything is possible, where desires, fears, and aggressions of all sorts are given full play, untrammeled by the exigencies of everyday life" (Smith, p. 120).

In his commentary of Shakespeare's original adaptation of the romance form to suit his own and his age's requirements, Frank Kermode maintains that even without turning to classical antiquity, it is possible to account for the new appetite for romances as a consequence of the popularity enjoyed by more recent works, including Spenser's magnus opus, as well as Philip Sidney's *The Countess of Pembroke's Arcadia* (1590). "These works," as Kermode explains, "are highly serious in their ethical and political intentions." As shown in the preceding segment of this chapter, there can be little doubt as to the seriousness of the ideological project underpinning *The Faerie Queene*. If this gravity of purpose is taken into account, "it may seem less surprising that Shakespeare could blend the improbabilities of romance plots with intentions evidently as profound" (Kermode, p. 8). As we shall see in the individual analysis of two Shakespearean romances, concerns of substantial ideological and historical significance traverse the fabulous events in which the plays may at first seem to glory unimpeded.

Kermode has also emphasizes the recurrence of the following conventions: "the recovery of lost royal children, usually princesses of great, indeed semi-divine, virtue and beauty," the inclusion of personae who, having been brought "near death," are then restored to the world of the living by means of "almost miraculous transformations," the use of reparative finales marked by "the healing, after many years of repentance and suffering, of some disastrous breach in the lives and happiness of princes," and the incorporation of "material of a pastoral character" (p. 6).

Shakespeare inserts the codes and conventions of the romance into dramatic structures of great diversity, the two plays examined in this study illustrating this proposition in an exemplary fashion. Both *The Winter's Tale* and *Cymbeline* share with the romance a preoccupation with the related topoi of loss and recuperation. Outlandish countries, remote isles, and raging seas are the most prominent of their recurrent settings. Magic, mystery, and wonder pervade the action even in the most realistic moments, as lost relations are found again, and, on occasion, even the (seemingly) dead re-enter the world of the living. The treatment of these key themes is consistently enlivened by a fascination with mistaken identities, and the practically endless narrative possibilities which this narrative stratagem entails.

In addition, the texts evince a passion for dramatic structures in which the mechanisms of meandering and deferral reign supreme, thus harking back to Chrétien de Troyes and his contemporaries, as well as more recent romance authors such as Ariosto and Spenser. The entire development of *The Winter's Tale* constitutes an extended deferment of the resolution to the crisis initiated by Leontes' "fit" in the play's opening. Similarly, *Cymbeline*'s action following the wager can be seen as a series of shifts from one episode to the next, one adventure to the next. In both plays, resolutions are accomplished by means of theatrical moments which strive to foreground their artificiality, and hence their relative arbitrariness, as if to suggest that without such self-conscious interventions on the playwright's part, the pattern of deferral could go on *for ever*.

Moreover, both *The Winter's Tale* and *Cymbeline* rely on inceptive incidents which appear to lack any obvious motivation. According to Peter Goldman, what Shakespeare seems to have found most appealing about the romance form is precisely its openness to the presentation of unforeseen circumstances, peppered with "absurd disjunctions and improbabilities" (Goldman): materials to which the playwright's legendary passion for irony would spontaneously warm. In *The Winter's Tale*, Leontes' sudden descent into the living hell of jealous rage is as powerful as it is, both at the theatrical and at the psychological levels, *because* it appears to be fundamentally devoid of any logical cause.

As Kermode points out, in Robert Greene's novel *Pandosto: The Triumph of Time* (1588), Shakespeare's chief source in the conception of *The Winter's Tale*, King Pandosto's jealous eruption is presented, like Leontes,' as being "without real foundation"; yet, it is "not, as in Shakespeare, merely fantastic" (Kermode, p. 27). This divergence between the source and its dramatic adaptation would seem to suggest that Shakespeare was eager to exploit to the maximum the romance's preference for wanton actions as a feature of the form which performance could profitably maximize. In lessening the element of "plausibility" found in Greene's fiction, Shakespeare causes Leontes' "jealousy to burst upon and destroy a harmonious situation like a natural calamity, a terrible disease" (p. 29)—in other words, he makes it look like a blight infiltrating and infecting the court *from the outside*.

In *Cymbeline*, likewise, Posthumus' succumbing to Iachimo's malicious narrative is effective, in both triggering the events to come, and in inviting reflection on complex affective issues, *because* of its apparent lack of motivation. To this extent, *The Winter's Tale* and *Cymbeline* echo the traditional romance's focus on actions which tend to be guided by the sheer desire for adventure. The forces unleashing the two plays' complications are gratuitous, just as the impetus behind the knight errant's peregrinations is often unconnected with any deeper motive, purpose, or rationale.

It is also striking that in *Cymbeline*, the ostensible absence of clear motivations behind the inceptive incident is complemented by a lack of introspection. As Cynthia Marshall contends, "the capacity for change is not accompanied by self-understanding.... Even the best developed characters seem peculiarly unaware of their actions, almost as though they were sleepwalking or drugged" (Marshall, p. 294). Relatedly, the drama lays special emphasis on "the role of fantasy in shaping human actions" (p. 295). Fantasy is a potentially regenerative faculty, which attests to the human power to affect reality through imagination rather than reason alone—that least reliable of instruments. Nonetheless, as *Cymbeline* emphasizes, it can also fuel deception and malevolence. The Machiavellian plot constructed by Iachimo to win the wager is woven on fantasies, and Cloten's self-identification with Posthumus, as he plans to violate Imogen while donning the estranged husband's clothes, is likewise sustained by a dangerous fantasy.

This aspect of the play is reinforced by its fascination with "sleeping characters" (p. 289). In two of *Cymbeline*'s most memorable moments, the heroine herself is presented as unconscious: first, in the scene in which Iachimo, performing a symbolic rape, penetrates her bedroom absconded in a trunk in order to fabricate convincing evidence of her marital unfaithfulness; and later, in the one where the ingestion of a narcotic brew she believes to be a tonic precipitates her into a state of deathlike insentience. Moreover, the play enters its climactic stage with the dream experienced by Posthumus as he slumbers in prison.

Cymbeline's use of sleeping personae should be assessed in the broader framework of its preoccupation with "the relative merits of activity and passivity," argues Marshall. This is evinced by the key questions it poses: "does history happen to us, or do we happen to it? Do individuals direct their own actions, or are they pawns within an encompassing structure? Are we ever entirely awake to life's meanings?" (pp. 289–290). It could be argued that the last of these questions pervades Shakespeare's entire corpus, the answer it tends to receive being a negative one, regardless of whether its outcome is tragic or comic.

All in all, Shakespeare's romances seem to suggests that actions lacking any obvious motivation are synonymous with the eruption of irrational and destructive forces whose impact proves devastating for individuals and communities alike. It is remarkable, however, that this state of affairs is counterbalanced by an alternative scenario in which the spirit of randomness provides the underpinning not so much of unjustifiable acts, as of serendipitous occurrences. This idea is encapsulated in Pisanio's captivating assertion, "Fortune brings in some boats that are not steer'd" (4.3.34).

Goldman also proposes that "when Shakespeare started writing tragicomic romance, he was probably responding to contemporary events, including a new fashion for tragicomedy, the popularity of masques, and the opening of the Blackfriars theater to the King's Men, with its more sophisticated audience and different styles of drama" (Goldman). Kermode confirms the significance of the new staging options afforded by this venue. "Shakespeare's company," states the critic, "from about 1609, were beginning to play at the Blackfriars, an indoor theatre, which catered for a richer audience than the great public playhouse across the river. This house would create a demand for plays which could exploit its superior facilities for music, scenery, and machinery." It is also necessary to recall that "this was the era of the great masques," courtly entertainments which capitalized, alongside the acting per se, on music, song, and dance, as well as sumptuous stage design and costumes. It is therefore feasible that the audiences patronizing the Blackfriars Theatre would have wished to see "the private theatre reflect the elaborate displays at Court" (Kermode, p. 7).

As shown later in this chapter, the deployment of emphatically theatrical effects in both *Cymbeline* and *The Winter's Tale* corroborate the contention that the performative opportunities offered by the Blackfriars Theatre would, at least in part, have influenced Shakespeare's decision to turn to the romance: a form, as argued throughout this book, which pivots on the self-conscious foregrounding of its fictionality—and, in Shakespeare's case, of the specifically dramatic structures underpinning the fiction's performance.

In both *The Winter's Tale* and *Cymbeline*, Shakespeare explores the very essence of theatricality by foregrounding throughout the artificial character of staged reality per se, and by laying arguably unprecedented emphasis on his theater's non-naturalistic elements through the incorporation of supernatural agencies and events. As emphasized throughout this study, one of the most salient features of the romance is its overt proclamation of fictionality. Shakespeare's metatheatrical flourishes in both *The Winter's Tale* and *Cymbeline* exemplify that propensity with special intensity. They accomplish this feat by literally *staging* the romance's eagerness to call attention to its fictionality by means of scenes in which enactment and performance are elevated to the status of pivotal themes—where they indeed become protagonists. At the same time, they deepen the sense of artificiality inherent in such scenes—and, by implication, of the entire dramatic constructs to which they belong—by recourse to the otherworldly as the timeless epitome of a resolutely non-mimetic world view.

Cymbeline contains numerous scenes ideal for spectacle, both sensational and solemn. The "funeral" staged for Cloten and Imogen/Fidele typifies this aspect of the play by providing directors with just the perfect opportunity for memorable spectacle. The scene's atmosphere is doubtlessly grave and awe-inspiring, but this mood is undercut by irony, since the supposedly deceased creatures are neither what nor who they seem. Fidele is not a youth, but a gracious and hapless damsel; nor is s/he dead, the physician from whom the evil Queen obtains her potions having inferred foul play upon her request for a lethal poison, and filled the phial with a drug inducing merely a deathlike torpor. Cloten is not, as Imogen believes him to be, her beloved husband; nor has he ventured into the forest in search of the exile Belarius and his charges, as the old man suspects.

The use of the word "dust" as one of the dirge's recurring images reinforces the scene's concern with the discrepancy between appearance and reality, epitomizing a murky world of elements which serve to obfuscate, rather than abet, human vision. Earlier in the play, "fog" is used to analogus ends to symbolize a lack of clarity in one's vision, and hence a pervasive sense of confusion. A good example is the scene in which Imogen complains: "I see before me, man. Nor here, nor here, / Nor what ensues, but have a fog in them / That I cannot look through" (3.2.79–81). According to Tony Tanner, "the 'fog' which centrally engulfs the heroine, Imogen, settles variously on them all, until they cannot see to see—to borrow Emily

Dickinson's powerful formulation. In no other play do so many characters seem so blind" (Tanner, p. lvi).

In fact, a ubiquitous sense of uncertainty affects all of the characters' perceptions, and often hazy interpretations, of their circumstances. This mood is associated with the play's employment, as its historical context, of a period of swift and constant change. Furthermore, insofar as Shakespeare's own age is marked by a pointed sense of disorientation, largely originating in the shift from the geocentric to the heliocentric conception of the cosmos, *Cymbeline*'s setting could be seen as a fictional correlative for an actual state of affairs of substantial momentum.

The play's topical significance is corroborated by its evocation of an enveloping atmosphere of fragmentation. As Judy Schavrien observes, "centrifugal forces work to disassemble identity of person as well as of couple, family, realm, and globe. Even the universe seems out of joint as malevolent or deeply misguided creatures dominate the outcome of action. The forces are both internal and external—psychological and sociopolitical, forces from Nature and from seemingly heavenly and hellish emissaries" (Schavrien, p. 122). This atmosphere of fragmentation is evident from the start, pervading the exchange through which the two Gentlemen apprise the audience of the background necessary to grasp the action's circumstances. "You do not meet a man but frowns. Our bloods / No more obey the heavens than our courtiers / Still seem as does the king" (1.1.1–3), states the First Gentleman. With these images, he seeks to portray the general feeling of dissatisfaction pervading the court, drawing a parallel between the personal and the social by intimating that people's bodies are no longer influenced, as they should, by heavenly laws, any more than courtiers bow to Cymbeline's own influence.

Just before falling asleep on the fateful night Iachimo infiltrates her private chamber, Imogen pleads: "To your protection I commend me, gods. / From fairies and the tempters of the night / Guard me, beseech you" (2.2.11–13). The princess' prayer is quite ironical when one reflects that the princess' words locate danger with otherworldly agents, such as a sprite or an incubus. However, her beliefs will soon to be contradicted with uncompromising brutality by the appearance on the scene of a *human* enemy whose malevolence far exceeds that of most (if not all) supernatural entities found in romance. The play harks back to earlier romances which likewise indicate that trouble of all kinds is more likely to be engendered by a human being, including oneself, than a supernatural agent. In Thomas Chestre's *Sir Launfal*, for example, the titular knight's misfortunes issue from the malice and vindictiveness of a mortal queen, not from the fairy lady who chooses him as her lover. To cite a further instance, Chrétien de Troyes' *Perceval, The Story of the Grail* intimates that the protagonist's pain stems from his own inadequate grasp of a code of conduct he struggles to master to scarce avail, rather than any obvious supernatural force.

It is also noteworthy that Guiderius' and Arviragus' longing to engage in martial exploits, a pursuit from which their secluded upbringing has barred them, harks back to Chrétien's characterization of Perceval. However, a big difference obtains between the two situations, for Perceval simply does not know how to be a knight, and is still far from learning at the point where Chrétien's own version of the story comes to an abrupt end. By contrast, Belarius' adoptive charges, who are in fact Cymbeline's lost sons, harbor so natural and spontaneous a penchant for noble conduct and heroic actions as to shine forth as chivalric paragons despite Belarius' efforts to keep them within the safe boundaries of a rustic existence whose greatest challenge is hunting. So passionate is the two youths' attraction to the prospect of great deeds that Belarius, when they ardently entreat him to let them join the British troops, has no choice but yield: "have with you, boys! / If in your country wars you chance to die, / That is my bed, too, lads, and there I'll lie. / Lead, lead. [*Aside.*] The time seems long; their blood thinks scorn / Till it fly out and show them princes born" (4.4.60–65).

Cymbeline abounds with instances of dramatic irony: the theatrical and rhetorical ruse whereby the audience is in a position to grasp the significance of situations and/or words offered on stage to which the characters themselves are oblivious. What is special about Shakespeare's use of this strategy in *Cymbeline* is his ability to elicit incongruent responses in the audience by inviting compassionate participation and detached scepticism at one and the same time. D. E. Landry points to this salient aspect of the play's handling of dramatic irony, stating that "in Imogen's waking next to Cloten and in the final recognition scene especially, the audience is both sympathetically engaged and ironically distanced." In the former, Shakespeare stages a "grotesque irony" (Landry, p. 78). In the latter, the action's comedic impetus derives from the presentation of a booty of concatenated disclosures so bountiful as to bring to mind a chain of "farcical associations" (Kermode, p. 29).

However, the ultimate irony does not reside so much with the content of either scene as much as with the mixed impressions they are likely to elicit in the audience. Indeed, as Landry stresses, "in both cases, the core of the narrative moves us; it is the palpable presence of the master dramatist pulling both affective and witty strings which holds us apart" (Landry, p. 78). The play's irony, therefore, replicates itself *within* its spectators, in that it holds the potential to produce a tantalizing sense of self-division in each member of the audience: a state induced by the simultaneous perception of the action's profundity and of its ludicrousness.

The play's appetite for irony is encapsulated in a line spoken in the closing act by the jailer guarding Posthumus. Commenting on the prisoner's longing for death, the jailer remarks: "What an infinite mock is this, that a man should have the best use of eyes to see the way to blindness!" (5.4.192–194). The idea that a man should employ his eyes best to perceive things like a blind man constitutes a succinct commentary on the often unfathomable discrepancy between appearance and reality so central to *Cymbeline* as a whole.

It is in *Cymbeline*'s views on misogyny that the play strikes some of its most starkly ironical chords. It is indeed deeply ironical that the (tragic) error conducive to the key complications we see in the play should be the result of the nefarious malice of one man (Iachimo) and the—potentially no less nefarious—gullibility of another man (Posthumus). Both men are sustained, in their respective attitudes, by the conviction that womanhood and fickleness—or frailty, as Hamlet would put it—are virtually synonymous. It is no less ironical that both the play's heroine and its villainess—i.e., its central female personae—should both prove unremittingly constant: Imogen in her loyalty to Posthumus, and the Queen in her attachment to the foolish Cloten. It is especially notable, with regard to the otherwise evil lady, that Cloten's disappearance leads to her death, while there is absolutely no indication that Cymbeline could ever die of grief when his own child goes awol.

The play's passion for irony is further attested to by its use of a hybrid textual form which blends fact ad fiction at will, thereby deliberately juxtaposing two theoretically incompatible frames of reference. This strategy alludes to the inherently arbitrary nature of *any* text which purports to offer a reliable and coherent account of historical events. "It is not that the sanctity of national history is being deliberately undermined," states Landry, "but that Shakespeare makes us aware that history *is* constructed, that both our personal and national myths must of necessity scaffold truth with an artificial, purposive design" (Landry, p. 77).

One of the most tantalizing ironies underlying *Cymbeline*'s action lies with the convergence of a story so rife with improbabilities and sudden revelations as to resemble the zaniest of fairy tales, and a subtext laden with political and ideological significance. The fabulous side of the play's approach to history is most evident in its flamboyant admixture of Roman antiquity and early modern Italy—or better, Italy as seen through English eyes in seventeenth-century England. The martial strand of *Cymbeline*'s intricate plot emphasizes its entanglement with the former, by focusing on the complex political, economic and diplomatic relations between Rome's imperial rule, and a nascent British nation. On the other hand, the character of Iachimo typifies the latter. "Iachimo's conduct," states Kermode, is clearly "un-Roman"—at least, we may add, vis-à-vis conventional perceptions of the ancient *caput mundi* and its breed. "He is a Sienese," continues Kermode, "and his Italian manners are appropriate to the wicked Italy of the Jacobean imagination; it was no part of the dramatist's purpose to portray a Tuscan of the time of Augustus" (Kermode, p. 18). As argued later, *The Winter's Tale* likewise abounds with deliberate anachronisms, and a comparable itch for historical hybridity.

On the other hand, *Cymbeline* harbors a political dimension which cannot be categorized as merely fabulous, insofar as it reflects specific ideological preoccupations coursing through Shakespeare's England at the time the romance was produced. This is borne out by its stance on contrasting interpretations of the law, vis-à-vis the project of consolidation of national identity and, by implication, the legitimation of England's expansionist and imperialist ambitions. On a pragmatic level, it could be argued that Shakespeare needed the fantastic component *in order to* create a dramatic mold suited to the presentation in public of controversial issues which could easily have incurred the harshest censorship. It is at this level that irony transcends its function as a mere trope, or rhetorical ruse, to function as the pivotal mechanism guaranteeing the dramatic text's *viability* (and fruition) qua theater.

It is therefore important, in assessing *Cymbeline*'s historical dimension, to grasp the meaning of its treatment of the relationship between power and the law with specific reference to Shakespeare's culture. As Brian C. Lockey explains, "King Cymbeline's initial attitude toward imperial Rome seems to be lifted from the pages of historiographers used by prominent common lawyers in order to illustrate the unchangeable nature of English law in the face of both foreign and 'domestic' threats." This perspective is reinforced by "statements made by the British queen and Cymbeline in the third act," which "reflect the common-law idea that Rome's conquest of Britain was partial." The titular monarch bolsters this proposition by arguing "for Britain's independence from Rome ... on the basis of a prior and separate British identity" (Lockey, p. 164). The protection of this identity is conditional on the "restoration and preservation of British legal traditions" (p. 165). As Cymbeline tells Lucius, the ambassador from Rome, his revolt against the Roman Emperor's authority is intended to achieve this very goal.

It is interesting that Shakespeare should have chosen to couch the protection of national identity not simply as a governmental priority, but also as a distinctively *legal* matter. This can be seen to reflect the "legal battles" of "the seventeenth century between common-law and civil-law courts.... Common-law jurists tended to view the civil-law courts" as inimical to the notion of Englishness per se, and one of the major "'foreign' threats to the common law's immemorial integrity." Civil-law representatives were thus demonized as "a contemporary incarnation of the ancient foreign invaders," who had in vain struggled to suppress the local approach to the legislature.

Shakespeare's handling of the relationship between civil law and common law constitutes a vital part of the play's ironical juxtaposition of the conventions of fabulous romance, and real-world political concerns. This hinges on the elaborate interweaving of two conflicting positions—the "discourses of absolutism and ancient constitutionalism"—into a single discourse: the "defense of British national integrity." This aspect of the play remains central to its historical import, even though in the end, *Cymbeline* refutes the king's "expression of nativism," positing the "anti–Roman stance" as synonymous with "tyrannical absolutism," and favoring instead a diplomatic policy of "reconciliation with Rome" (p. 166). The protection of a pre–Roman national identity remains, by implication, a noble goal. Yet, Rome's presence in Britain is presented as an ultimately unavoidable reality. It could in fact be argued that Rome is the Other whose presence is necessary for a distinctively British identity to assert itself.

The idea that Britain's infiltration by Rome is somewhat unavoidable is corroborated by Iachimo's invasion of Imogen's bedchamber. In purely functional plot terms, the scene is necessary to the advancement of the villain's evil strategy, and hence of the complications which fill the play's main body. On the figurative plane, however, it symbolizes the penetration of "the innermost enclosure of supposedly impenetrable British soil." Moreover, the scene reminds us that Rome's presence in Britain is ubiquitous in broadly cultural, rather than just political or martial terms, by underlining the pervasiveness of images of classical derivation in the decor of the princess' bedroom, and drawing attention to her choice of Ovid's work as an apposite bedtime read. In this perspective, the scene indicates that Iachimo "is not the first Roman presence in Imogen's bedroom" (O'Hanlon).

Cymbeline is not merely concerned with the construction of a sense of national identity for Britain *as a whole*: on the contrary, the identity it aims to shape is specifically Anglo-Saxon (as opposed to Celtic). Galen O'Hanlon argues that the romance, "set as it is on the frayed edges of the early Roman Empire," portrays a vivid picture of a "court in the process of fashioning a colonial identity separate from but connected to the centre of power in Rome. The colonial framework also extends to the relationship between England and Wales—the latter of which has been usefully emptied of Welsh people in order to give a fittingly wild backdrop to the childhood of Britain's future kings" (O'Hanlon).

The Welsh setting, in this regard, cannot be construed merely as an appropriate backdrop for the staging of a pastoral romance. In fact, it carries political implications of considerable magnitude. The scenes set in Wales draw attention to the anglicizing project pursued by the English rulers at the time the play was first performed. Ronald Boling substantiates this proposition, arguing that in *Cymbeline*, "Rome is to Britain what in Shakespeare's time England was to Wales. *Cymbeline*'s Britain plays a double role, empire to Wales but colony to Rome: as *Cymbeline*'s Wales is anglicized, so *Cymbeline*'s Britain is Romanized" (Boling, p. 35). It is also important to recall that Wales holds a special place in Arthurian lore, as do the Celtic traditions underpinning the style and themes of many chivalric romances.

The conflict between the idea of an original British identity, and the inescapable reality of Roman presence in Britain, is couched not merely as a political issue but also as a *gendered* issue. Jodi Mikalachki pursues this line of reasoning in her analysis of *Cymbeline*'s nationalism, proposing that the emergence of an English nation is conditional on "virile bonding": the establishment of a pointedly masculine community through the expulsion of deviant femininity, emblematized by the Queen, and the enthronement of a tame version of femininity, of which Imogen is constructed as the exemplar (Mikalachki, p. 264).

Thus, as O'Hanlon points out, "insular nationalism" is associated primarily with the figure of the spiteful Queen, responsible for initiating Britain's insurrection. Even though she "invokes a male presence in the kings," in advocating the necessity of mutiny, she underscores "the 'natural bravery' of the isle," which alludes to "an image of aggressive femininity." By contrast, "the King's submission to Rome," dramatized at the play's close, marks the triumph of a fundamentally male concept of authority. The opposition is matched by the different tones and registers with which the advocator of each side is connected. Thus, while the Queen's discourse is pervaded by "shrill rhetoric," Lucius statements are distinguished by a sense of "calm assurance," as evinced by "the simplicity with which he places Cymbeline firmly beneath Caesar" (O'Hanlon).

The Queen's speech in Act 2, scene 1, strives to advance the myth of Britain as an inviolable fortress: a regal enclosure "which stands / As Neptune's park, ribbed and palèd in / With rocks unscalable and roaring waters, With sands that will not bear your enemies' boats / But suck them up to the' topmast" (3.1.21–25). It could be argued that the urge to lay such resounding emphasis on Britain's impregnability lies not so much with a firm belief in its reality, as on a latent dread of invasion or desecration. This ironical rupture between apparent and implied meanings is not the sole irony traversing the reprehensible dame's position. Indeed, it is somewhat paradoxical that she should view Imogen's own impenetrability (by her repulsive son Cloten, that is) as a crime, when this same quality is regarded as her country's prime virtue. Clearly, in the Queen's outlook, there is a radical disjuncture between the princess and her father's kingdom.

Posthumus appears to embrace a diametrically opposed view of the situation, explicitly comparing the two at the beginning of the final act, as he resolves to discard his Italian costume, attire himself as "a Briton peasant" (5.1.24), and join Cymbeline's forces to meet his end in the protection of the country of his wronged beloved, whom he believes dead at Pisanio's hand as per his own iniquitous instructions. "'Tis enough," he declares, "That, Britain, I have killed my mistress. Peace, / I'll give no wound to thee" (5.1.19–21). In the guilt-ridden Posthumus' mind, fighting for Britain, and thus proclaiming the realm's territorial integrity, becomes a way of asserting Imogen's own purity and inviolability: the very virtues he has doubted. The identification of spouse and nation may also be viewed as a fantasy of wish-fulfillment, insofar as Posthumus' words suggest that restoring Britain's independence from Rome is a way (at least symbolically) of restoring the dead Imogen.

The splintered nature of *Cymbeline*'s world is reinforced by Shakespeare's deployment of the fraught romance centered on Posthumus and Imogen as a means of foregrounding what David M. Bergeron terms "self-division" (Bergeron, p. 31). To substantiate his thesis, the critic notes that the play's protagonists "move in different directions," Imogen "busily cutting herself off from her royal family and he in search of his family." In the process, both characters strive to negotiate "an internal division" (p. 32). In Posthumus' case this is borne out by his struggle to come to terms with is the unresolved tension between contrasting aspects of his personality, which he interprets in pointedly gendered terms. The uncompromising strategy through which he attempts to put an end to the conflict is simply to brand all of his flaws, both actual and potential, as essentially feminine. Imogen, by contrast, must "explore through disguise the masculine part of herself" (p. 33).

Overcoming self-divisions, *Cymbeline* intimates, is not only vital to the attainment of a person's identity. In fact, it is also the means—especially if one happens to be a member of a royal family by birth or legitimate marriage—by which a nation constructs its collective identity. The individual's effort to heal one's self-division therefore becomes a metaphor for the healing of an entire realm of its political tensions and dynastic insecurities. Just as the individual's capacity to overcome his or her self-division is instrumental in ensuring the private realm's serenity, so the nation's capacity to overcome its own internal fractures is key to the prevention of political disintegration. In this context, "the poignant reunion of father and daughter, the acceptance of Posthumus by Cymbeline, and the revelation of the lost sons all point to peace and harmony in the private life of the royal family, thereby opening the prospect for peace in the kingdom. These actions heal divisions and self-divisions and assure the kingdom's future through orderly familial succession" (p. 36).

With its integration of the private and public domains, *Cymbeline* articulates a contemporary preoccupation with the importance of "orderly familial succession" to the establishment of a stable realm. James I's ascent to the English throne was held to have put an end to a protracted period of genealogical uncertainty. Not only did the new monarch appear to have finally "solved the succession problem": no less crucially, "he also brought with him a wife and three royal children—the first royal *family* to control the English throne in nearly a century" (p. 34). Hence, *Cymbeline*'s celebration of the concurrence of familial concord and political stability reflects an actual cultural scenario of uncommon magnitude.

Cymbeline's dénouement, even as it luxuriates in the romance's proverbial proclivity for absurd coincidences and sudden revelations, must be grasped in the light of these socio-political issues. Indeed, the resolution it offers fully vindicates the contention that the smooth transmission of power from one generation to the next is vital to the creation and maintenance of both stability and concord. At the same time, the play's genealogical concerns encapsulate its ultimate irony. The core of the action seems to use the kingdom's material circumstances merely as a backdrop for the articulation of the vicissitudes undergone by an intimate romance. In this respect, it could be said to make the public subservient to the private. The finale, however, mocks this interpretation of *Cymbeline*'s priorities, as Shakespeare intimates that the resolution of familial conflicts centered on individuals is by no means a private matter, but rather the instrument whereby a splintered society may achieve a cohesive and lasting identity.

As a title, "*The Winter's Tale*" alludes to two vital aspects of the play's identity as both an artifact and an affective reality. On the one hand, it throws into relief the play's standing as a piece of fiction: a "tale." On the other hand, it intimates that this fiction has been conceived according to codes and conventions pertinent to the evocation of a specific mood. Not only does it highlight the play's status as a fictional construct, therefore: it also defines this construct's tenor as germane to "winter." Both the word and its implied antonym carry climatic connotations, which directors may wish to exploit in their interpretation of the play's multi-layered setting, and in their choice of palettes, costumes, and props. At the same time, however, such terms symbolize specific emotional dispositions and spiritual destinies.

There are two key moments in the play in which winter is referred to overtly to evoke both the act of storytelling and a mental condition. Firstly, Mamilius states: "A sad tale's best for winter: I have one / Of sprites and goblins" (2.1.25–26); "There was a man—... Dwelt by a churchyard" (2.1.29–30). The doomed prince does not get to live long enough to develop the narration, though the play does tell a "winter's tale" on the boy's behalf in its elaboration of the transition from tragedy to pastoral. Secondly, Paulina refers to winter to alert Leontes to the unpardonable nature of his offences, visualizing his fate as a narrative laden with abysmal despair: "A thousand knees / Ten thousand years together, naked, fasting, / Upon a barren mountain, and still winter / In storm perpetual, could not move the gods / To look that way thou wert" (3.2.208–212).

While an attraction to unfamiliar lands defines the play's geographical identity, its historical features evince a penchant for the hybrid and the incongruous. In this respect, *The Winter's Tale* embodies the romance's characteristic proclivity for irony by deliberately cultivating temporal—and hence cultural—inconsistencies which leave the spectator amused and puzzled by turns, depending on the tone of the scene in which they are located. A contextual jumble which audiences keen on uncomplicated naturalism would feasibly deem absurd, the play oscillates between the Hellenic and the Christian eras, and their respective mores and value systems, the ancient world of a semi-mythical Sicily and Shakespeare's own England.

Leontes consults the Apollo's Delphic oracle, and references to a clearly polytheistic pantheon pepper both Hermione's and Perdita's speeches. However, as Watts points out, the play also alludes to "the Christian doctrine of original sin," while Autolycus makes reference to the Biblical tale of the "Prodigal Son," and "Camillo mentions Jesus and Judas." In addition, the artist held to have executed Hermione's statue, Giulio Romano, was an "employee of Pope Leo X," and reported to have passed away "as recently as 1546." The play's mixed frame of reference is further reinforced by of the assertion that "Hermione is daughter of the Emperor of Russia." By being left pointedly undefined, this world evokes a timeless aura of mystery. Bohemia, on the other hand, is rooted in the here and now through one of the play's most amusing incongruities: the country's use of a "currency" consisting of "pounds and shillings." Moreover, the courtly portions of Sicilia and Bohemia alike contrast sharply with the world of the shepherds, the country people, and Autolycus. The rogue, in particular, employs with mesmerizing proficiency a discourse, comprising "songs, tricks and thieves' slang," which "belongs distinctively to Shakespeare's day" (Watts, p. 10).

The audience is informed at an early stage in the action that there is "Great difference betwixt our Bohemia and your Sicilia" (1.1.4). The contrast between the two countries is no doubt stark, the former being introduced as the province of jealous cruelty and guilt perpetual, and the latter as the nest of regeneration and growth. However, given Shakespeare's arguably unmatched penchant for irony, one could scarcely expect his polarization of the two lands to be so total as to preclude the existence of parallels which serve to undermine the opposition. The most striking of these consists of the intimation that Polixenes is as capable of tyrannical conduct and murderous drives as Leontes. When Florizel's love for a low-born girl is disclosed, the Bohemian monarch's response is as illogical as Leontes' reaction to the thought that his wife might be an adulteress.

Sicilia and Bohemia do not constitute a pair of mutually excluding realities because they are both implicated in the same cycle of birth, death and rebirth which defines the play's time-space as a whole. Furthermore, neither realm can transcend humanity's vulnerability to destructive forces, regardless of whether it blindly gives in to nefarious delusions, or strives to achieve reconciliation and balance. The ironical agency of serendipity ensures that in both lands, harmony might ensue even from the most muddled, conflictual, and seemingly hopeless of tangles. The same seasonal cycle embraces the whole of nature, and it is only logical, in a sense, to expect the same discordant rhythms to permeate the world in all its facets. This is ultimately what the play throws into relief most forcefully.

Watts underscores the idea that all aspects of the romance partake of the same underlying reality. "The thematic structure of *The Winter's Tale*," states the critic, "is one in which age, corruption and destruction are contrasted with youth, love and creation, so that eventually a predominantly harmonious (but marginally discordant) resolution can be attained. We are reminded that age, corruption and destruction are manifest not merely in individuals, and the courtly world, but in greater nature too: in wintry blasts, lethal storms, and predatory creatures; fulness, love and sexuality are associated with the natural bounty of spring and summer, with the regenerative aspects of the seasonal cycle, and with the perennial benign activities of the countryside" (Watts, pp. 15–16). Watts' use of the phrase "but marginally discordant" deserves special recognition, in view of its implicit stress on Shakespeare's eschewal of definitive resolutions, and hence on the play's ironical spirit.

It is as a result of the play's cultivation of a persistent, albeit often latent, sense of disharmony that its redemptive forces do not gain full dominance even when the tragic spirit coursing the play's early acts ceases to prevail. According to Thomas McFarland, *The Winter's Tale* as a whole can indeed be regarded as a "winter pastoral," insofar as even the sheep-shearing festival set in Bohemia, supposedly held in summertime, is infused with troubling undercurrents (McFarland). In fact, as Humphrey Tonkin points out, the rustic episode teeters "on the edge of catastrophe, Polixenes being ready to tear it apart whenever he chooses to do so." As is often the case with pastoral settings generally, the fête offers the soil in which the seeds of resolution and renewal might begin to germinate. Yet, this potential is not actualized within the pastoral world itself. All of the key characters must first journey to Sicilia—the land marked by Leontes' spiritual *winter* regardless of the island's actual climate—before any harmony may be found (Tonkin, p. 28).

Working at various levels throughout *The Winter's Tale*, the force of irony makes itself felt most vibrantly in the tension between the law of the Sicilian court, and the forestal world's own idiosyncratic laws, which signal a temporary disruption of courtly decorum. Intimated by the terrifying storm attendant on Antigonus' arrival on the shore where he is to abandon his hapless charge, the disturbance of courtly order is brought to the fore with unequivocal, albeit somewhat ludicrous, directness in the stage direction, "Exit, pursued by a bear" (3.3.56).

As Helen Cooper remarks, this line has become "notorious" to the extent that "modern theatregoers" are almost bound to see it as "random and meaningless." This reaction is, to some extent, justified, if one considers that the sentence "is not prepared for by the previous action of the play." In fact, its foundations lie with "the coding and resonances that the motif brought with it" when the play was first performed: factors of which its original viewers would be well aware, even if they are "long lost to modern readers or audiences" (Cooper 2008, p. 2). Indeed, various versions of a romance in which an infant is snatched away by a bear in a forest had been in circulation for centuries by the time *The Winter's Tale* was written and staged, constituting a story which, to Shakespeare's contemporaries, was as familiar as classic fairy tales are to us.

Adding further humor to the line's tenor, Tonkin notes: "we do not know when the Bear intrudes on the proceedings, how long he has been standing there. This bear, second only to Winnie-the-Pooh in literary fame, breaks through the melodramatic tension of the occasion with feral abruptness. Indeed, in his ferocity he perhaps resembles the suddenness of Leontes' rage" (Tonkin, p. 47). The savage animal's irruption therefore exemplifies what Jeanne Addison Roberts pithily terms "the Wild," disrupting the courtesy of civilized existence (Roberts).

In the course of the sheep-shearing festival, where Perdita plays the role of "Mistress o'th'Feast" (4.4.68) as the rustic equivalent of a courtly patroness, the girl declares that her garden hosts no products of artificial cross-breeding, which she regards as a perversion of nature's own laws. Polixenes refutes her stance by arguing that there is nothing unnatural about the hybrid plants Perdita disapproves of, because their cultivation is made possible by nature itself: "nature is made better by no mean / But nature makes that mean; so, over that art / (Which you say adds to nature) is an art / That nature makes" (4.4.89–92). In the Bohemian king's perspective, art is capable of enhancing nature by holding "the mirror up to nature," as famously put in *Hamlet* (3.2.23). The exchange between Perdita and Polixenes turns out to carry darkly ironical connotations, insofar as the prospect of his royal offspring's union with the putative shepherdess (itself a form of cross-breeding) is precisely what throws the Bohemian ruler into a paroxysm of fury which, as noted earlier, is akin to Leontes' jealous explosion at the play's start in both unreasonableness and intensity. The rural scene's irony is compounded by the fact that Perdita is *not*, in fact, a wench of humble birth.

Polixenes' views on art reflect a Renaissance aesthetic stance influenced by Neoplatonism. In Plato's work, and most pointedly in the *Republic*, art is "condemned as a mystifying illusion and as the copy of a copy. Indeed, art is said to imitate the forms of nature and since nature is already a second-rate copy of the Pure Forms or Ideas, it is automatically relegated to the conditions of a shadow of a shadow" (Cavallaro, p. 158). In the Neoplatonist reading of art's relation to reality, conversely, art does not imitate mere appearances. On the contrary, it has the power to reascend to the Pure Forms themselves. In this perspective, "lawful art mocks not by naturalistic imitation," as Mary L. Livingston points out, "but by mirroring the higher principle of natural order" (Livingston, p. 352).

According to Mary D. Garrard, Renaissance artists inspired by such principles held that their "art was not to imitate the mere phenomena of nature (*natura naturata*) but, rather, its higher invisible principles (*natura naturans*)," and that their works, therefore, could offer refined forms which could "successfully compete with Nature herself" (Garrard, p. 71). As a result, the conscientious and truly *inspired* representation of nature in an artwork was deemed to harbor the potential to enlighten the beholder, instead of yielding third-hand imitations of nature's splendors.

Aristotle's aesthetic theories develop a cognate perspective, arguing that "art does not imitate the particulars of nature but actually represents general and universal characteristics. This makes it more dependable than history itself. Aesthetic pleasure is generated by the realistic representation of objects, so that even supposedly ugly things end up possessing beauty in virtue of their accurate depiction of reality" (Cavallaro 2001, pp. 158–159). Aristotle's aesthetic positions are also relevant to *The Winter's Tale*, and to the redemptive thrust of the statue scene in particular, insofar as "Aristotle ... praises art's ability to evoke powerful emotions through the principle of catharsis ('purification,' 'cleansing'). People's exposure to feelings and passions of a universal nature will help them come to terms with universal facets of human experience and achieve a deeper understanding of the world" (p. 159). The statue scene, examined in depth in the ensuing segment, could be read as a cathartic event in the Aristotelian sense of the term.

As Tonkin explains, "Perdita's view of nature is that art can only corrupt it," whereas Polixenes' avers that "to perfect nature is simply to use an art that is in turn derived from nature. In the context of the play, both positions are deeply ironic." Indeed, the girl's position "seems to undermine her situation as a shepherdess vis-à-vis Florizel," while "Polixenes' belief in the virtues of such cross-fertilization of stock would seem to favor her and weaken the arguments that he is soon to use when he reveals himself. Thus, Polixenes' explanation, that over art is nature, inadvertently justifies Florizel's love for Perdita" (p. 53).

The play's preoccupation with the relationship between art and nature reaches its apotheosis in the statue scene. The dramatic and affective impact of this singular dramatic episode pivots on a subtle interaction between nature and art. Nature is invested with the power to imitate art, and the art thus engendered is accorded, in turn, the capacity to morph into nature. The first part of the spectacle displays a breathing woman in the guise of a lifeless statue (here nature becomes art); the second part shows a statue coming to life (here art becomes nature). As Livingston points out, on this subject, "the 'statue's coming alive enacts dramatically the theory of art implied in Polixenes' defense of art: the magical metamorphosis of 'stone' into life symbolizes the workings of the art which 'itself is nature'" (Livingston, p. 351).

If irony's greatest power is its knack of throwing into relief life's ubiquitous uncertainty, then the statue scene at the close of *The Winter's Tale* is a veritable paean to irony. The play's ironical disposition is announced in the very first act, as the Bohemian lord Archidamus declares that Leontes' and Polixenes' friendship is such that "there is not, in the world, either malice or matter to alter it" (1.1.29–30). The supreme irony achieved in the climactic scene capitalizes on a simple—yet, by virtue of its very simplicity—uniquely effective strategy: neither the characters nor the audience are provided with definitive answers to the question of Hermione's status vis-à-vis the domains of life and death.

It may well be the case that Hermione never died, and Paulina has been hiding her for sixteen years: this is the most "realistic" option available. However, it is equally feasible, in the romance's idiosyncratic logic, for Hermione to have indeed perished of grief at the announcement of Mamilius' own demise, and for the animation of her statue to constitute a portent of sorts. (It is worth recalling, in this respect, that evidence pointing to the queen's departure is potent. Not only does Leontes see her corpse: Antigonus is visited by her ghost, and in Shakespeare's opus, specters are not, as a rule, anything other than the products of actual deaths.)

The intriguing comments on the issue of Hermione's absence for the main part of the play proffered by Gemma Jones, who played Hermione in Ronald Eyre's production of the play at the RSC in 1981, deserve note in this context: "whether she died and was born again; whether she lived in that removed home and nightly cried herself to sleep; whether she was indeed turned to stone? If asked to comment.... I say, 'She stopped.' She removed herself from life until the time was ripe for her re-emergence. 'I have preserved myself,' she says to Perdita—in a sort of Zen-like aspic" (Jones, p. 162).

According to Peter Goldman, "one of the major difficulties of the statue scene is that the earlier scene in which she died very clearly and emphatically indicated that Hermione was dead.... The dramatic lacuna is not accidental, nor is it simply a cheap trick to increase the wonder of the final scene. On one level, Hermione is indeed dead. Shakespeare's insistence on the fact of her death suggests that this final scene is an allegory of art." With "the reanimation of Hermione through art," Shakespeare alludes to humanity's ongoing "need for a public 'sacred.' What's real in the final scene is not Hermione's literal resurrection, but rather what it means, the peaceful presence of the community to itself" (Goldman).

Extrapolating from Goldman's argument, it could be argued that the statue scene typifies those special moments in which individuals are allowed to become absorbed, in symbolic form, in a collective dimension. This is obviously fictitious (just as the contents on which religious ceremonies thrive always are), because no human can escape the reality of his or her singularity. Yet, that imagined collective dimension is useful to the extent that it enables people to transcend, albeit temporarily, the boundaries of the self through the activation of a heightened sense of commonality and harmony. Moments of this kind are most effective when those who partake of their alternate reality can enjoy their illusion while—indeed *by*—recognizing that it is an illusion.

The romance, as a form, is ideally suited to capture such moments by virtue of its special relationship with fictionality: i.e., its frank admission to the consummately imaginary status of its stories. It is able to make us feel the sense of cohesion which those moments are meant to evoke without for a second pretending that they are anything other than artificial—and *arty*. Relatedly, it enables us to acknowledge not only their social function as cohesive tissues, but also, and more importantly in the present context, to appreciate their status qua art.

The statue scene can be read as the culmination of a death anxiety, associated specifically with the female gender, which permeates the play as a whole. This is already evident in the early dialogue where Polixenes waxes lyrical about his and Leontes' youth, suggesting that prior to their introduction to the fair sex, they were free to enjoy a state of total innocence. Women, by implication, are branded as harbingers of sinful knowledge. When Hermione objects by exclaiming "Grace to boot! / Of this make no conclusion, lest you say / Your queen and I are devils," (1.2.80–82), she calls attention to the cultural reality of Shakespeare's England at the time *The Winter's Tale* was first performed. At this time, the dreaded specter of witchcraft loomed large, and the horrors attendant on the persecution of those deemed to be involved in its practice held palpable reality for playwrights and theater-goers alike. The equation of witches to devils would be founded on the popular belief that copulation with Satan was among the perverse creatures' favorite pursuits.

As Leontes' madness escalates, Paulina herself is explicitly equated to a "a mankind witch" (2.3.68), and a "gross hag" (2.3.108). The most harrowing connection between Leontes' and the historical witch hunters' methods lies with his decree that the infant Perdita herself should be consigned to "the fire" (2.3.141). When, later in the play, Polixenes also succumbs to insane passions in opposing Florizel's marriage to Perdita, he calls the girl a "fresh piece / Of excellent witchcraft" (4.4.416–417).

Just as witch hunters, in their fatal dogmatism, were incapable of any misgivings regarding their assumptions, often taking as evidence the flimsiest of delusions and rumors, so Leontes does not question for a moment the veracity of his convictions. When he claims that Camillo knows about the adulterous liaison, for example, he declares that this knowledge is "past doubt" (1.2.266) when, in fact, he has no rational basis on which to found his accusation. Leontes therefore deems it inconceivable that in doubting his assertions, Camillo might be insinuating that he is "muddy," "unsettled" (1.2.323). Likewise, when Camillo leaves Sicilia with Polixenes, instead of poisoning the Bohemian ruler as instructed, Leontes is only able to see his erstwhile advisor's "flight" as evidence for his assistance in the growth of the illicit union. It just does not—*cannot*—occur to him that the escape could have anything to do with the lethal nature of his own orders.

Given the wiccaphobia so rampant in Jacobean society, a trend complicated by the monarch's insalubrious fascination with the world of witchcraft, the statue scene could easily have come across as so audacious a piece of theater as to verge on blasphemy. Indeed, the statue disclosed by Paulina in the play's dénouement has all the qualities of a work of magic, insofar as sorcerers have often, over the centuries, been credited with the capacity to create objects capable of acquiring autonomous motion and the gift of language. It is not surprising, therefore, that Paulina should proclaim as firmly as she does that her actions are within the bounds of propriety. While frankly admitting that she has the power to make the statue move, she is concerned that those present might suspect that she is being "assisted / By wicked powers" (5.3.90–91). She then urges "those that think" that what she is performing "is unlawful business" (5.3.96) to "depart" (5.3.97), and stresses again that her "spell is lawful" once Hermione has descended from her pedestal, and approached her husband (5.3.105).

Leontes himself dispels any insinuation that Paulina's actions might partake of sorcery, embracing the notion of "magic" as "an art / Lawful as eating" (5.3.110–111). It is also worth noting, in this regard, that when Leontes addresses the statue directly earlier in the scene, declaring "Oh royal piece: / There's magic in thy majesty" (5.3.38–39), he is ascribing magical powers to the *statue itself*, not to Paulina as potential witch. It is nonetheless undeniable that Leontes gets quite agitated when the statue moves, anxious to ascertain whether what he is witnessing is magic or art—neither of which it really is, strictly speaking. Paulina claims it is a miracle, but the statue's motion is not a miracle either.

In fact, it is the result of the deft layering of multiple meanings wherein the boundary between truth and untruth is progressively eroded. On one level, the so-called miracle amounts to plain deception, since the statue is actually a real woman posing as the artwork of a dead woman. At the same time, it is a theatrical ruse sustained by masterful stagecraft, akin to formalized performances such as the masque or the intermedio. Thus, though not a work of magic in the literal sense, its dramatic caliber as a superlative simulation of a feat of magic makes it akin to legerdemain. As a performance, or miniature play-within-a-play, the statue scene transcends the "reality" of the action by offering an undiluted celebration of the power of fiction to engender alternate realities. It thus captures the *essence of fiction* at its most self-consciously proficient.

These layers of meaning are so closely interlocked that it is well-nigh impossible to separate one from the other with any degree of finality, in much the same way as it is hopeless to establish where life ends and non-life begins, where real-life ends and play-acting begins. As a blurring of the boundary between reality and illusion with respect to both life and death, the statue scene echoes the trial scene, and specifically the exchange between the unjustly accused queen and her deranged spouse, where Hermione states, "My life stands in the level of your dreams, / Which I'll lay down," and Leontes ripostes: "Your actions are my dreams'" (3.2.80–81).

Its interpretation as a piece of theater does not altogether clear the statue scene of its latent association with magic. This is because it was not uncommon, in Shakespeare's time, to regard figures embroiled in the pseudo-reality of theater—such as dramatists, impresarios and stage managers—as conjurers. As B. J. Sokol reminds us, "there was a wide range of opinion in the Renaissance on the work of magical makers of illusion. They were frequently portrayed as evil, especially when engaged in erotic magic." Ironically, however, "praise was heaped on artists who inspired erotic responses." This is especially true of theorists given to idealize without reservations "the work of masters like Praxiteles or Michelangelo and Pontormo which caused spectators to 'fall in love.'"

Whether "artworks inspiring love" are commended or demonized is determined by the use to which they are put. This explains why Paulina is at first reluctant to let Leontes "kiss the statue." On the one hand, she is concerned that the act might lead the king to indulge in a "fetishistic confusion of art with life." On the other hand, she wishes to protect him from the no less nefarious trap of "Petrarchan idolatry, or a perversely pleasurable grieving over an unobtainable and absent love." This form of blind worship is fueled by the courtly-love convention which places the female object of desire on an inaccessible pedestal, and enjoins the lover to admire such an object from afar without ever presuming to possess it. This strategy, as noted in Chapter Two, can be explained in a psychoanalytical key as an effort to formalize, and hence negotiate, the legendary insatiability of human desire in all its forms.

Paulina's "gallery," states Sokol, "provides for the true artistic virtues of conveying quality and form but prohibits the false ones of conveying quantity and sense." This perspective is inspired by a wish to elevate art above the strictures of the material world, and locate it instead with a domain of incorporeal forms akin to Plato's Ideas. In this regard, it echoes the teachings of Neoplatonism. At the same time, it requires the artwork's beholders to disengage themselves from the empirical dimension, associated with the crude yearning to consume the object's palpable substance, and endeavor instead to penetrate its ineffable spiritual core. What Paulina expects of the king is a preparedness to "touch more than outward shapes, see more than outward colours," and grasp the power of "art to symbolise inner life." This is the prerequisite of his capacity "to learn to love" (Sokol, p. 158).

Nevertheless, it must be emphasized that Shakespeare's pairing of artistic creation and love does not pivot on the idealization of the transcendent power of art generally found in Neoplatonism. This is borne out by the fact that the statue, while functioning as the emblem of the type of artifice ideally suited to inspire love, is not exempt from the flaws of matter. On the contrary, it associates art with the corporeal dimension through its display of details so vivid as to defy the cold purity of marble—and, by extension, the refined reality of an artwork meant to capture timeless perfection. It alerts the viewer to the mutability of the flesh—and, by implication, to the perishability of anything human—by incorporating *wrinkles* which Hermione's visage did not exhibit at the time of her death. On the factual level, this is simply due to the statue not being a statue at all but a real person. On the symbolic one, however, it carries deeper resonance as the distillation of an aesthetic sensibility indisposed to condemn materiality a priori as synonymous with sin.

Ultimately, we might as well accept that the "transformation" staged in the play's climax is an arbitrary occurrence unfolding in blunt defiance of reason and logic—and, more importantly, that it is *meant* to be viewed as arbitrary: as a metonymic distillation of the arbitrariness which pervades human life at each turn, and which irony strives to encapsulate through its unparalleled emphasis on the incongruous and the inconclusive.

Bibliography

Because of the intrinsically volatile character of the world wide web, it cannot be guaranteed that all of the websites explored while producing this book are still extant, and that the URLs provided in this bibliography are therefore available and accessible today.

Ariosto, L. [1516; revised 1521 and 1532.] *Orlando furioso*. Translated by W. S. Rose. Translation published 1823–1831. http://sacred-texts.com/neu/orl/index.htm

Armstrong, D. 2003. *Gender and the Chivalric Community in Malory's Morte d'Arthur*. Gainesville, FL: University Press of Florida.

Ashe, G. 1997. "Origins." In *The Arthurian Handbook*, Second Edition, edited by N. J. Lacy, G. Ashe G. and D. N. Mancoff. New York: Garland.

Auerbach, E. 1957. *Mimesis: The Representation of Reality in Western Literature*. Translated by W. R. Trask. Princeton, NJ: Princeton University Press.

Bakhtin, M. 1984. *Rabelais and His World*. Translated by H. Iswolsky. Bloomington, IN: Indiana University Press.

Barber, R. [1979.] 1991. *The Arthurian Legends: An Illustrated Anthology*, edited by R. Barber. Woodbridge, Suffolk and Rochester, NY: The Boydell Press.

_____. 2000. "Chivalry and the *Morte Darthur*." In *A Companion to Malory*, edited by E. Archibald and A. S. G. Edwards. Cambridge: Brewer.

_____. 2003. "Chivalry, Cistercianism and the Grail." In *A Companion to the Lancelot-Grail Cycle*, edited by C. Dover. Cambridge: Brewer.

_____. 2010. "Lancelot-Grail." http://www.boydellandbrewer.com/content/docs/Lancelot_Grail_Article.pdf

Barthes, R. [1967.] 1977. "The Death of the Arthur." In *Image/Music/Text*. Translated by S. Heath. London: Fontana Press.

_____. [1973.] 1975. *The Pleasure of the Text*. Translated by R. Miller. With a Note on the Text by R. Howard. New York: Hill & Wang.

Baumgartner, E. 2003. "The *Queste del saint Graal*: from *semblance* to *veraie semblance*." Translated by C. Dover. In *A Companion to the Lancelot-Grail Cycle*, edited by C. Dover. Cambridge: Brewer.

Beer, G. 1970. *The Romance*. The Critical Idiom. London and New York: Routledge.

Benson, L. D. 1968. "Art and Tradition in *Sir Gawain and the Green Knight*." In *Twentieth Century Interpretations of Sir Gawain and the Green Knight*, edited by D. Fox. Englewood Cliffs, NJ: Prentice-Hall.

Bergeron, D. M. 1987. "Images of Rule in *Cymbeline*." *Journal of Dramatic Theory and Criticism*. Spring 1987. University of Kansas.

Bloomfield, M. H. 1970. "*Sir Gawain and the Green Knight*: An Appraisal." In *Critical Studies of Sir Gawain and the Green Knight*, edited by D. R. Howard and C. K. Zacher. Notre Dame, IN and

London: University of Notre Dame Press.
Bogdanow, F. 1972. "The Love Theme in Chrétien de Troyes's 'Chevalier de la Charrette.'" *The Modern Language Review*, Vol. 67, No. 1, January 1972, pp. 50–61. http://www.jstor.org/stable/3722385
Boling, R. J. 2000. "Anglo-Welsh Relations in *Cymbeline*." *Shakespeare Quarterly* 51: 33–66.
Bostock, P. 1989. *Poststructuralism, postmodernism and British academic attitudes: with special reference to David Lodge, Malcolm Bradbury and Gabriel Josipovici*. British Library. http://www.amazon.co.uk/Poststructuralism-postmodernism-British-academic-attitudes/dp/B001ON0P5W/ref=sr_1_8?ie=UTF8&qid=1417372874&sr=8-8&keywords=paddy+bostock
Bowers, R. H. 1970. "*Gawain and the Green Knight* As Entertainment." In *Critical Studies of Sir Gawain and the Green Knight*, edited by D. R. Howard and C. K. Zacher. Notre Dame, IN and London: University of Notre Dame Press.
Brandsma, F. 2010. *The Interlace Structure of the Third Part of the Prose Lancelot*. Cambridge: D. S. Brewer.
Bridgwood, R. 2010–2011. "The Depiction of Lancelot in Chrétien de Troyes' *The Knight of the Cart* and Malory's 'Book of Sir Lancelot and Queen Guinevere' in *Le Morte Darthur*." The University of Nottingham, School of English Studies. INNERVATE—Leading Undergraduate Work in English Studies, Volume 3, pp. 480–487. ISSN: 2041-6776.
Briggs, K. 1976. *A Book of Fairies*. London: Penguin.
Brooks-Davies, D. 1977. *Spenser's Faerie Queene: A Critical Commentary on Books I and II*. Manchester: Manchester University Press.
Bruckner, M. T. 2008. "*Le Chevalier de la Charrette*: That Obscure Object of Desire, Lancelot." In *A Companion to Chrétien de Troyes*, edited by N. L. Lacy and J. Tasker Grimbert. Cambridge: Brewer.

_____. 2000. "The shape of romance in medieval France." In *The Cambridge Companion to Medieval Romance*, edited by R. L. Krueger. Cambridge: Cambridge University Press.
Bulfinch, T. [1858.] 1997. *The Age of Chivalry. The Illustrated Bulfinch's Mythology*. Illustrations by G. Caselli. New York: Macmillan.
Busby, K. 1993. *Chretien de Troyes: Perceval (Le Conte du Graal)*. Critical Guides to French Texts, 98. London: Grant & Cutler.
Calvino, I. 1995. *Orlando furioso di Ludovico Ariosto raccontato da Italo Calvino*. Milan: Mondadori.
Carson, A., Mother, O.S.U. 1970. "The Green Chapel: Its Meaning and Its Function." In *Critical Studies of Sir Gawain and the Green Knight*, edited by D. R. Howard and C. K. Zacher. Notre Dame, IN and London: University of Notre Dame Press.
Castiglione, B. [1528.] 2002. *The Book of the Courtier: The Singleton Translation*, edited by D. Javitch. Translated by C. S. Singleton. New York: W.W. Norton.
Cavallaro, D. 2001. *Critical and Cultural Theory. Thematic Variations*. London and New Brunswick, NJ: The Athlone Press.
_____. 2011. *The Fairy Tale and Anime*. Jefferson, NC: McFarland.
Cazelles, B. 1996. *The Unholy Grail: A Social Reading of Chrétien de Troyes's "Conte du Graal."* Stanford, CA: Stanford University Press.
Chase, C. J. 2003. "The Gateway to the Lancelot-Grail Cycle: L'Estoire del Saint Graal." In *A Companion to the Lancelot-Grail Cycle*, edited by C. Dover. Cambridge: Brewer.
Chestre, T. 2000. *Sir Launfal*. Translated by James Weldon. *Middle English Series*. Cambridge, Ontario: In parentheses Publications. http://www.yorku.ca/inpar/launfal_weldon.pdf
Choi, Y. 2010. "*Sir Launfal*: A Portrait of a Knight in Fourteenth Century England." *Medieval and Early Modern English Studies* Vol. 18, No.1, 1–28.

Chrétien de Troyes. 2008a. *Lancelot, or, the Knight of the Cart.* In *Arthurian Romances By Chrétien de Troyes.* Translated by W. Comfort. Digireads.com Publishing.

———. 1999. *Perceval, The Story of the Grail.* Translated by B. Raffel. New Haven and London: Yale University Press.

———. 2008b. *Yvain, or, the Knight with the Lion.* In *Arthurian Romances By Chrétien de Troyes.* Translated by W. Comfort. Digireads.com Publishing.

Coghlan, R. 1993. "Introduction." In *The Illustrated Encyclopaedia of Arthurian Legends* by R. Coghlan. Shaftesbury, Dorset, Rockport, MA, and Brisbane, Queensland: Element.

Cole, J. 2007. *Ceremonies of the seasons: Exploring and Celebrating Nature's Eternal Cycle.* London: Duncan Baird Publishers.

Combes, A. 2003. "The *Merlin* and its Suite." Translated by C. Dover. In *A Companion to the Lancelot-Grail Cycle*, edited by C. Dover. Cambridge: Brewer.

Comfort, W. 2008. *Arthurian Romances By Chrétien de Troyes.* Translated by W. Comfort. Digireads.com Publishing.

Conway, D. J. 2005. *The Ancient Art of Faery Magick.* Berkeley, CA: The crossing Press.

Cooper, H. 2008. *The English Romance in Time. Transforming Motifs from Geoffrey of Monmouth to the Death of Shakespeare.* Oxford and New York: Oxford University Press.

———. 1998. "Introduction." *Le Morte Darthur: The Winchester Manuscript.* Oxford: Oxford University Press.

Cramer, S. 2010. "Otherworld Journeys: Death and Rebirth." http://vault.hanover.edu/~battles/arthur/Otherworld.html

Cupitt, C. 1998. "The Magic of *Sir Orfeo.*" http://www.oocities.org/area51/hollow/2405/orfeo.html#12

The Death of Arthur. 2000. Translated by N. J. Lacy. In *The Lancelot-Grail Reader.* New York and London: Garland Publishing.

Delacroix, C. 1998. "Medieval Romance & the Fairy Tale." *All About Romance.* http://www.likesbooks.com/wb4.html

Derrida, J. 1988. "Structure, sign and play in the discourse of the human sciences." In *Modern Criticism and Theory*, edited by D. Lodge. London and New York: Longman. Originally printed in Derrida, J. 1978, *Writing and Difference.* Translated by A. Bass. London: Routledge & Kegan Paul.

Dini, C. 2014. *Ariosto: Guida all'Orlando Furioso.* Rome, Italy: Carocci editore.

Diverres, A. 1970. "Some Thoughts on the Sens of *Le Chevalier de la Charrette.*" *Forum for Modern Language Studies*, Vol. 6, pp. 24–36.

Dover, C. 2003. "Towards a Modern Reception of the *Lancelot-Grail Cycle.*" In *A Companion to the Lancelot-Grail Cycle*, edited by C. Dover. Cambridge: Brewer.

Duggan, J. J. 1999. "Afterword." In *Perceval, The Story of the Grail.* Translated by B. Raffel. New Haven and London: Yale University Press.

Dunn, E. C. 1918. "The Drawbridge of the Graal Castle." *Modern Language Notes* 33.7. *JSTOR.* Web. 8 March 2010.

Eckhardt, C. D. 1974. "Arthurian Comedy: The Simpleton-Hero in *Sir Perceval of Galles.*" In *The Chaucer Review: A Journal of Medieval Studies and Literary Criticism* 8:3, pp. 205–220.

Edwards, E. 2001. *The Genesis of Narrative in Malory's Morte Darthur.* Cambridge: D. S. Brewer.

———. 2000. "The Place of Women in the *Morte Darthur.*" In *A Companion to Malory*, edited by E. Archibald and A. S. G. Edwards. Cambridge: D.S. Brewer.

Everett, D. 1968. "The Alliterative Revival." In *Twentieth Century Interpretations of Sir Gawain and the Green Knight*, edited by D. Fox. Englewood Cliffs, NJ: Prentice-Hall.

Fisher, S. 2000. "Women and men in late medieval English romance." In *The Cambridge Companion to Medieval Romance*, edited by R. L. Krueger. Cambridge: Cambridge University Press.

Flusser, V. "Key Words," edited by A. Müller-Pohle and B. Neubauer. http://www.equivalence.com/labor/lab_vf_glo_e.shtml

Fox, D. 1968. "Introduction." In *Twentieth Century Interpretations of Sir Gawain and the Green Knight*, edited by D. Fox. Englewood Cliffs, NJ: Prentice-Hall.

Friedman, J. B. 1970. *Orpheus in the Middle Ages*. Cambridge, Massachusetts: Harvard University Press.

Frye, N. 1990. *The Secular Scripture: A Study of the Structure of Romance*. New Edition. Cambridge, MA: Harvard University Press.

Fuchs, B. 2004. *Romance*. The New Critical Idiom. New York and London: Routledge.

Garrard, M. 1992. "Female portraits, Female Nature." In *The Expanding Discourse: Feminism and Art History*, edited by N. Broude and M. D. Garrard. New York: Westview Press.

Gaunt, S. 2000. "Romance and other genres." In *The Cambridge Companion to Medieval Romance*, edited by R. L. Krueger. Cambridge: Cambridge University Press.

"The General Prologue." An Interlinear Translation. The Middle English text is from *The Riverside Chaucer*, edited by L. D. Benson. Available on *The Geoffrey Chaucer Page*. http://sites.fas.harvard.edu/~chaucer/teachslf/gp-par.htm

Genette, G. 1988. "Structuralism and literary criticism." In *Modern Criticism and Theory*, edited by D. Lodge. London and New York: Longman.

Goldman, P. 2011. "*The Winter's Tale* and Antitheatricalism: Shakespeare's Rehabilitation of the Public Scene." *Anthropoetics* 17, Volume XVII, number 1. Fall 2011. http://www.anthropoetics.ucla.edu/ap1701/1701goldman.htm

Green, D. H. 1979. *Irony in the Medieval Romance*. Cambridge, London, New York, New Rochelle, Melbourne and Sydney: Cambridge University Press.

Hahn, T. 2000. "Gawain and popular chivalric romance in Britain." In *The Cambridge Companion to Medieval Romance*, edited by R. L. Krueger. Cambridge: Cambridge University Press.

Haidu, P. 1968. *Aesthetic Distance in Chrétien de Troyes: Irony and Comedy in Cligès and Perceval*. Genève: Librairie Droz.

Herron, T. 2013. "Spenser and Raleigh." *Centering Spenser—A Digital Resource to Kilcolman Castle*. East Carolina University. http://core.ecu.edu/umc/Munster/settlement_R&S.html

Hibbard Loomis, L. 1970. "*Gawain and the Green Knight*." In *Critical Studies of Sir Gawain and the Green Knight*, edited by D. R. Howard and C. K. Zacher. Notre Dame, IN and London: University of Notre Dame Press.

The History of The Holy Grail. 2000. Translated by C. J. Chase. In *The Lancelot-Grail Reader*. New York and London: Garland Publishing.

Howard, D. R. 1968. "Structure and Symmetry in *Sir Gawain*." In *Twentieth Century Interpretations of Sir Gawain and the Green Knight*, edited by D. Fox. Englewood Cliffs, NJ: Prentice-Hall.

Huizinga, J. 1972. *The Waning of the Middle Ages*. Translated by F. Hopman. Middlesex: Penguin Books.

Hunt, T. 2008. "*Le Chevalier au Lion*: Yvain Lionheart." In *A Companion to Chrétien de Troyes*, edited by N. L. Lacy and J. Tasker Grimbert. Cambridge: Brewer.

Jameson, F. 1975. "Magical Narratives: Romance as Genre." *New Literary History*, Vol. 7, No. 1. "Critical Challenges: The Bellagio Symposium," pp. 135–163. Autumn 1975.

Jirsa, C. 2008. "In the Shadows of the Ympe-Tre: Arboreal Folklore in *Sir Orfeo*." *English Studies* 89.2: 141–151.

Jones, G. 1989. "Gemma Jones: *Hermione*." In *Players of Shakespeare 1: Essays in Shakespearean Performance by Twelve Players with the Royal Shakespeare Company*, edited by P. Brockbank. Cambridge: Cambridge University Press.

Kaeuper, R. 2000. "The societal role of chivalry in romance: northwestern Europe." In *The Cambridge Companion to Medieval Romance*, edited by R. L.

Krueger. Cambridge: Cambridge University Press.

Kaske, C. V. 2006a. "Introduction." In *The Faerie Queene—Book One*, edited, with introduction, by C. V. Kaske. Indianapolis, IN: Hackett Publishing Company.

_____. 2006b. Notes to *The Faerie Queene—Book One*, edited, with introduction, by C. V. Kaske. Indianapolis, IN: Hackett Publishing Company.

Keats, J. 1884. "The Eve of St. Agnes." *The Poetical Works of John Keats*. http://www.bartleby.com/126/39.html

_____. 1818. "Letter to Richard Woodhouse, October 27, 1818." http://www.john-keats.com/briefe/271018.htm

Kelly, D. 2008. "Narrative Poetics: Rhetoric, Orality and Performance." In *A Companion to Chrétien de Troyes*, edited by N. L. Lacy and J. Tasker Grimbert. Cambridge: Brewer.

Kenny, L. I. 2013. "Carnival, Pagan and Christian symbolism in Sir Gawain and the Green Knight." http://www.academia.edu/6168460/Carnival_Pagan_and_Christian_Symbolism_in_Sir_Gawain

Ker, W. P. 1957. *Epic and Romance: essays on medieval literature*. New York: Dover Publications.

Kermode, F. 1963. *The Final Plays*. London: Longmans Green.

Kibler, W. and Carroll, C. 1991. "Introduction." In *Arthurian Romances* by Chrétien de Troyes. Penguin Classics. Translated by W. Kibler and C. Carroll. London: Penguin.

King, S. 1993. *Danse Macabre*. London: Warner Books.

Krueger, R. L. 2000. "Introduction." In *The Cambridge Companion to Medieval Romance*, edited by R. L. Krueger. Cambridge: Cambridge University Press.

Lacan, J. 1985. "God and the *Jouissance* of Woman." In *Feminine Sexuality: Jacques Lacan and the école freudienne*, edited by J. Mitchell and J. Rose. New York: W. W. Norton.

_____. 1972. "Of Structure as an Inmixing of Otherness Prerequisite to Any Subject Whatsoever." In *The Structuralist Controversy*, edited by R. Macksey and E. Donato. Baltimore: Johns Hopkins University Press.

Lachaud, F. 2002. "Dress and Social Status in England before the Sumptuary Laws." *Heraldry, Pageantry and Social Display in Medieval England*, edited by P. Coss and M. Keen. Woodbridge, Suffolk: Boydell.

Lacy, N. J. 1980. *The Craft of Chrétien de Troyes: an Essay on Narrative Art*. Davis Medieval Texts and Studies, 3. Leiden: Brill.

_____. 1997. "Early Arthurian Literature." In *The Arthurian Handbook*, Second Edition, edited by N. J. Lacy, G. Ashe G. and D. N. Mancoff. New York: Garland.

_____. 2000a. "The evolution and legacy of French prose romance." In *The Cambridge Companion to Medieval Romance*, edited by R. L. Krueger. Cambridge: Cambridge University Press.

_____. 2000b. "Introduction." In *The Lancelot-Grail Reader*. New York and London: Garland Publishing.

_____. and Ashe, G. 1997. "Preface to the First Edition." In *The Arthurian Handbook*, Second Edition, edited by N. J. Lacy, G. Ashe and D. N. Mancoff. New York: Garland.

Lacy, N. J., Ashe, G. and Mancoff, D. N. 1997. "Perceval." Entry in "An Arthurian Glossary." In *The Arthurian Handbook*, Second Edition, edited by N. J. Lacy, G. Ashe and D. N. Mancoff. New York: Garland.

Landry, D. E. 1982. "Dreams as History: The Strange Unity of *Cymbeline*." *Shakespeare Quarterly* Vol. 33, No. 1. Spring 1982, pp. 68–79. Shakespeare Folger Library.

Lardo, C. 2010. *I mostri dell'Orlando Furioso, specchi della natura umana*. Florence, Italy: Le Lettere.

Läseke, S. 2011. "'With fairi forth y-nome': The Representation of the Fairy World in *Sir Orfeo*." *Medievalists.net*. http://www.medievalists.net/2011/01/29/with-fairi-forth-y-nome-the-represe ntation-of-the-fairy-world-in-sir-orfeo/

Lear, J. 2011. *A Case for Irony*. The Tanner Lectures on Human Values. Cambridge, MA, and London: Harvard University Press.

———. 1998. "The Examined Life. A philosopher grapples with Socrates and with his own individuality." Review of *The Art of Living. Socratic Reflections From Plato to Foucault*, by A. Nehamas. Berkeley: University of California Press. *The New York Times on the Web*, October 25. http://www.nytimes.com/books/98/10/25/reviews/981025.25lear2t.html

Leverage, P. 2011. "Is Perceval Autistic? Theory of Mind in the *Conte del Graal*." In *Theory of Mind and Literature*, edited by P. Leverage, H. Mancing, S. Schweickert and J. Marston William, pp. 133–151. West Lafayette, IN: Purdue University Press.

Lewis, C. S. 1958. *The Allegory of Love*. Oxford: Oxford University Press.

Livingston, M. L. 1969. "The Natural Art of *The Winter's Tale*." *Modern Language Quarterly* 30: 340–355.

Lockey, B. C. 2009. *Law and Empire in English Renaissance Literature*. Cambridge: Cambridge University Press.

Lodge, D. 1985. *Small World: An Academic Romance*. London: Penguin.

Loomis, R. S. [1963.] 1992. *The Grail: From Celtic Myth to Christian Symbol*. London: Constable.

Loponen, M. "Faerie Folklore in Medieval Tales—an Introduction." http://www.academia.edu/300335/Faerie_Folklore_in_Medieval_Tales_an_Introduction

Lot, F. 1918. *Étude sur le "Lancelot" en Prose*. Paris: Édouard Champion.

Malory, T. 1896. *Selections from Malory's Le Morte D'Arthur*, edited by A. T. Martin. London and New York: Macmillan.

Mann, J. 2000. "Malory and the Grail Legend." In *A Companion to Malory*, edited by E. Archibald and A. S. G. Edwards. Cambridge: Brewer.

Marriott, S. 2006. *The Ultimate Fairy Handbook*. London: MQP Publications.

Marshall, C. 2003. "*Cymbeline*: A Modern Perspective." In *Cymbeline*, edited by B. A. Mowat and P. Werstine. Folger Shakespeare Library. New York London, Toronto, and Sydney: Simon & Schuster Paperbacks.

Matthews, J. 1993. "Foreword." *The Illustrated Encyclopaedia of Arthurian Legends* by R. Coghlan. Shaftesbury, Dorset, Rockport, MA and Brisbane, Queensland: Element.

Mauss, M. [1925.] 2000. *The Gift: The Form and Reason for Exchange in Archaic Societies*. Translated by W. D. Halls. New York: W. W. Norton & Company.

McCarthy, T. 1991. *An Introduction to Malory*. Woodbridge, Suffolk: D. S. Brewer.

McCullough, A. 2006. "Criminal Naivety: Blind Resistance and the Pain of Knowing in Chrétien de Troyes's *Conte du Graal*." *Modern Language Review* 101, pp. 48–61.

McFarland, T. 1972. *Shakespeare's Pastoral Comedy*. Chapel Hill: University of North Carolina Press.

McGinn, C. 2004. *Mindsight—Image, Dream, Meaning*. Cambridge, MA and London: Harvard University Press.

Mertes, K. 1988. *The English Noble Household 1250–1600: Good Governance and Politic Rule*. Oxford, UK: Basil Blackwell.

Mikalachki, J. 1995. "The Masculine Romance of Roman Britain: *Cymbeline* and Early Modern English Nationalism." *Shakespeare Quarterly* 46: 301–322.

Mitchell, B. 1964. "The Faery World of *Sir Orfeo*." *Neophilologus*, 48, 156–9.

Nehamas, A. 1998. *The Art of Living. Socratic Reflections From Plato to Foucault*. Berkeley: University of California Press. Extract in: http://www.nytimes.com/books/first/n/nehamas-art.html

Nietzsche, F. [1882.] 2001. *The Gay Science*. Translated by J. Nauckhoff and A. Del Caro. Cambridge: Cambridge University Press.

Nietzsche, F. [1886.] 2003. *Beyond Good and Evil*. Translated by R. J. Hollingdale. London: Penguin Books.

O'Connell, M. 1977. *Mirror and Veil: The*

Historical Dimension of Spenser's Faerie Queene. Chapel Hill, NC: The University of North Carolina Press.

O'Hanlon, G. 2015. "Notions of nationhood in Shakespeare's *Cymbeline*." https://www.litencyc.com/prize/Essays 2011/essay3.doc

Parker, P. 1979. *Inescapable Romance*. Princeton, NJ: Princeton University Press.

Patch, H. R. 1918. "Some Elements in Mediaeval Depictions of the Other World." *PMLA*, Volume 33. January 1.

Pearsall, D. 2003. *Arthurian Romance: A Short Introduction*. Oxford: Blackwell Publishing.

Pickens, R. T. 2008. "*Le Conte du Graal*: Chrétien's Unfinished Last Romance." In *A Companion to Chrétien de Troyes*, edited by N. L. Lacy and J. Tasker Grimbert. Cambridge: Brewer.

Poulson, C. 1999. *The Quest for the Holy Grail: Arthurian Legend in British Art 1840–1920*. Manchester and New York: Manchester University Press.

Propp, V. 2014. "Fairy Tale Transformations." In *Modern Genre Theory*, edited by D. Duff. Abingdon, Oxon and New York: Routledge.

The Quest for the Holy Grail. 2000. Translated by E. J. Burns. In *The Lancelot-Grail Reader*. New York and London: Garland Publishing.

Quint, D. 1985. "The Boat of Romance and Renaissance Epic." In *Romance: Generic Transformations from Chrétien de Troyes to Cervantes*, edited by K. Brownlee and M. Scordilis Brownlee. Hanover, NH: University Press of New England.

Rabine, L. W. 2002. "The Establishment of Patriarchy in *Tristan and Isolde*." In *Tristan and Isolde: A Casebook*, edited by J. Grimbert Tasker. Routledge.

Refini, E. 2008. "L'isola-balena tra 'Furioso' e 'Cinque Canti.'" In *Italianistica*, XXXVII, 3.

Rider, J. 2000. "The other worlds of romance." In *The Cambridge Companion to Medieval Romance*, edited by R. L. Krueger. Cambridge: Cambridge University Press.

Rilke, R. M. 1996. "Letter to Witold von Hulewicz." In *Selected Letters 1902–1926*. Translated by R. F. C. Hull. Cited in *The Inner World* by M. Warner. London: National Touring Exhibitions/South Bank Centre.

Roberts, J. A. 1991. *The Shakespearean Wild: Geography, Genus, and Gender*. Lincoln, NE, and London: University of Nebraska Press.

"Romance." *Online Etymology Dictionary*. http://www.etymonline.com/index.php?term=romance

"Romance." *Oxford Dictionaries*. http://www.oxforddictionaries.com/definition/english/romance

"Romances of Chivalry." *Spain Then and Now*. http://www.spainthenandnow.com/spanish-literature/romances-of-chivalry/default_68.aspx

Sánchez Martí, J. 2000. "The Representation of Chivalry in *The Knight's Tale*." *Revista Alicantina de Estudios Ingleses* 13:1, pp. 161–173. http://rua.ua.es/dspace/bitstream/10045/5356/1/RAEI_13_13.pdf

Saunders, C. 2004. "Chaucer's Romances." In *A Companion to Romance*, edited by C. Saunders. London: Blackwell. Extract: *Blackwell Reference Online*: http://www.blackwellreference.com/public/book.html?id=g9780631232711_9780 631232711

———. 1993. *The Forest of Medieval Romance: Avernus, Broceliande, Arden*. Cambridge: D. S. Brewer.

———. *Magic and the Supernatural in Medieval English Romance*. Cambridge: D. S. Brewer.

Saussure, F. de. [1916.] 2013. *Course in General Linguistics*. Translated by R. Harris. London: Duckworth.

Schavrien, J. 2013. "Shakespeare's *Cymbeline* and the Mystical Particular: Redemption, Then and Now, for a Disassembled World." *International Journal of Transpersonal Studies*, Vol. 32, Issue 2, pp. 122–140. Palo Alto, CA: Sophia University.

Schlegel, F. [1800.] 1968. *Dialogue on Poetry and Literary Aphorisms*. Translated by E. Behler and R. Struc. University Park: Pennsylvania State University Press.

Schweke, J. 2006. *Women's roles in Arthurian literature*. Norderstedt, Germany: GRIN Verlag GmbH.

Seaman, M. 2000. "Thomas Chestre's *Sir Launfal* and the Englishing of Medieval Romance." *Medieval Perspectives* 15: 105–119.

Shemek, D. 1998. *Ladies Errant: Wayward Women and Social Order in Early Modern Italy*. Durham, NC: Duke University Press.

"Sir Orfeo." *Wikipedia*. https://en.wikipedia.org/wiki/Sir_Orfeo

Smith, B. R. 1991. *Homosexual Desire in Shakespeare's England*. Chicago: University of Chicago Press.

Sokol, B. J. 1994. *Art and Illusion in The Winter's Tale*. Manchester and New York: Manchester University Press.

Spearing, A. C. 1990. "Marie de France and Her Middle English Adapters." *SAC* 12: 117–156.

_____. 1968. "View Points." In *Twentieth Century Interpretations of Sir Gawain and the Green Knight*, edited by D. Fox. Englewood Cliffs, NJ: Prentice-Hall.

Speirs, J. 1968. "*Sir Gawain and the Green Knight*." In *Twentieth Century Interpretations of Sir Gawain and the Green Knight*, edited by D. Fox. Englewood Cliffs, NJ: Prentice-Hall.

Spenser, E. [1590.] 2006. *The Faerie Queene—Book One*, edited, with introduction, by C. V. Kaske. Indianapolis, IN: Hackett Publishing Company.

Stern, E. 2002. "A Touch of Medieval: Narrative, Magic and Computer Technology in Massively Multiplayer Computer Role-Playing Games." University of Southern California, School of Cinema & Television eddoATc-level.cc http://ic.media.mit.edu/courses/mas878/pubs/stern-cgdc02-touch-of-medieval.pdf

Stevens, J. 1973. *Medieval Romance. Themes and Approaches*. London: Hutchinson & Co.

Stoppino, E. 2012. *Genealogies of Fiction. Women Warriors and the Dynastic Imagination in the "Orlando Furioso."* Fordham University Press.

The Story of Merlin. 2000. Translated by R. T. Pickens. In *The Lancelot-Grail Reader*. New York and London: Garland Publishing.

Talbot Donaldson, E. 1968. "View Points." In *Twentieth Century Interpretations of Sir Gawain and the Green Knight*, edited by D. Fox. Englewood Cliffs, NJ: Prentice-Hall.

Tanner, T. 1996. "Introduction." In *Romances*, edited by S. Barnet. London: Everyman's Library.

Thiher, A. 1987. *Words in Reflection*. London: Chicago University Press.

Tonkin, H. 2003. "Five Lectures on Shakespeare's Romances: *Pericles, Cymbeline, The Winter's Tale, The Tempest*." President's College, University of Hartford. Spring 2001. http://uhaweb.hartford.edu/tonkin/pdfs/romancesfivelectures.pdf

Tolkien, C. 1995. *Sir Gawain and the Green Knight, Pearl* and *Sir Orfeo*, edited by C. Tolkien. Translated by J. R. R. Tolkien. London: HarperCollins Publishers.

_____. 1965. *Tree and Leaf*. Extract. In "What is a Fairy Tale?" *SurLaLune*. http://www.surlalunefairytales.com/introduction/ftdefinition.html

Trachsler, R. 2003. "A Question of Time: Romance and History." *A Companion to the Lancelot-Grail Cycle*, edited by C. Dover. Cambridge: Brewer.

Tsai, B. 2013. "Appropriating the Classical Underworld: The Otherworld and its Spectacle in *Sir Orfeo*." *Limina: A Journal of Historical and Cultural Studies*. Special Volume: *Receptions*. http://www.academia.edu/7785698/Appropriating_the_Classical_Underworld_The_Otherworld_and_its_Spectacle_in_Sir_Orfeo

Twitchell, J. B. 1988. *Dreadful Pleasures*. Oxford: Oxford University Press.

Vance, E. 1987. *From Topic to Tale: Logic and Narrativity in the Middle Ages*. Minneapolis: University of Minnesota Press.

Vinaver, E. 1966. *Form and Meaning in Medieval Romance*. The Presidential Address of the Modern Humanities Research Association. Modern Humanities Research Association.

Vonnegut, K. 1981. *Palm Sunday*. London: Granada.

Wace. 1938–1940. *Le Roman de Brut*, edited by I. Arnold. 2 vols. Paris: Champion.

Warner, M. 2000. *No Go the Bogeyman*. London: Vintage.

_____. 2006. *Phantasmagoria*. Oxford: Oxford University Press.

Watts, C. 2004. "Introduction." In *The Winter's Tale*, edited by C. Watts. Wordsworth Classics. Ware, Hertfordshire: Wordsworth Editions.

Weston, J. L. [1920.] 2013. *From Ritual to Romance*. CreateSpace Independent Publishing Platform.

Wilde, F. S. 1887. *Ancient Legends, Mystic Charms and Superstitions of Ireland*. London: Penguin.

Wise, N. 1979–1989. Review of *Perceval le Gallois* by Eric Rohmer, 1978. *Film Quarterly* 33:2, Winter.

Zaczek, I. 2005. *Fairy Art: Artists & Inspirations*. London: star Fire Publishing.

Index

Ariosto, L. 2, 4, 17, 66, 152–167, 172, 175, 183
Armstrong, D. 119–120, 121, 122, 124
Ashe, G. 6, 7, 9–10, 31, 63, 78
Auerbach, E. 16–17, 28, 59

Bakhtin, M. 141
Barber, R. 10, 11, 12, 14, 15, 18, 25, 45, 95, 96, 108
Barthes, R. 39–40, 50–51, 97, 155
Baumgartner, E. 105
Beardsley, A. 9
Beer, G. 37, 38, 40
Benson, L. D. 142–143
Bergeron, D. M. 193–194
Bloomfield, M. H. 140–141
Bogdanow, F. 71
Boiardo, M. M. 163, 164
Boling, R. J. 192
Boron, R. de 17, 18
Bostock, P. 39
Bowers, R. H. 141–142
Brandsma, F. 99
Bridgwood, R. 69–70
Briggs, K. 134
Brooks-Davies, D. 172, 176, 177
Bruckner, M. T. 4, 61, 69, 74, 88–89
Bulfinch, T. 55
Busby, K. 82, 89, 91

Calvino, I. 20, 39, 86, 153, 155–156, 160, 161, 164, 166
The Canterbury Tales 2, 114–115
Carroll, C. 57–58
Carson, A. 139
Castiglione, B. 169
Castle Dor 8
Cavallaro, D. 134, 199
Cazelles, B. 108
Le Chanson de Roland 36, 40, 163, 164
Chase, C. J. 97
Chaucer, G. 2, 4, 15, 114–115, 127, 142, 144, 150

Chestre, T. 2, 127–131, 187–188
Choi, Y. 127, 128–129
Chrétien de Troyes 1, 2, 4, 14, 15, 17, 20, 25, 36, 45, 46, 57–92, 95, 96, 99, 103, 106, 108, 112, 128, 132, 137, 139, 147, 150, 156, 168, 183, 188
Clarke, A. C. 34
Coghlan, R. 10, 17, 18, 21, 22
Cole, J. 140
Combes, A. 97–98
Comfort, W. 6, 29–30, 45, 52, 58
Conway, D. J. 135
Cooper, H. 11, 24, 116, 117, 151, 180, 197–198
Cramer, S. 76
Cupitt, C. 136
Cymbeline 2, 181–194

The Defence of Guinevere 22
Delacroix, C. 130
Derrida, J. 48, 53, 59
Dini, C. 156, 161–162
Diverres, A. 71
Dover, C. 112
Duggan, J. J. 90
Du Maurier, D. 8
Duncan, J. 9
Dunn, E. C. 76

Eckhardt, C. D. 78
Edwards, E. 119, 120–121
Eliot, T. S. 9, 20
Étude sur le "Lancelot" en Prose 41
Everett, D. 144

The Faerie Queene 2, 167–180
Fisher, S. 148
Flusser, V. 33
Fox, D. 143–144
Friedman, J. B. 136
Frye, N. 14, 55–56
Fuchs, B. 152

217

Index

Garrard, M. 199
Gaunt, S. 37, 73, 74, 103
Gawain Poet 2, 137–151
Genette, G. 26–27
Gerusalemme Liberata 172
Goldman, P. 183, 185, 201
Green, D. H. 170

Hahn, T. 90–91, 102–103
Haidu, P. 46, 78–79, 81, 82, 90, 91
Herron, T. 171
Hibbard Loomis, L. 143, 144, 148
Howard, D. R. 140
Huizinga, J. 136
Hunt, T. 60–61, 62

Idylls of the King 22–23

Jameson, F. 53
Jirsa, C. 136
Jones, G. 200

Kaeuper, R. 54
Kaske, C. V. 170, 174, 177
Keats, J. 5, 51, 144
Kelly, D. 25, 71
Kenny, L. I. 140
Ker, W. P. 29
Kermode, F. 182, 183–184, 185, 188, 190
Kibler, W. 58–59
King, S. 34
Krueger, R. L. 4

Lacan, J. 42–44, 69
Lachaud, F. 129
Lacy, N. J. 7, 9, 13, 45, 59–60, 78, 82, 100, 102, 109, 116
Lancelot-Grail Cycle 2, 16, 18, 20, 31, 41, 93–113
Lancelot, or, the Knight of the Cart 2, 25, 36, 60, 69–77, 84, 99, 106, 132
Landry, D. E. 188–189
Lardo, C. 164–165, 166
Läseke, S. 132
Lear, J. 49, 51–52
Leverage, P. 78
Lewis, C. S. 47, 119
Livingston, M. L. 199, 200
Lockey, B. C. 190
Lodge, D. 38, 39, 159
Loomis, R. S. 31–32
Loponen, M. 132–133
Lot, F. 41

Malory, T. 2, 21, 93, 115–125, 127, 128, 142, 150, 179
Mancoff, D. N. 78
Mann, J. 123
Mann, T. 50
Marriott, S. 135
Marshall, C. 184, 185

Mauss, M. 149
McCarthy, T. 93, 116, 117–11
McCullough, A. 78
McFarland, T. 197
McGinn, C. 32
Mertes, K. 128, 129
Mikalachki, J. 192
Mitchell, B. 132
Morris, W. 22
Le Morte d'Arthur 2, 115–125, 142

Nehamas, A. 49–50
Nietzsche, F. 165

O'Connell, M. 172, 173, 175, 176
O'Hanlon, G. 191, 192, 193
Orlando Furioso 2, 4, 17, 66, 153–167, 172, 175
Orlando Innamorato 163, 164

Parker, P. 41–42
Patch, H. R. 76
Pearsall, D. 10, 11, 13, 14, 15, 20–23, 28, 29, 72, 94, 113, 125, 148–149, 150, 175, 178
Perceval, the Story of the Grail 2, 17, 46, 61–62, 63, 76, 77–92
Pickens, R. T. 89
Poulson, C. 116–117, 119, 178, 179
Propp, V. 130–131

Quiller-Couch, A. 8
Quint, D. 76–77

Rabine, L. W. 15–16
Refini, E. 165
Rider, J. 35, 68–69, 75, 104, 132
Rilke, R. M. 33
Roberts, J. A. 198

Sánchez Martí, J. 115
Saunders, C. 114, 131, 179, 180, 181
Saussure, F. de 153
Schavrien, J. 187
Schlegel, F. 33
Seaman, M. 129
Shakespeare, W. 1, 2, 46, 114, 179, 180–205
Shemek, D. 156–157
Sir Gawain and the Green Knight 2, 137–151
Sir Launfal 2, 44, 127–131, 132, 135, 149, 172, 187–188
Sir Orfeo 2, 75, 131–136, 149
Smith, B. R. 182
Sokol, B. J. 204
Spearing, A. C. 128, 137–138
Speirs, J. 138–139
Spenser, E. 2, 4, 21, 23, 151, 167–180
Spiess, A. 9
Stern, E. 34
Stevens, J. 4–5, 45, 63–64
Stoppino, E. 158–159
Strassburg, G. von 9

Talbot Donaldson, E. 138
Tanner, T. 186–187
Tasso, T. 172
Tennyson, A. 8, 22–23
Thiher, A. 154
Tolkien, C. 138
Tolkien, J. R. R. 126, 145
Trachsler, R. 93
Tsai, B. 132
Twitchell, J. B. 35

Vance, E. 36
Vinaver, E. 41, 42, 48, 77, 124–125, 161
Vonnegut, K. 24

Wace 12–13
Warner, M. 34, 36
The Waste Land 20
Waterhouse, J. W. 8, 9
Watts, C. 182, 196, 197
Weston, J. L. 19, 20, 139
Wilde, F. S. 133
The Winter's Tale 2, 180, 181, 183, 184, 185, 186, 195–205
Wise, N. 77

Yvain, or, the Knight with the Lion 2, 14, 20, 25, 36, 60, 62, 64–69, 85, 106, 131, 150, 172

Zaczek, I. 135–136

www.ingramcontent.com/pod-product-compliance
Lightning Source LLC
Chambersburg PA
CBHW032054300426
44116CB00007B/728